Marvelous Minds

Marvelous Minds
The discovery of what children know

Michael Siegal

Professor and Marie Curie Chair in Psychology
University of Trieste, Italy, and

Professor of Psychology,
University of Sheffield
UK

OXFORD
UNIVERSITY PRESS

Great Clarendon Street, Oxford OX2 6DP

Oxford University Press is a department of the University of Oxford.
It furthers the University's objective of excellence in research, scholarship,
and education by publishing worldwide in

Oxford New York

Auckland Cape Town Dar es Salaam Hong Kong Karachi
Kuala Lumpur Madrid Melbourne Mexico City Nairobi
New Delhi Shanghai Taipei Toronto

With offices in

Argentina Austria Brazil Chile Czech Republic France Greece
Guatemala Hungary Italy Japan Poland Portugal Singapore
South Korea Switzerland Thailand Turkey Ukraine Vietnam

Oxford is a registered trade mark of Oxford University Press
in the UK and in certain other countries

Published in the United States
by Oxford University Press Inc., New York

A catalogue record for this title is available from the British Library

Data available

Library of Congress Cataloging in Publication Data

Data available

Typeset by Cepha Imaging Private Ltd., Bangalore, India
Printed in Great Britain
on acid-free paper by
Biddles Ltd., King's Lynn, Norfolk

ISBN 978-0-19-920705-3 (Pbk.)

10 9 8 7 6 5 4 3 2 1

Contents

Preface

What is the nature of children's knowledge? Without sacrificing the essential details, my aim in this book is to summarize the evidence to as wide an audience as possible. These findings have to do with children's grasp of the thoughts and beliefs of others and how these may differ from one's own and from reality, the shape of the earth and its movement in the cosmos, the importance of food, health, and hygiene, processes of life and death, and number and arithmetic. Another issue is the extent to which the knowledge of atypically developing children – especially those who have been diagnosed with autism – departs from that of their typically developing counterparts.

For each instance, we need to consider the fundamental question of why children apparently have so much difficulty showing what they know, as anyone who has worked with them will testify. Is it, for example, because at an early stage of development they are restricted to considering appearances rather than underlying realities and are incapable of insight into the minds of others and the invisible properties of objects? Or is it because they have difficulties in being able to understand the purpose and relevance of the questions that adults ask and they come up with answers that do not reflect the depth of what they can and do know? At the heart of this controversy is the extent to which, in certain areas of their knowledge, children can be deemed to have some limitation or deficit in their early understanding – a deficit that is so resistant to factual information that it cannot be overcome through early exposure to opportunities for learning and needs to be undergo a radical change.

In order to resolve the controversy and to discover what children genuinely can and do know, we need to steer between two mistakes: concluding that children have knowledge when they do not – a "false positive" – and concluding that children do not have knowledge when they actually do – a "false negative." Of course judgments about what children know are not the only ones that are vulnerable to conclusions based on false positive or false negative results. For example, adults make these mistakes all the time in relationships. They make the false positive mistake of choosing a person to be a suitable partner when he or she would actually not be. They also make the false negative mistake of refusing to accept a person as a suitable partner when he or she actually would be.

Presumably adults are often strong enough to cope with their mistakes. But false positive or false negative decisions about what children can and do know could have indelible consequences for their future welfare. Children may be thrown into stressful learning environments where they are over their heads or, alternatively, they may be cut off from all sorts of possibilities that allow them to reach their most effective potential. In the latter case, consideration needs to be given – as it will be in the chapters that follow – to "conversationally enriched" techniques of explicit questioning that better enable children who are inexperienced in conversation to understand the purpose and relevance of questions about what they know.

There also needs to be consideration given to cultures that provide maximal support for children at an early age so that their knowledge in certain areas is soon apparent and also to be mindful of conditions where this support crumbles so that children's understanding, and even that of adults, falters. On the one hand, all we need is the knowledge of a group of children in a culture somewhere to suggest what knowledge is within the grasp of children more generally. Such findings suggest that negative results in other cultures that appear to point to limitations in children's knowledge may amount to false negatives that, in some cases, may result instead from inexperience in following questions in conversation or restricted early opportunities for learning. On the other hand, children's understanding can be fragile when there is little or no cultural support. In this case, differences between children and adults seem to diminish. In anecdotal incidents that follow the chapters in the book, I have sought to illustrate the importance of the cultural context for everyday knowledge.

I would like to thank people in America, Australia, Britain, and elsewhere who have helped to facilitate and stimulate my work: Mark Blades, Peter Carruthers, Dick Eiser, Tim German, Erland Hjelmquist, Paola Iannello, Stephen Laurence, Antonella Marchetti, Ayumi

Matsuo, Liz Milne, Peter Newcombe, Gavin Nobes, Georgia Panagioaki, Clair Pond, Annika Dahlgren Sandberg, Virginia Slaughter, Steve Stich, Tyron Woolfe, Amir Amin Yazdi, and especially my frequent collaborators Candida Peterson, Luca Surian, and Rosemary Varley. I would also like to express my appreciation to Martin Baum at Oxford University Press for his guidance with the manuscript. For hospitality during my visits to Greece as moderator of the psychology course at City College, the Sheffield campus in Thessaloniki, I am indebted to Aggelos Rodafinos and his staff. For organizing my welcome to Italy, thanks are due to Silvia Barbieri, Nicola Bruno, Walter Gerbino, Riccardo Luccio, Chiara Passolunghi, Carlo Semenza, and Maria Tallandini, and I am very grateful to participants in the Trieste weekly postgraduate seminar series: Bruno Bianchi, Radosveta Dimitrova, Laura Iozzi Corinna Michelin, Tommaso Pecchia, Sandra Pellizzoni, Laura Iozzi, Alice Gherzil, Denis Razem, and Elena Salillas. Much of my work described here has been carried out with the generous support of the Nuffield Foundation, Leverhulme Trust, the European Union Sixth Framework Marie Curie research program, and the Fondazione Benefica Kathleen Foreman-Casali. It has also benefited from discussions at workshops sponsored by Sheffield Hang Seng Cognitive Studies Centre, particularly the AHRC Culture and the Mind Project.

My mother Sonia passed away after the completion of the first draft. This book is dedicated to her memory.

MS

August 2007

Credits

p. 16 "Wildlife Watch" from *The Guardian,* 20 September 2000. Reproduced by permission.

p. 26 Photograph of children using Nicaraguan Sign Language courtesy of A. Senghas.

p. 29 "Sally-Anne" illustration reproduced with the kind permission of the artist, Axel Scheffler

p. 30 "Fishing" task illustration reproduced from M. Siegal & R. Varley (2002). Neural systems underlying theory of mind. *Nature Reviews Neuroscience, 3,* 463–471.

pgs. 32–33 Illustrations of puppet and observer in infant ToM tasks from V. Southgate, A. Senju, and G. Csibra (2007). Action attribution through anticipation of false beliefs by two-year-olds. *Psychological Science,7,* 587–592, copyright Wiley-Blackwell 2007. Reproduced by permission.

p. 36 Illustration of irony detection story from A. T. Wang, S. S. Lee, M. Sigman, and M. Dapretto (2006). Developmental changes in the neural basis of interpreting communicative intent. *Social, Cognitive, and Affective Neuroscience, 1,* 107–121, copyright Oxford University Press 2006.

p. 50 Child's drawing of the earth courtesy of G. Nobes.

p. 52 This illustration was published in S. Vosniadou and W. F. Brewer (1992). Mental models of the earth: A study of conceptual change in childhood. *Cognitive Psychology, 24,* 535–585, copyright Elsevier 1992.

p. 53 This illustration was published in A. Samarapungavan, S. Vosniadou, and W. F. Brewer (1996). Mental models of the earth, sun and moon: Indian children's cosmologies. *Cognitive Development, 11,* 491–521, copyright Elsevier 1996.

p. 68 Illustrations of possible earth models from G. Nobes, A. E. Martin, and G. Panagiotaki (2005). The development of scientific knowledge of the earth. *British Journal of Developmental Psychology. 23,* 47–64. Copyright British Psychological Society. Reprinted by permission.

p. 69 Illustrations of adult models of the earth courtesy of G. Panagiotaki.

p. 75 Photograph courtesy of G. Taylor

p. 80 *Fracastoro, Girolamo.* [Photograph]. Retrieved August 2, 2007, from Encyclopedia Britannica Online: http://www.britannica.com/eb/art-10774

p. 82 Illustration from K. Inagaki and G. Hatano (2002). *Young children's thinking about the biological world.* New York: Psychology Press, p. 91. Reproduced by permission from Routledge /Taylor & Francis Group, copyright 2002.

p. 85 Adult drawings of germs reproduced by kind permission of C. J. Nemeroff.

p. 86 Germ illustration reproduced from M. Siegal and C. C. Peterson (eds.) (1999). *Children's understanding of biology and health.* New York: Cambridge University Press. Artist, Sophia Rose.

p. 91 Illustration of mother sipping a drink courtesy of A. Hejmadi.

p. 94 Illustration of germ transmission from V. Curtis, S. Cairncross, and R. Yonli, R. (2000). Domestic hygiene and diarrhoea – pinpointing the problem. *Tropical Medicine and International Health, 5,* 22–32. Wiley-Blackwell Publishers. Reproduced by permission.

p. 124 Illustration of "infant arithmetic" reprinted by permission from Macmillian Publishers Ltd: *Nature, 358,* 749–750, copyright 1992.

p. 125 Material used to examine monkeys' numerical understanding from E.M. Brannon and H. S. Terrace (1998). Ordering of the numerosities 1–9 by monkeys. *Science, 282,* 746–749. Reprinted by permission from AAAS.

p. 126 Solutions to bracket equation problems from R. Varley, N. Klessinger, C.A.J. Romanowski, and M. Siegal (2005). Agrammatic but numerate. *Proceedings of the National Academy of Sciences, 102,* 3519–3524. Copyright by The National Academy of Sciences of the United States of America, all rights reserved.

p. 128 Illustration of a possible context for answers on number conservation problems reprinted by permission from Taylor & Francis from M. Siegal, (1997). *Knowing children: Experiments in conversation and cognition, Second edition.* Hove, UK: Psychology Press, p. 26.

p. 135 This quotation was published in C. L. Smith, G. E. A. Solomon, and S. Carey (2005). Never getting to zero: Elementary school students' understanding of the infinite divisibility of number and matter. *Cognitive Psychology, 51,* 101–140, copyright Elsevier 2005.

p. 147 This illustration was published in L. Mottron, L. and S. Belleville (1993). A study of perceptual analysis in a high-level autistic subject with exceptional graphic abilities. *Brain and Cognition, 23,* 279–309, copyright Elsevier 1993.

p. 157 Illustration of brain activation in response to voices adapted by permission from Macmillian publishers: *Nature Neuroscience, 7,* 801–802, copyright 1992.

p. 158 Reproduced with the kind permission of A. J. Barker

p. 163 Courtesy of the MRC Institute of Hearing Research, Nottingham. Reproduced by permission.

p. 171ff. Parts of Chapter 8 were adapted from M. Siegal and L. Surian (2004). Conceptual development and conversational understanding. *Trends in Cognitive Sciences, 8,* 534–538.

p. 181 Illustration of frogs and napkins in a garden path sentence task reproduced with the kind permission of L. Meroni.

Chapter 1

Kids, appearance, and reality

One has all the goodness and the other all the appearance of it.
Jane Austen, *Pride and Prejudice*

Among all animal species, humans have unique intelligence. Yet humans are not alone in demonstrating what they know. Dogs, for example, can respond to many names for things. In fact, there are reports that one border collie named Rico can respond to dozens and dozens of terms. Rico can retrieve toys and balls upon request. He can even use an unfamiliar name that he never heard before to retrieve a new object in contrast to other objects that have been named before. Dogs like Rico also enjoy play and tickling.' This certainly the case of Shannie, part border collie, who is often in our neighborhood, and is pictured below at rest and at play.

Human children share with dogs the ability to associate names with objects. They enjoy play and tickling. But from a very early age, kids display very much more. They engage in conversations with others as speakers and listeners. They can experiment with things that they encounter in their environment in a variety of different ways. They can make spontaneous generalizations, such as "Birds fly."[3] They can also understand that the appearance of an object does not necessarily correspond to its real invisible properties. They are often concerned to find out why the world works as it does. In fact, children's interest in the organization and functioning of the human brain and body, the genetic basis of life, the workings of the earth, sun, and the rest of the cosmos, and the nature of time and space are so fundamental to human welfare that we would scarcely question its importance. To know the cause of things is not simply the obsession of professional scientists but a concern for everyone. Yet how do we as adults ever get to such an understanding?[3] What is there in the development of children's marvelous minds that allows them to have insight that culminates in such sophisticated reasoning – reasoning that animals such as dogs lack?

Developmental psychologists who study changes with age in kids' thinking and behavior are divided on this pivotal question. For example, there are those who are inclined toward the position that was proposed by the Swiss researcher Jean Piaget (1896–1980). Over a career lasting more than 60 years, Piaget contended that children initially are not able to identify cause-and-effect relations.[4] He used the term "preconceptual" to describe their early understanding. According to his analysis, children under the age of about 7 years focus "egocentrically" or "one-sidedly" on a single aspect of their sensory world. They often rely on appearance rather than underlying reality in judging and reasoning about the numbers of objects in a row and the amount of volume of liquid in a glass. Critically, for young children, the number of objects is based on how they appear. Take two rows of candies set out with each candy in a row in "one-to-one correspondence" with a candy in the other row:

When asked, even 3-year-olds normally report that there are there are the same number of candies in each row. If one of the two rows is lengthened and they are asked again whether the number in each row is the same or whether one row has more, children under 7 years often maintain that the number of candies is now larger in the longer row:

According to the Piagetian view, they focus one-sidedly on increased row length and ignore the decreased density. Similarly, for young children, pouring juice from a short, thick glass to a tall, thin one increases the amount there is to drink; they focus one-sidedly on the tallness of the glass and ignore its smaller width. This appearance-led one-sided perspective on the world is so widespread that, according to a Piagetian analysis, children rely on appearance rather than underlying reality in their characterization of the shape and position of the earth, sun, and stars and in their categorization of substances as edible irrespective of their contact with invisible impure substances.

Without question, Piaget devised ingenious methods for studying children. His ideas about children's understanding have exerted a dominant influence over developmental psychology in the twentieth century – an influence that persists to this day in courses and textbooks on child development and education. Some have even gone so far to claim that "assessing the impact of Piaget on developmental psychology is like assessing the impact of Shakespeare on English literature, or Aristotle in Philosophy – impossible." However, this is a misleading analogy. Shakespeare and Aristotle are towering figures in the fields of literature and philosophy but that does not dissuade scholars from rightly analyzing their impact on intellectual discourse. Indeed, Piaget's theory has not gone unchallenged.

First, there are those who believe that young children are not simply swayed by appearances but that they possess coherent, though naive, theories of the world. According to this account, children have are "conceptually impoverished" or have a "conceptual deficit." They develop by discarding their early naive theories in favor of more sophisticated ones that they encounter later. In the process, they go through a form of "conceptual change" in their knowledge of the world.[5]

This process is viewed as very much akin to that which takes place in the beliefs of adult scientists once the dominant paradigm – the accepted way of going about the process of carrying out science – has been overthrown by the presence of anomalous evidence that grows ever impossible to ignore, creating what amounts to a scientific revolution. Conceptual change can be painful in that children, like scientists, tend to cling to previous contradictions and presuppositions rather than admit to a new view.

Second, there are those who may be seen as nativists – maintaining that children do have an innate core or skeletal notion of scientific ideas involving cause-and-effect relations – an adaptive specialization that involves a core preparedness for acquiring knowledge.[6] Development in children's understanding is built upon this core. This approach can be traced all the way back to Plato's dialog between Socrates and Meno's slave boy, illustrating that our learning can involve recollecting what we already know. One nice modern way of putting it, as observed by David and Ann Premack in their enlightening book *Original Intelligence,* is that this process is guided by modules, or innate devices, that channel children's learning in domains that are fundamental to human knowledge. Children's modular intuitions develop as they grow older and are tailored to solving specific problems, protecting them from holding false hypotheses about the nature of objects in the physical world and the beliefs of others in the mental world. In this sense, development based on modular learning can take the form of "enrichment" in children's knowledge rather than a radical conceptual change that breaks with previous naive theoretical convictions that are incompatible or incommensurable with a mature understanding.

The nature of conceptual change varies across specific areas. A radical or "nonconservative" change may be likely to take place in some areas. For example, in the key area of numerical reasoning, children's thinking may undergo a nonconservative conceptual change when coming to grips with fractions.[7] They need to relinquish their theory that the domain of numbers is restricted to the integers used for counting in order to accommodate fractions as infinite sets of numbers that fill in the gaps between the integers. Nevertheless, there are many varieties of conceptual change in other areas of knowledge that may simply take the form of theory revision or differentiation through adding or deleting instances of a key concept. It may also take the form of a "local" incompatibility or incommensurability – one that requires a section of previous theorizing in a particular area of knowledge to be overthrown, rather than a complete reconceptualization.

In this book, based on evidence from studies carried out in America, Australia, Brazil, Britain, Canada, Ecuador, France, Germany, India, Iran, Italy, Japan and many other countries, I aim to show that children's understanding in certain key areas of knowledge can be seen in terms of these two options to Piaget – particularly the second one. At least from the time that they can speak, and mostly likely even as babies without language, children have a core or skeletal notion of the nature of the world. Changes in their understanding can often be seen in terms of a progressive enrichment in their knowledge about the world. In certain key areas, children's early naive understanding may not undergo a radical conceptual change because (1) their knowledge is not as naive as some psychologists and educators have assumed or because (2) children do not initially have a prior model or theory in certain specific areas of knowledge – no entrenched presuppositions – in the first place. In this connection, the depth of children's potential for understanding is greater than parents, teachers, and psychologists have often estimated.

But how can this be? Is this in itself a naive view? Don't kids often offer silly, uninformed answers about the world around them? Aren't they prone to judge on the basis of superficial appearances rather than underlying reality? Aren't they apt to judge the shape of the earth by its flatness, food by its outward color or sweet appearance, the characteristics of plants and animals by physical resemblance, and life and death as controlled by some mysterious inner force, or a force that comes from the supernatural? How can young children understand the world if they can't even count beyond 3, 5, or 10!

Of course, children often say and do things that are consistent with the "classical" analysis provided by Piaget that is in tune with the intuitions of many parents and teachers. However, as is starting to be acknowledged in many child development and education courses, we know now that this simple estimate of what children know is quite wrong and that many of the interview questioning techniques that have been used to determine children's knowledge do not come anywhere close to reliably determining what they know. As I will aim to show in this book, to a considerable extent, children's apparent failure on tests of their knowledge in various areas reflects limitations in their ability to interpret questions. In the case of young children aged 3–7 years who, unlike babies, can talk, these limitations in many – but not all instances – may be seen in terms of a lack of understanding of the implications of conversations as these are intended by interviewers who are striving to determine the course of children's development. Kids are mystified about the purpose and relevance of interviewers' questions – their answers might not then always reflect ignorance that amounts to a conceptual deficit in a particular domain of knowledge. Instead, children need to come to grips with the conversational environment. Since what children say and do in response to questions may not reflect the depth of their actual or potential knowledge of the world around them, it is the discovery of new methods of how to question children that should be headline grabbing, rather than the range of failing answers on the many tests that have been devised to determine what they know. Children may in fact know more at an early age about reality and the phenomenal world of appearances – displaying a capacity for understanding that is liable to be overlooked.

What do children know about the distinction between reality and the world of appearances?

In one of my favorite Piaget books, *Play, Dreams and Imitation*, there are many examples of how children confuse appearance and reality. In one instance, Piaget reports that his daughter Jacqueline, at 2 years 7 months of age, confuses the identity of her baby sister, Lucienne, in a new bathing suit with a cap: "Jacqueline asked, "What's the baby's name?" Her mother explained that it was a bathing costume, but Jacqueline pointed to Lucienne herself and said, "But what's the name of that?" (referring to Lucienne's face) and repeated the question several times. But as soon as Lucienne had her dress on again, Jacqueline exclaimed very seriously, "It's Lucienne again," as if her sister had changed her identity in changing her clothes." According to Piaget's interpretation of this exchange between Jacqueline and her mother, children do not understand that persons and objects retain their real underlying identity despite changes in appearance.

Piaget originally reported this type of observation in 1951, and it has been echoed since in many studies outside his native Switzerland. For example, in one investigation of children's ability to distinguish appearance from reality, American 3-year-olds were reported to believe that a cat could be easily disguised to turn into a dog. In this work, children aged 3–6 years were shown a cat named Maynard whom they were allowed to pet.[8] When asked, all the children knew that Maynard was indeed a cat. Then the children saw the experimenter put a mask over Maynard's head – a mask of a fierce-looking dog. The experimenter remarked, "Look, it has a face like a dog. What is this animal now?" It seemed that in contrast to the 6-year-olds, many of the 3-year-olds now believed that Maynard had become a dog. They would no longer pet him and did not recognize that under his skin he had a cat's bones and a cat's stomach.

If children think that changes in appearance not only mask but also actually change the identity of an animal, might they also think that even their own identity can be changed through changing their appearance? Might they, for example, think boys can become girls and girls can become boys simply by dressing as the opposite sex?

Inspired by Piaget, there have been numerous studies that have attempted to interview children along just these lines to determine their understanding of the permanence of gender. In one such interview, children aged 3–5 years were asked a series of 14 questions and "counterquestions" to determine whether they would understand that their gender remains constant over time and that they will remain boys or girls despite wearing the clothes or playing the games of the opposite sex.[9] There were nine questions on their knowledge of gender identity – for example, "Are you a girl or boy?" – two on gender stability – for example, "When you were a little baby were you a boy or a girl? When you grow up will you be a mummy or daddy?" – and three questions on gender consistency – for example, "If you wore (opposite sex of subject) clothes would you be a boy or a girl? If you played (opposite sex of the subject) games, would you be a girl or a boy?." The counterquestions were designed to probe the certainty of the children's original responses (such as, "If you played (opposite sex of subject) games, would you be a (opposite sex of subject's first response)?"). Children seem to find the identity questions (given first) easier than the stability questions (given second). The consistency questions (given last) are most difficult and are often answered incorrectly by 3-year-olds and even by some children as old as 5 years.

Considerable theoretical significance has been attached to these responses.[10] It has been maintained that, since young children center on the perceptual appearances rather than the invariant features of a transformation, they base their judgments of gender on changes in games and clothes. Once children have achieved a stable concept of gender, they know that, for example, a boy will remain a boy even if he wears girls' clothing or plays girls' games. In efforts to live up to a self-definition as a boy or girl, children seek out sex-appropriate activities.

Historically, it has long been recognized that children answer questions put to them in this way. But why? Do their answers truly reflect the absence of a conceptual understanding or do these answers reflect problems in children's understanding of the purpose and relevance of questions designed to determine what they know? The pace of progress in research on child development and education has not been particularly rapid in the past 30 years or so, but I do believe that very significant progress has now been made.

Preconceptual or truly conceptual: studies of the child's conversational skills and the appearance–reality distinction

It was John Flavell at Stanford University in California, author of the powerful book *The Developmental Psychology of Jean Piaget*, who independently assessed the ability of 3- and 4-year-olds to understand the distinction between appearance and reality. In a series of intriguing articles from 1983 through to 1999, Flavell and his colleagues arrived at the conclusion that, by the age of 4 years, children have substantial knowledge of the appearance–reality distinction, although below this age they display the confusions originally described by Piaget.[11]

Flavell's team devised tests to determine whether children can distinguish between the true nature of a substance and its appearance under, for example, colored filters or masks and costumes. For example, in one task, a female interviewer showed children milk in a glass with a red filter wrapped around it. She asked the children, "What color is the milk really and truly? Is it really and truly red or really and truly white? Now here is the second question. When you look at the milk with your eyes right now, does it look white or does it look red?" Less than half of 3-year-olds tested in this way correctly identified the milk to *look red* but to *be white* really and truly. By contrast, most 4-year-olds gave correct answers.

In another of Flavell's studies, 3-year-olds saw an adult named Ellie put on a disguise as a bear. An interviewer asked them, "When you look at her with your eyes right now, does she look like Ellie or does she look like a bear? Here is a different question. Who is over there really and truly? Is she really and truly Ellie, or is she really and truly a bear?" The numbers of right answers given by the 3-year-olds were no better than what would be expected by chance. They made two types of errors in about equal proportions. Children would either say that Ellie both looked like and truly was a bear – called by Flavell "phenomenism" errors – or that she looked like and truly was Ellie – called "realism" errors. The 4-year-olds, unlike the 3-year-olds, largely avoided either type of error. They mostly gave appearance responses to "looks like" questions about appearance and reality responses to "really and truly" questions about reality.

The answers of the 4-year-olds provide far more support for children's understanding than Piaget would allow in kids so young, but when it comes to 3-year-olds, Flavell and his colleagues interpret their findings squarely to support Piaget's claim that young children often believe "if a situation is what it is, it is so because it cannot be otherwise." They proceed to speculate that, owing to limitations in their development, children cannot see that their parents can still love them even when they themselves feel unloved, or that children cannot help but be frightened by masks or shadows in their bedroom, even though they have been told that these are not dangerous.

However, familiarity with the naive strategies that very young children use to interpret the meaning and purpose of an adult's questions suggests the possibility that 3-year-olds are just not getting the point of the exercise. Possibly their realism errors reflect their evaluation of the deception depicted in the situation, for example, their belief that Ellie was not disguised well as a bear. Alternatively, their phenomenism errors may reflect their playful evaluation that Ellie was disguised so well as a bear that Ellie not only looked like a bear but also had really and truly become a bear. If so, the answer that Ellie both looks like and really is Ellie is not a genuine realism error and the answer that Ellie both looks like and really is a bear is not a genuine phenomenism error. Instead of a conceptual failure to grasp the distinction between appearance and reality, their answers may instead simply reflect a failure to share the implication that the interviewer's questions had a scientific purpose: to determine what children know about the distinction between appearance and reality.

Certainly, children's proficiency at fantasy and imagination demonstrates that they can conceive of world in a manner other than it is. If children under 7 years are given "contrary fact problems" in which they are told, "All cats bark. Rex is a cat" and then asked, "Does Rex bark?" most will reply "Of course not!" The reply is much the same if told, "All fishes live in trees. Tot is a fish" and asked "Does Tot live in water?" However, if shown a play world in which cats bark and fish live in trees, most children – even many 2-year-olds – will answer correctly.[12]

Consistent with these observations, it has been shown in relation to Flavell's pioneering work that even children as young as 2 years can describe the appearance and display the real function of objects in the context of a show-and-tell game.[13] Moreover, 3-year-olds display an understanding of the appearance–reality distinction when asked to respond in the course of natural conversation to an interviewer's request. In these studies, children are given deceptive objects such as a blue birthday candle covered by a blue crayon wrapper so that it looked like a crayon though in reality it was a candle and a gray, irregular piece of sponge that looked like a rock. They are also provided with nondeceptive objects: a red crayon, a white birthday candle, a granite rock, and a yellow sponge. At a nearly perfect success rate, children can pick out the correct object when the experimenter asked questions about appearance ("I want you to take a picture of Teddy with something that looks like a crayon. Can you help me?") and reality ("I want a sponge to clean up some spilled water. Can you help me?"). In fact, 2-year-olds show considerable flexibly in naming objects and even infants aged 12–18 months often flexibly categorize objects by varying their answers to an interviewer's requests.[14] By contrast, 3-year-olds often respond incorrectly when questioned using Flavell's procedure. In this instance, one possibility is that children may have interpreted the purpose and relevance of appearance–reality questioning as a request to evaluate the effectiveness of a deception rather than as a request to determine whether they can distinguish between appearance and reality.

In any event, what children tell their interviewers and friends is at odds with Piaget's theory. It has been shown that children as young as 4 years and, in some instances, as young as two do have knowledge of the distinction between appearance and reality. This is of course not to make the ludicrous claim that children never conflate appearance with reality. As any parent will testify, children do this every day when they pretend in play. In their enthusiasm, children can often engage in fantasy that overtakes their knowledge of the appearance–reality distinction. I am driven now to own up to an incident from my parenting days. I was looking after my older daughter Susanna when she was 3-year-old (she is now a 27-year-old lawyer). Susanna liked to play with her new safety scissors. Her favorite doll Tilly had a long fringe along her forehead and Susanna decided that Tilly needed a haircut, although I have no conclusive proof whether Susanna held the assumption that Tilly's hair would grow back one day. Then having cut Tilly's hair, Susanna decided to cut the fringe of the little boy who was her playmate. Having taken my eyes off Susanna and her friend for just 10 minutes, I came back into the room to find locks of Tilly's hair intertwined on the floor with that of the boy. Susanna calmly told her horrified father, "I cutted Tilly's hair and cutted off the boy's hair too," leaving me struggling with an explanation to the boy's parents when they came to pick him up.

So on the one hand, in their everyday actions, very young children do clearly distinguish between appearance and reality. On the other hand, we have incidents like the Tilly haircut episode, together with systematic experiments on children's knowledge of the appearance–reality distinction, that have led many to conclude that 3-year-olds do after all have a fundamental conceptual deficit in distinguishing appearance and reality. What are the reasons for this discrepancy? Why do 3-year-olds who are adept at using appearance–reality knowledge in their everyday actions have so much difficulty on the tasks such as devised by Flavell and his colleagues? Is it a matter of memory – that children simply cannot keep in mind both the appearance and reality of objects at the same time? Is it that the appearance of an object is so vivid that children cannot help but let it intrude on their reasoning about its real qualities? Or is it, as I have suggested, the conversational understanding of young children that leads them to answer in a way that suggests they have little or not grasp of the distinction between appearance and reality.

The critical findings here have been reported in 2003 and 2006 by Gideon Deák at the University of California, San Diego.[15] In one experiment, Deák and his research team gave 3-year-olds appearance–reality tasks along the lines of those used by Flavell. For example, they presented children with a box that looked like a rock and asked, "What does this look like to you? [That's right/Actually] it looks like a rock. But really and truly it's not a rock … it is a hiding place. See? You can open it and put pennies inside. What is it really and truly? [That's right/Actually] it is a hiding place, but it looks like a rock."

The test questions were, "What is this really and truly? Is it really and truly a rock or really and truly a box? When you look at this right now, does it look like a box or does it look like a rock?"

As in Flavell's studies, children gave many realism and phenomenism answers to such questions in claiming that the box that looked like a rock was in fact a box in both appearance and reality or a rock in both appearance and reality. However, Deák and his colleagues reasoned that the nature of the questioning itself is quite obscure. Therefore the children were given a task involving an "overlap" between the correctness of appearance and reality questions to see whether children are simply repeating their answer (rock–rock or box–box) because they don't realize that test questions merit truly different answers. For example, they were shown a bear holding a key and asked test questions not just about appearance and reality but instead about the relation between objects, "What does this look like? Does it look like a key or does it look like a bear? What does it have? Does it have a key or does it have a bear?" The questions then were about the simultaneous presence of two items rather than about the appearance and reality of one item. For the 3-year-olds tested, there was a strong relation between answers on the appearance–reality tasks and the overlapping control tasks. Children who perseverated in their answers, giving either realism or phenomenism responses on one type of task, often did so on the other, especially if they were children who had yet to acquire an advanced vocabulary.

Then in a follow-up study, Deák and his team looked systematically at a host of other factors that may underlie children's errors on appearance–reality tasks, including memory and their ability to suppress or "inhibit" intrusive labels for objects. They found that a poor performance on tests of memory or inhibition had no relation with such errors. Instead, these were associated with children's specific pragmatic knowledge about how to respond to questions. Children who had difficulties on appearance–reality tasks also perseverated on pairs of questions that had nothing to do with appearance and reality. For example, children were just shown a drawing of a tree and flower and asked two questions, "Is the one that grows tall the tree or the flower?" and "Or is the one that smells good the tree or the flower?" Despite the strong conversational implication that there should be different answers to such questions, some 3-year-olds perseverated and answered both questions with "tree" or "flower" and went on to make appearance–reality errors. Such children also were likely to indicate that questions that have ambiguous or indeterminate answers have instead one single answer. For example, they say that they know the color of a Lego piece that will be retrieved from a box of different-colored Legos.

These results suggest that 3-year-old kids' lack of success on appearance–reality tasks does reflect a lack of experience with the point of the conversation initiated by the interviewer. If asked two questions about appearance and reality that involve deciding between choices of appearance and reality, they may be unclear that the questions are really new and different and that each of the two questions requires a newly reasoned answer – one that does not depend on the other. Moreover, they may simply not consider that a question may have more than one answer. If this is the case, then children may stick with their first answer until provided with feedback or until asked a new question altogether.

Moreover, the quality of this feedback is crucial. Consider the instance of questions about gender constancy. In response to the question, "Are you a girl or boy?" even a 3-year-old boy will say "boy." In response to the question, "When you were a little baby were you a boy or a girl? When you grow up will you be a mummy or daddy?" a boy will say that he was a boy as a baby and will grow up to be daddy. Finally, the boy will be asked the questions, "If you wore girls" clothes, would you be a boy or a girl? If you played girls' games, would you be a girl or a boy?" By this time, the boy may be wondering what the purpose of all this is. He may see these questions as silly and switch his answer to give a silly or cute answer to try to please the questioner. Indeed testing young children for their understanding using what would seem to be the simplest of tests is not at all straightforward and can lead to unanticipated answers. Although by the age of three and possibly earlier, children are skilled at distinguishing reality from pretending, they may not readily identify the purpose and relevance of pretense in answering questions.[16]

For example, efforts have been made to use 3-year-olds' knowledge of the distinction between appearance and reality to test their understanding of what it means to lie in contrast to making a mistake. On one occasion when I was "piloting" the questions we would ask children in a study, one of my students interviewed 3-year-old Sophie. She gave Sophie a slice of moldy bread and two teddy bears, one bear who was an "onlooker" and so could witness a deception in contrast to the other bear who had his back turned. To determine Sophie's attitude to the bread, the interviewer said, "Here's a slice of moldy bread. Is it okay or not okay to eat? Sophie duly replied, "Not okay."

Then the interviewer continued, "Let's put some breakfast spread over the mold so we can't see it." She then said to Sophie, "This bear didn't see the mold on the bread. He told a friend (at this point, he produced a stuffed animal toy) that it was okay to eat. Was that a mistake or a lie? This bear did see the mould on the bread. He told a friend that it was okay to eat. Was that a lie or a mistake?" Instead of answering the question as intended, Sophie told the interviewer, "Give them back. Those are my bears!"

In fact, the majority of 3-year-olds when given this type of food scenario do accurately distinguish between a lie and a mistake.[17] At the same time, there is considerable variability among the many kids like Sophie in their ability to "read" questions and to understand the conversational context in which they are asked. All children when they begin talking may start out to some extent with a naive theory of conversation. This theory does not recognize the possibility that a speaker may intentionally portray deceptions in order to test what children know. It is also the case that young children are not especially practiced in shifting the focus of their attention and coming up with answers that are simply the opposite of what they are used to saying. They may need more time than do older children and adults to come up with the opposite answer. Once they become experienced in participating in conversation that may make use of deception as well as humor, sarcasm, and irony, they may come to relinquish this theory to take into account that alternative interpretation of a speaker's message. Children who are especially experienced in language – bilingual or even trilingual children – are ones who may be particularly advanced in shifting their attention in their answers to questions (including ones about the appearance and reality of objects in the world), and those children who have late access to language such as late-signing deaf children may be disadvantaged. In either case, this advancement should at least in part occur through a development in conversational understanding that enables children to interpret questions as intended, to express what they know, and to gain knowledge about the world.

To distinguish between appearance and reality is often a sober challenge for adults – let alone children and animals. For example, adults in many cultures have particular difficulty in dealing with death. When beloved persons or animals have died, it is hard to accept that they not only look dead but that they really are dead and will never again be alive. The fact of death awakens us to the reality of own mortality, which all too often overlooked or unspoken in the cultures of Western industrial countries. We may go so far as to impute the ability to reflect on mortality to our pet animals as well. An unusual example is provided by a newsclipping from the 2000 Sydney Olympic Games:

Wildlife watch

'Those Olympic athletes just love their funny Australian animals. American shooter Cindy Gentry bought a kangaroo pelt last year, but "when I unrolled it out of the suitcase," says Gentry, "my little labrador, who's about the same color, looked at me like, 'oh gosh, am I next?'"

As death is a process for which we often search for an explanation, the distinction between appearance and reality is commonly blurred. In this sense, we must consider the expected standard for children's understanding of the distinction between appearance and reality in relation to that which is achieved by adults.

What develops in children's understanding: a working model

So there is nothing that we know about children up to now that rules out an early incipient understanding of the distinction between appearance and the phenomenal world of appearances – a distinction that is so basic to the detection of cause and effect relations. On the contrary, children's understanding of this distinction is part of their early core knowledge.

It is time now to reassert and to build upon the working model of development that I examined in an earlier book: that young children have a substantial core *implicit* knowledge or truly conceptual competence.[18] In certain key areas, this knowledge is indeed guided by modules that are tailored to solving specific problems, protecting them from holding false hypotheses about the nature of objects in the physical world and the beliefs of others in the mental world. Alternatively, there are some areas in which, rather than possessing an initial naive theory of the world, children have no entrenched presumptions or prior model or theory. Their knowledge is not naive; it is simply nonexistent or fragmented and thus it is open to instruction from parents, teachers, and the media. However, in either case, children's capacity for understanding may not be revealed in conversations with investigators because the measures designed to test what children know require language interpretation skills that are beyond their grasp or experience, or because children are not familiar with the settings of questions they are asked to answer. On many tests of what they can and do know, children may lack plans or procedures to translate what they know into an explicit correct response that corresponds at least to their implicit, skeletal knowledge. Even if children do have these procedures, they need to interpret and share the meaning and purpose of questions in the way intended by an interviewer.

If children's development is not necessarily restricted by conceptual limitations or a one-sidedness of their understanding in the manner proposed by Piaget and they do have knowledge of the distinction between appearance and reality, there is the challenge of discovering what children know. An alternative account is needed for young children's lack of success in their responses to interviewers' questions on tests of their understanding. The model proposed here is that children frequently can succeed if these tests are formulated in a "child-friendly" language within contexts that provide the experience and support to facilitate their correct answers.

In the pages that follow, I will describe recent and new evidence for a core understanding in various areas of knowledge and the nature of the conceptual change that their understanding might undergo in the process of their development. This evidence demonstrates that even very young children really and truly do have marvelous minds.

Chapter 2 will proceed to examine the extent to which children understand how the minds of others work. In particular, do children at the age of 3 or 4 years living in countries as diverse as Britain and Iran display a "theory of mind" in understanding how the actions of other children can be predicted on the basis of beliefs and emotions that may be different than their own? Can this theory be expressed in children's reasoning independently of abilities in language?

Chapter 3 concerns children's knowledge of the first exact science: astronomy. It will address the questions: Do children begin by believing that the shape of the earth is flat and that the sun revolves around the earth? Or are they capable of understanding that the earth is a round sphere that revolves around the sun? This chapter will examine studies of children's understanding of astronomy and geography carried out in many different countries including America, Australia, Britain, and Sweden.

Biology is a fundamental area of human knowledge. It involves an understanding of the determinants of our appearance and behavior, biological processes such as breathing and sleeping, as well the knowledge that substances that may look good to eat may not be so in reality. Questions to be explored in Chapter 4 will include: Do children understand that physical attributes such as eye color have a biological origin whereas food preferences, for example, are culturally determined? Can they understand the microscopic basis of contamination and the transmission of illness? Can they identify processes of food purification? Answers come from children in America, India, and elsewhere.

Life and death are matters that concern children at a very young age. The death of a loved one or a pet can be very disturbing. At some point children inevitably need to confront the issue of the prerequisites for life and the causes of death. Chapter 5 will thus address the question of to what extent young children in different countries such as America, Ecuador, and Germany understand the creation of life and the permanence of death.

To characterize and act upon the world of objects, children in every culture count. Counting is as natural as walking and talking – an adaptive specialization for numerical problem solving. But are children's number abilities tied to understanding the meaning of the words that we use for counting? Is children's early theory of number limited to the discrete whole numbers that are used for counting or might they be prompted to accommodate their theory to take into account numerical relations – fractions, decimals, and proportions – that fill in the gap between integers? What about children in aboriginal cultures such as those found in Brazil and Australia who acquire a language with few words for counting. Are people in such cultures limited in their mathematical reasoning? Chapter 6 will be devoted to a consideration of these issues.

A frequent and justified refrain is that not all kids are the same. Some in fact are very different. In Chapter 7, the capacity for knowledge will be examined in children with autism.

The eighth and final chapter will examine universals in early human development. In doing so, it will draw together work on precocious knowledge found in studies of children in different cultures, and focus on ways of questioning children to discover what they know. It will stress the impact of early access to language and conversation on children's knowledge in areas as varied as psychology and theory of mind, cosmology, biology, health and hygiene, the life and death process, and number and arithmetic, and it will examine different interpretations for the quality and rate of learning in terms of methods of questioning children.

Clearly a terrorist!

It is easy to find anecdotal evidence to show that adults, of varying degrees of sobriety, also have problems distinguishing between appearance and reality under some of the normal conditions of everyday living. For example, there is the joke set in Ireland – although it could occur any place – where there are two men sitting at a bar[19]. One asks where the other comes from. "Cork," he says. "Well, I never! I'm from Cork myself. What school were you at?" "St Columba's." Would you believe it? So was I! When did you leave?" "1971 ...." And so on. Another customer arrives and asks the barman what is going on. He replies, "Nothing special. The O'Reilly twins are drunk again."

Clearly a terrorist! *(cont.)*

I also have been involved in an appearance–reality mix up with an Irish connection. Writing my thesis required me to go around different schools in Oxford in order to ask children questions about whether they would like to rely on adults or other children for advice about solving certain problems. It turned out that the answers had to do with the perceived intellectual and moral virtues of the proposed advisors rather than status as an adult or child.

An unkind person suggested I looked like the Halloween man dressed in an orange raincoat and a black scarf. I might indeed have appeared strange to some as I walked into a pub that I will call The Fox (not its real name) exhausted from a day's cycling and testing. I parked my bicycle outside and walked in accompanied with my bag of testing materials. I asked for half a cider, not noticing the perturbed look of the lady behind the bar. The pub itself seemed strange as a gathering point for sailors – most unusual, as Oxford is about as far away from the sea as you can get in England.

About 10 minutes later, two policemen came in and asked me to come out with them. I asked them if I could leave my things in the pub. Surprisingly, they asked me to bring them out with me. Then they frisked me by their squad car and opened up my bag. All they saw was cartoon pictures of kids and adults.

They shook their heads and said sorry. Then I went back in the pub. Everyone inside was laughing and I was offered a free whole pint of cider. They had thought I was an Irish terrorist! My purpose

Clearly a terrorist! *(cont.)*

was to blow up the pub full of sailors with the bomb I had hidden in my bag.

But since when does everyone who does not speak with an English accent sound Irish? There may be some affinity between Scottish and Canadian accents (like mine) but Irish – never. Trying to hide my embarrassment, I walked out. I never went back to the Fox again.

Chapter 2

Language, conversation, and theory of mind

The mind is its own place, and in itself / can make a heaven of hell, a hell of heaven.
John Milton, *Paradise Lost*, Book 1, lines 254–5

Closely related to the knowledge of the distinction between appearance and reality is the possession of a "theory of mind" (ToM). This involves the understanding of a basic psychology – how the beliefs, feelings, and intentions of others can differ from one's own and from reality. A ToM leads us to understand the unexpected outcome of actions that are not in accordance with our desires.

From the very first time that they come into contact with language as babies, children are exposed to discussions about beliefs, feelings, and other mental states that are relevant to ToM. Just as is the case for language, ToM reasoning is present universally in all human cultures, because just as virtually everyone talks, or in the case of the deaf, signs, everyone is concerned about what is in the minds of others. We strive to determine whether the knowledge of others faithfully represents, or is a distortion of, the real state of affairs in the world that we sense around us. It is impossible to overemphasize the centrality of ToM in human civilization because ToM is necessary for the appreciation and transmission of culture in the form of novels, theatre, and song, and more generally for the maintenance of family and social life.

Shakespeare himself was no slouch in the ToM department. His theatrical expertise evidently shone through in his personal life. A story often told about Shakespeare concerns a deception about a deception.[1] It involves Richard Burbage, the leading actor in the original performances of many Shakespearean plays, including *Richard III*.

Burbage was so charismatic that a female fan suggested to him that they meet up when her master was out of town. She asked him to arrange a signal when he arrived at her house. Burbage told her that he would tap at the door three times and announce, "It is I, Richard the Third." Unfortunately for Burbage, Shakespeare overheard the arrangements for the deception and was curious enough to find out where the lady lived. Before the appointed time for the secret rendezvous, Shakespeare acted Burbage's part. He used the signal to gain entrance to the lady's house and to benefit from her charms (no wonder since it was he who had written *Romeo and Juliet*). Then Burbage came to her door and repeated the signal. Shakespeare put his head out of the window and told him to go away, as William the Conqueror had reined before Richard III.

We are all not so sophisticated in the exercise of ToM as was Shakespeare. However, as will be seen, the core ToM ability to recognize that others can have beliefs that differ from reality is present in all human cultures. Although this mechanism is linked to engagement in conversations with others, it is independent from the acquisition of language in the form of vocabulary and syntax. In this chapter, we examine parallels between language and ToM reasoning. Then we consider how access to conversations with others supports ToM.

Language

Language is a human attribute acquired spontaneously without formal instruction. Amazingly, brain imaging studies show that newborns learn sounds for speech even while they are sleeping, and that babies' responses to language at 2 months occur in the same left hemisphere brain areas as for adults. At 2 months also, babies prefer speech to nonspeech sounds. In the first few years of human development, virtually all children acquire the grammar of their native language. In fact, the grammar of language is mandatory in that we cannot stop ourselves from acquiring it.[2]

One influential view on language acquisition is that the structure of children's language is triggered only by exposure to a linguistic input that is highly limited and fragmented – an indication of the fundamental innateness of grammar. According to the "poverty of the stimulus" account advocated by the MIT linguist Noam Chomsky and many others, the acquisition of grammar proceeds automatically in a modular fashion, largely independently of nonverbal intelligence. Despite wide variations in their language environment, children in every culture acquire aspects of grammar in a fixed order at about the same time in their development. They make sense of a language input that is compatible not only with the grammar of their own native language but with the grammar of many others. The errors that they do make are highly predictable and often reflect what would be grammatical in another language. Further, it has long been established that children are not corrected for the grammaticality of their language but for whether or not what they say appears to be truthful. That children's grammar unfolds largely in the absence of feedback on whether their grammar is well-formed or not is further testament to its innate, biological foundations. We acquire language in the form of words and rules that allow us to generate an infinite number of sentences that we have never uttered or heard before and to judge these sentences as grammatical. To take an example from Chomsky, all native English speakers would agree that "Colorless green ideas sleep furiously" adheres to English grammatical rules, though they would not be likely to have come across it before.[3]

Evidence from deaf children who are cut off from speech input strengthens this account. About 10 percent of children who are born without hearing have parents who are deaf. These parents typically communicate using a sign language. Profoundly deaf infants born to deaf parents display manual babbling using a reduced set of the phonetic units in American Sign Language much in the way that hearing children babble using the sounds of their native spoken language. So babbling is tied to the abstract structure of language rather than to input from speech.

Communication between the deaf and hearing reveals still more about the nature of language. Hearing babies exposed to the sign language of their deaf parents produce low frequency hand movements inside a tightly restricted space in front of the body. These movements correspond to the signing space in sign languages. Moreover, across cultures, deaf children display similarities in the linguistic structure of their gestural communication despite differences in the spoken language of their hearing parents. The spontaneous gestures of American deaf children resemble those of Chinese deaf children rather than those of their own mothers. These involve language-making skills that do not require a language model to be activated: segmenting sentences into words, setting up a system of contrasts in morphology, and building structures that govern the syntax or grammar of language.[5]

Further support for the emergence of language without a language-making model has come from a recent study of Nicaraguan deaf children exposed to a highly degraded language environment. This investigation has shown that deaf children can act spontaneously and largely independently of an adult model to create a functional scheme of meaningful signs in order to communicate effectively. Ultimately, newer generations of deaf children who have grown up alongside users of the original scheme have been shown to use Nicaraguan Sign Language, a mature sign language that has emerged over the past 25 years.[6]

Moreover, research on deaf children in input-deprived language environments points to an optimal or critical period for language acquisition. Persons who become deaf after having already acquired spoken English during childhood are often more proficient in learning a sign language than those born profoundly deaf into a hearing family who received little linguistic experience as infants, toddlers and preschoolers before exposure to a sign language at school. Furthermore, deaf persons who are exposed early in childhood to a natural sign language are generally able to learn a second language, such as spoken English, better than those who have not been exposed to language until later.[7]

In very rare cases when children are not exposed to any language whatsoever, they do appear irreparably impaired in their later language learning. Two cases in particular, one that is 200 years old and the other only 20, demonstrate the potential difficulties of learning language if not exposed to language input during infancy – a period that has often been hypothesized to be a critical period for language development to proceed normally.

First there is the case of Victor, known as the "Wild Boy of Aveyron," that occurred shortly after the French Revolution. Victor was sighted in 1797 in the woods of Aveyron in south central France, captured in 1799, and brought to Paris to be socialized at the Institute for Deaf Mutes. It was estimated then that he was a 12- or 13-year-old. Consistent with the noble aims of the post-revolutionary era that were based on the notion that children's development could be transformed by changing their social environment, a young doctor named Jean-Marc Itard set out to educate Victor. Over a five-year period, Itard made heroic efforts to educate Victor who disappointingly could only recognize a few words and never learned to communicate with others normally.[8]

Then there is the more recent case of Genie, termed a "modern day wild child." Genie spent the greater part of her childhood in extremely deprived conditions without exposure to language. Her days were spent chained to a potty and at night she was tied up in a sleeping bag. A UCLA psycholinguist, Susan Curtiss, carried out an extensive study of Genie's language and nonverbal intelligence and found that Genie clearly did not have normal language.[9] In particular, she did not produce WH questions in the manner of normal children. There were no questions in the form of "Who's that? What's that? Where is she going? Genie could not use the third person pronouns, "he," "she," and "they" and confused "you" and "me." Curtiss concluded,

> Genie fails to acknowledge questions, statements, request, summonses, and so forth, much of the time … She appears to be conversationally incompetent. Verbal interaction with Genie consists mainly of someone's asking Genie a question repeatedly until Genie answers, or of Genie's making a comment and someone else's responding to it in some way.

In neither the case of Victor nor Genie was it possible to study their development during the hypothesized critical period for language during infancy. Brain damage at birth or early autism could have accounted for their language impairment, rather than lack of access to language. Nevertheless, as Itard noted, Victor must have possessed the intelligence to enable his survival in the forest. As Curtiss found, Genie had an exceptional ability to do well on tasks that require spatial intelligence such as drawing and completing patterns in mazes. Given the level of their nonlinguistic abilities, it seems entirely plausible that Victor or Genie would not have shown such severe disproportionate language impairment should either have had early exposure to a normal language environment.

ToM reasoning

Does a poverty of stimulus account extend to the course of ToM reasoning in young children? To answer this question, we turn to the wealth of studies on ToM reasoning shown by children's responses on tasks designed to determine whether they can identify how a person with a false belief can initially be deceived about the location or identity of an object.

One example concerns the "Sally-Anne" task involving unexpected locations for objects. In this task (as illustrated on the page opposite), children are told about Sally, a story character with a false belief about the location of a ball. The character is described as having placed the ball in a box but, when she is away, another story character called Anne moves it into a different location. The test question concerns where Sally – who has not witnessed the deception and therefore has a false belief – will look for her ball.

A second example is the "Smarties" task involving the misleading contents of containers. Here children are shown a Smarties tube (M&M candies in the US) that, when opened, is revealed to contain pencils. The test question concerns what another person – who again has not witnessed the deception and therefore has a false belief – will think is in the tube.

Several forms of misleading contents tasks have been developed with a view toward minimizing the requirement that children need advanced vocabulary and grammar to pass ToM tasks. The "fishing"

this is Sally   this is Anne

Sally puts her ball in the basket

Sally goes away

Anne moves the ball to her box

where will Sally look for her ball?

task is one such example. Here children are provided with pictures and asked to determine which of the four alternatives are correct in indicating a boy's false belief. Consider the illustration on the next page. As shown in the top left panel, a flap depicting reeds conceals the end of the line of the boy's fishing rod. The reality of the situation is shown through removal of the flap revealing the boy has caught a boot (top right panel). The boy's false belief is shown by removal of the flap that this time reveals a fish (bottom left panel). Once children lift and replace the flaps, they are shown a separate picture of the boy (from the original picture, bottom right panel) with a blank thought bubble above his head. Next to this picture are four small pictures. Two of these are distracter items: one shows the content of the boy's belief and the other shows the actual object. To determine whether they can recognize

whether a person can have a belief that differs from reality, children are asked to indicate which of the four pictures shows what the character is thinking and which shows the actual object concealed by the flap.

Most 3-year-olds and many 4-year-olds perform poorly on Sally-Anne, Smarties, or fishing (thought picture) tasks,[10] leading some to claim that young children have a conceptual deficit in their ToM reasoning that requires a nonconservative or radical conceptual change (often termed a "theory-theory" view). Exposure to conversational opportunities that allow insight into mental states appears to place children on an accelerated timetable so that they may solve the tasks 6–12 months earlier. Much work has shown that the more children are exposed to talk about beliefs, emotions, and other mental states, the earlier they succeed on ToM tasks.[11]

In some cultures, children do not have much exposure to conversations about beliefs and other mental states. Yet even so, the large majority of normal 4- to 5-year-olds in all cultures studied so far succeed on ToM tasks.[12] Given the wide variation in conversational experience across cultures, these findings are consistent with a poverty of stimulus analysis: that some minimal early access to mental state knowledge – knowledge that others have beliefs that differ from one's own and from reality – "triggers" ToM reasoning. Just as children are not taught the concepts of noun, verb, and grammatical subject during their spontaneous acquisition of language, they are not taught the concept of belief. Instead, in talking to others, they receive information on the truth or falsity of the correspondence between a person's desires (for example, to find an object) and beliefs (where it is located).

Such types of ToM tasks have their limitations, however. Accurate responses do not only require false belief understanding but also concern language comprehension and the ability to follow the implications of the test questions.[13] For this reason, many efforts have been made to simplify the tasks. Even children aged 3 years can often answer correctly if provided with explicit questioning designed to overcome language and conversational demands that are implicit in the tasks. For example, on Sally-Anne tasks, children need to recognize that the purpose of the questioning is to determine whether they can detect how others' beliefs may be initially false. Therefore they are required to follow the implications of test questions intended by the experimenter that the standard question, "Where will a person (with the false belief) look for the object?" means "Where will the person look first?" Nevertheless, 3-year-olds are inexperienced in conversation with others as they have themselves only recently started to talk. For this reason, they may not recognize these implications even though they may understand the concept of a false belief. Instead, they may assume that the purpose of the questioning is more straightforward: to test whether they can predict the behavior of others in achieving a goal. If so, the question, "Where will Sally look for her marble?" may simply be interpreted as "Where does Sally have to look (or go to look) for her marble in order to find it?"

By the age of 3 years, most children respond correctly on ToM reasoning tasks if these are framed in a way that overcomes the likelihood that children misinterpret the purpose and relevance of the test questions. Studies in the US, Italy, Australia, and Iran have shown that asking children to say where will Sally look first for her marble clarifies that the question refers to Sally's initial false belief about the location and how she will be mistaken at first.[14] On this test question, most (though not all) 3-year-olds answer correctly. These studies challenge the position that ToM reasoning goes through a radical conceptual change between 3 and 5 years. What apparently seems to be evidence for conceptual development in children's answers to "standard" test questions really amounts to growth in children's conversational understanding.

Further evidence that children's performance on standard false belief tasks is likely to underestimate their knowledge comes from research with babies in American, British, and Italian "babylabs." In these studies, infants and toddlers aged from 15 months to 2 years have been shown videos of a person or a cartoon character who has a false belief about the location of object and yet still nonetheless searches for the object in its real location. In such circumstances, children look reliably longer at the unexpected event than they did when the character, as expected, searched in the believed location. On this basis, it may be concluded that even before language is established, infants and toddlers are capable of identifying how the mind mediates behavior in that they pay unusual attention to a scenario that violates this expectation.

For example, in a study carried out in the Birkbeck College babylab in London by Victoria Southgate, Atsushi Senju, and Gergely Csibra, 2-year-olds were shown video clips involving a puppet who concealed a ball in one of two locations in front of a person who wore a visor to conceal her eye gaze. As illustrated on the opposite page, the children were first familiarized to two events in which (A) the puppet places the ball in the left box and (B) then in the right box (as indicated by the white arrows).

After each time the ball was hidden, the doors were illuminated and a person, while smiling, reached through the corresponding window to retrieve the ball. In the test trials, the puppet initially placed the ball in the left box. In the "False Belief 1" condition (C), the puppet then moved the ball to the right box, after which the person turned around and the puppet removed the ball from the scene. In the "False Belief 2" condition (D), the person turned around and then the puppet moved the ball to the right hand box and then removed it from the scene. For both test trial types, after the puppet has removed the ball, the actor turned back to the scene and the doors were illuminated. The 2-year-olds focused their attention at the correct window – in anticipation of where the person with the false belief would look for the ball – rather than the incorrect window or elsewhere. Such children may well have benefited from access to conversation that they receive even in early infancy. Mothers' references to beliefs and other mental states that they direct at 6-month-olds are a good predictor of their children's later success on ToM tasks.

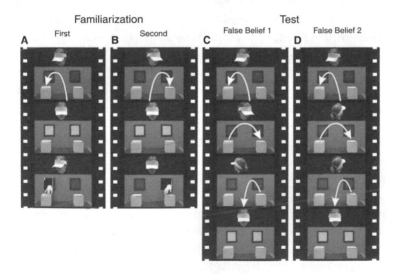

At Rutgers University in New Jersey, the psychologist and cognitive scientist Alan Leslie has proposed that healthy children are innately endowed with a theory of mind mechanism (ToMM) that is part of the core architecture of the human brain, and operates as functionally specialized module for learning about mental states. Leslie and his colleagues propose that the core theory of mind knowledge that beliefs may be true or false is "introduced into the cognitive system by a mechanism, analogously to the way that color concepts are introduced by the mechanisms of color vision." According to this account, "the child does not build theories of what color is nor discover theories of particular colors. Instead the mechanisms of color vision serve to introduce color representations and to lock the representations to appropriate referents in the world." Therefore changes in children's performance on standard Sally-Anne ToM tasks in children between the ages of 3 and 4 years reflect not a developing ToM but a developing selection processor (SP) mechanism dependent on growth in their ability to focus their attention on the range of alternatives from which it is necessary for children to choose the correct answer. At first, children often operate on the basis of a "very simple ToM." This is built on the premise that others' beliefs correspond to reality – these usually do in the real world. To answer correctly, children need to shift their attention to share the purpose and relevance of the ToM task in order to demonstrate their knowledge that others' beliefs can be false and do not correspond with reality.[16]

Development of the SP involves the ability to "inhibit" a very simple ToM in following the conversational implications of dialogues that concern the link between false beliefs and behavior. This process involves executive functioning (EF) abilities that allow us to consider and shift our attention to inhibit the choice that beliefs correspond to reality (as these usually do) and to select instead the alternative that a false belief will lead to an undesired consequence.[17] Such abilities are called upon in the everyday lives of adults across a wide variety of situations, and sometimes are not summoned up as quickly as we would like. A shortfall in our EF can occur when driving a car, for example, when there is a need to use an indicator on the right of a steering wheel in a new car to signal a turn whereas for years in previous cars this was to use an indicator on the left. In such cases, the old reaction to use the left indicator may persist for many weeks or months with the fairly trivial but annoying consequence of momentarily activating the windshield wipers on a sunny day. By contrast, a switch to driving on the left after having driven on the right demands an especially quick EF reaction – one that, if unsuccessful, can be followed by especially harmful consequences. Finding appropriate destinations even when walking also demands EF. There is a story about a scientist who was so deep in thought about an experiment that he walked home to his ex-wife rather than to his present wife simply out of an inability to shift his attention to a new situation!

In the case of EF and ToM in young children, changes in brain development have been proposed as the substrate that accompanies their growing ability to inhibit the choice that beliefs truly corre-spond to reality and to entertain the possibility that beliefs are false. These changes have been hypothesized to include rapid growth in the right frontal cortex as well in other right hemisphere structures such as the right temporal–parietal junction. As damage to the right hemi-sphere in adult patients is often accompanied by inability to follow the implications of a speaker's message in conversation and to answer correctly on Sally-Anne type ToM tasks, it is tempting to entertain the hypothesis that brain maturation in the right hemisphere during early childhood underpins the development of EF and the expression of ToM reasoning and conversational understanding generally that occurs with increasing age.[18]

It has been pointed out that ToM reasoning extends to the under-standing of critical aspects of communication such as irony. To realize that a message is intended to be ironic requires insight into the speaker's belief that, despite what he or she says, the anticipated outcome of an action has not materialized. Recently, in a functional magnetic resonance imaging study, a UCLA team led by A. Ting Wang investigated brain activation in children aged 9–14 years and adults associated with viewing cartoons with either a sincere or an ironic ending.[19] Both children and adults easily judged remarks in these cartoons as sincere or ironic. Children and adults decided in response to the question, "Did Dina (one of the two cartoon charac-ters, on the next page) mean what she said?" that the ending shown in the bottom left was sincere and the one in the bottom right was ironic.

'Bryan and Dina are blowing up balloons.'

'Bryan keeps blowing his till it is huge. Dina says. "Nice going!"

'Bryan keeps blowing his till it pops. Dina says. "Nice going!"

However, while both groups were proficient at detecting irony, there were clear differences in the pattern of brain activation that accompanied their decisions. Overall, in their detection of irony, activation of frontal brain areas (the medial prefrontal cortex and left inferior frontal gyrus) as well as the superior temporal sulcus in the right hemisphere was stronger in children than in than adults. By contrast, activation of certain posterior occipitotemporal regions (the right fusiform gyrus, extrastriate areas and the amygdala) was stronger in adults than in children. In children compared to adults, it may be more necessary to recruit frontal regions to reconcile the discrepancies between the literal and intended meaning of ironic statements. The greater activation of certain posterior regions in adults may reflect the "automatization" of reasoning about the mental states underlying ironic remarks. Although EF was not examined in the Wang study, the results are consistent with the hypothesis that efficient processing of the intended meaning of messages involves maturation of frontal and right hemisphere substrates. A challenge for future research is to specify the role of EF mechanisms in interpreting speakers' messages as these are intended in both typically developing children and those who appear to have a specific impairment in their pragmatic abilities.

Signposts to development: ToM in deaf children

What happens in the unusual case when children are cut-off from conversations about beliefs and other intangible mental states? Would there then be a persistent impairment in ToM reasoning? Research with deaf children has started to address this question.

Approximately 90 percent of congenitally deaf children are raised in hearing families. These children have no easy means of communication with hearing family members and other children, especially about topics like mental states that may have no concrete referent. Given that developing a ToM may be dependent on hearing other people talk about mental states, it would seem that the restricted conversational world of some deaf children might result in difficulties that are specific to understanding the (invisible) thoughts of others. These children typically acquire a sign language mainly outside the family and are "late signers."

By contrast, roughly 10 percent of deaf children are born into families with a deaf communicative partner who uses a sign language, and can be regarded as "native signers." As they have access to language even before school, owing to the presence in their household of at least one fluent user of a sign language, they should resemble typically developing hearing children in their ToM performance. This prediction is in line with the observation that deaf preschoolers with deaf parents converse as readily about nonpresent ideas, objects and events in sign, as do hearing children in speech with hearing parents.[20]

Previous studies have shown that, on key tests of ToM reasoning, deaf children of hearing parents persistently lag several years behind hearing children of hearing parents, even when care has been taken only to include children of normal intelligence and social responsiveness in the deaf samples. However, such studies have been limited to ones in which children have been given language based Sally-Anne or Smarties type tasks and measures of the children's language that have relied only on rough estimates by teachers of the children's proficiency at sign language. Therefore the late-signing deaf may not have scored well on ToM tasks because of language difficulties rather than late access to conversations about others' beliefs and how these may be false.

To investigate this issue, I was fortunate to enlist a deaf native signing PhD student, Tyron Woolfe, together with Stephen Want, who was a postdoctoral fellow fresh from his studies at Oxford University. In a study involving communication with the deaf, we had to improvise to maintain communication among the three of us. Tyron's native language is British Sign Language (BSL) but he can lip-read spoken British English and use spoken British English in a one-on-one situation in conversations with hearing persons. Since Tyron could not easily read lip-read me, a person who does not speak British English, and my sign language is not very well developed, I found myself speaking first in my version of English to Stephen who then, in British English, spoke to Tyron who then could lip-read Stephen and respond to both of us in spoken English. At the end of the three years of Tyron's research, it was no surprise that we had also exchanged about 5000 email messages, even though Tyron was located in an office just across the corridor from mine.[21]

Tyron, Stephen, and I planned out a study of deaf children on false belief tasks using "thought pictures" such as the fishing task that, as seen above, minimizes the need for verbal comprehension. We also directly assessed deaf children's language skills using a test of receptive ability in the syntax and morphology of BSL that was newly developed at the time. We sought to determine whether or not a difference in performance on pictorial tasks would emerge between late and native-signing deaf children, and whether this difference would disappear when the children's abilities in BSL, as well as in nonverbal intelligence, were controlled.

Compared to the late signers, the native signers in our studies excelled in their ToM performance though they were actually younger in age and were no more proficient in sign language as shown on the BSL. So the possibility that native signers may be advantaged on ToM because of their proficiency at sign language was ruled out. About 75 percent of the time they were successful on the ToM tasks, whereas less than 20 percent of the answers given by the late signers were correct. In contrast to late-signing deaf children, both normal hearing and native signing deaf children appear to enjoy an early conversational access that triggers the expression of ToM reasoning.

Another possibility is that nonverbal intelligence, such as that involving the ability to match object patterns, would explain the difference between the two groups of deaf children in our investigation. However, on measures of nonverbal intelligence as well as BSL proficiency, there were no significant differences. Therefore, the finding that native signing children excel at ToM compared to their late-signing counterparts can be seen to point to the powerful impact of early access to conversation. In contrast to deaf late-signing children, deaf children for whom sign is their native language have early opportunities to converse about the beliefs of others and to formulate an understanding of how these can be false, facilitating their performance on measures of ToM reasoning.[22]

Although there appear to be no significant differences between the deaf and hearing in the quality of attachment and mother–toddler interaction, deaf children of hearing parents receive much less communication than is the case for deaf children of deaf parents. Hearing mothers of deaf 2- and 3-year-olds do direct more visual communication to their children than do hearing mothers of hearing children, but they still communicate primarily through speech to which the children do not often attend. By contrast, through visual communication, deaf mothers of deaf children can match the responsiveness of hearing mothers of hearing children.

Further work is required to determine whether hearing families who strive to acquire a sign language early can serve to boost ToM in the deaf child. As a number of studies have shown, most hearing parents do not have sufficient proficiency in manual communication to optimize social interactions with their deaf children, and to converse freely about imaginary or unobservable topics such as others' beliefs. Moreover, they will often use the oral mode to converse with other hearing family members, innocently limiting a deaf child's access to informal conversations that may encourage insight into ToM reasoning as well as other aspects of social understanding. In our investigation, the level of BSL attained by hearing family members of late-signing deaf children was highly variable. One 8-year-old late signer who failed the ToM tasks had family members who nevertheless were all actively learning BSL.[23]

Similarly, the schools of late signers cannot be relied upon to provide a substitute for the kinds of conversations about the unobservable beliefs of others. Though attending signing all-deaf schools should prompt deaf children to engage in more conversations in a sign language, the sign language fluency of adult figures in schools is variable and hence the quality of communication is not uniform. For late signers attending mainstreamed schools, adults who have the responsibility to translate information to a sign language for deaf children (and to use complementary forms of visual communication) are often only present for the translation of curricular material, and not for informal conversations in school that have the potential to stimulate development reflected in ToM reasoning. Few hearing children are taught to sign and, for those who do, this is usually extremely limited and is a mode of communication that is not used among their hearing peers.

Our results converge with research on ToM in hearing children pointing to the importance of conversational awareness in successful task performance. In studies that I described earlier in this chapter, specifying that the ToM test question is intended to refer to how a person with a false belief will *initially* be misled – rather than to the revised true belief of a person once a deception is discovered – prompts hearing children to produce correct responses. However, in contrast to hearing children, late-signing deaf children do not improve significantly on ToM tasks when the intention of the test question is explicitly "conversationally supported" along these lines, suggesting that the expression of ToM reasoning benefits from exposure to language and conversations about mental states during an early optimal or sensitive period.[24]

This pattern points to the importance of delineating two types of abilities in conversation. First is the ability to understand the pragmatic implications of questions (e.g. that they refer to an initial, rather than a final search). A failure to follow these implications can mask hearing children's conceptual understanding, and that understanding only becomes apparent once the need to make specific conversational implications about the purpose and relevance of the task is removed. Second, there is the awareness involved in understanding the general shared grounding for communication in the mutual beliefs, knowledge, and assumptions underpinning conversational exchanges. Deaf late-signing children are liable to be cut off from the early exchanges about similarities and differences in mental states with parents and siblings that are familiar to hearing children and native signers. Above all, they are isolated from experience with the structure of well-formed conversation. As maintained by Paul Harris of the Harvard Graduate School of Education, this experience alerts normal hearing children by the age of 3 years that speakers are persons with knowledge who store and seek to provide information about the world.[25]

Indeed there is a substantial link between mothers' use of mental state verbs such as thinking, believing and feeling when their children are only 6 months of age and their performance on ToM tasks as preschoolers once they have started to talk. The results of some Swedish research underscore this point that the groundwork for children's expression of ToM reasoning is established in infancy. Sweden prides itself on its advanced social policy concerning deaf children. This mandates that deaf children in Sweden be allowed access to Swedish Sign Language (SSL) at the age of 2 years and onwards and that hearing parents, grandparents, and siblings be all granted free lessons in SSL to communicate with a deaf child in the family. Yet Swedish deaf children of hearing parents are still delayed users of a sign language. They also show protracted delays in performance on ToM measures, presumably as the groundwork for having insight into mental states normally occurs in the first two years of life while the child is largely preverbal. In fact, a team in Aberdeen, Scotland, led by Philip Russell have found that problems in answering ToM test questions linger in deaf children of hearing parents even at the age of 13–16 years of age. These problems are shared by deaf adults in Nicaragua who have had late access to Nicaraguan Sign Language.[26]

A possibility that remains to be tested is that deaf children with hearing parents who presumably lack early input about mental states do not respond as well as deaf children with deaf parents on attentional ToM tests designed for babies and toddlers who are at a very early stage in their language development. It may be that, even at 15 months to 2 years of age, deaf children of deaf parents who are exposed to sign language from birth do not differ in their attention on ToM tasks. By contrast, they display an advantage over deaf children of hearing parents who are have no early access to either a sign or spoken language.

Thus ToM is not simply a matter of vocabulary and proficiency in speaking grammatically. Rather, it is the end result of a social understanding facilitated by early conversational experience. This experience may start to take place even before children themselves acquire language and become active participants in dialogues with others. In the case of deaf late-signing children, limitations in conversational knowledge involving the general shared grounding for communication may prevent children from answering correctly when asked test questions on ToM tasks.

However, it would be going much too far to claim that late-signing children are completely without insight into the beliefs of others. For example, it has been shown that late signers aged 8–13 years have the ability to attribute mental states such as thinking, believing and feeling correctly in describing stories about hypothetical situations involving relationships with others.[27] In this respect, we simply need to know more about the processes by which children come to share others' beliefs in the conversational networks of deaf late and native signing children. There is a need to explore how the actual quality of communication between the deaf and their conversational partners influences their ToM understanding as well as their self-esteem and life satisfaction.

So far though, the pattern of results supports a poverty of stimulus account for the acquisition of ToM reasoning in normal children. This acquisition hinges upon receiving the requisite environmental input within a critical period in early development—a process that parallels the acquisition of grammar. Just as children require some minimal access to language for grammar to develop, they seem to require at least some minimal access to conversational opportunities to display normal ToM reasoning skills. Therefore as is the case for language, the developmental trajectory of ToM reasoning may be affected when the requisite input is not received within an early critical period, as is the case for late-signing deaf children. This is possibly also the case, as shown in some meticulous Swedish studies, for some nonvocal children with cerebral palsy who also cannot easily engage in conversations that necessarily involve mental states.[28]

In this sense, it is instructive to contrast the ease of using gesture to refer to concrete objects, such as "bees" with mental states such as "beliefs." Children can point to bees – and concrete referents in general – to communicate messages. However, they cannot rely on such "ostensive" acts to point and communicate about false beliefs. In Alan Leslie's analysis, to be able to share the meaning of a false belief, children need to exercise their capacity to inhibit the response that arises from a very simple ToM – one that operates under the premise that beliefs and reality truly correspond as these very often do. This process takes place within conversational exchanges with others about the nature of the inner worlds of mental states. Children in conversation are regularly faced with situations in which speakers may hold different beliefs or perspectives. Indeed, to participate appropriately in conversation, children have to keep these differences in mind. The full expression of these differences in what children say may require extensive exercise, and it is just the daily involvement in conversation that may give children the opportunity to practice the inhibitory skills required on ToM reasoning tasks.

Mind over grammar: the relation between ToM reasoning and language grammar

At this point, it is necessary to consider another interpretation of the relation between performance on ToM reasoning tasks and language measures besides that of access to conversation. Some have claimed that the grammar of language enables children to entertain propositions that involve the simultaneous representation of alternative state of affairs, such as the consequences of behavior by individuals who hold true or false beliefs. More specifically, it has been maintained that it is the acquisition of sentence complementation in the grammar of language that enables children to reason out solutions to false beliefs. By this account, ToM reasoning is dependent on the possession of syntactic structures such as those known as "sentence complementation" that permit the embedding of false propositions within true statements ("Mary knows that John [falsely] thinks chocolates are in the cupboard"). In this sense, grammar provides the "representational template" to reason out about ToM problems. The BSL Receptive Skills Test that was given to the signing children in our investigation does not directly assess the syntax of sentence complementation.

Therefore we cannot rule out this possibility on the basis of our own work.

It is likely that a certain level of syntax and semantics is necessary for ToM performance but, nevertheless, many young children are adept at syntax and semantics but still do poorly on ToM tasks. However, the position that syntax, at least in the form of sentence complementation, is the basis for theory of mind reasoning, does seem implausible in that there appears to be no specific role for complementation in children's performance on measures of their understanding of false beliefs. Many 3-year-olds who fail ToM tasks spontaneously produce sentence complements in their speech. They correctly answer questions involving sentence complementation if those sentences take the structure [person]-[pretends]-[that x] (e.g., "He pretends that his puppy is outside"). By contrast, 3-year-olds do poorly when given sentences that take the form [person]-[thinks]-[that x] (e.g., "He thinks that his puppy is outside"). Both use the same complements yet children only pass when "pretend" is used. Although training in sentence complementation enhances performance on ToM tasks, these training studies may in fact involve exposure to discourse that may foster conversational understanding that in turn promotes success on false belief tasks. In this light, the syntax of sentence complementation falls short of providing a complete account of ToM performance, at least on pictorial "fishing" tasks.[29]

Converging evidence comes from studies of adults following brain damage who have become aphasic and have lost grammar though retaining their ToM reasoning ability.[30] Though such patients have a language-configured mind that could be seen to support ToM development, their performance is consistent with the dissociation between grammar and ToM in childhood. Finally, there are many instances of sign languages and spoken Aboriginal Australian languages in which there is no sentence complementation. Instead of clausal complements such as "John told everyone that Mary washed the car," users of such languages instead employ "clausal adjunct" forms such as "Mary having washed the car, John told everyone (it)." If complementation in this sense were necessary to instantiate ToM reasoning, no ToM would be possible in these language groups.

Grammar may thus be seen as a "co-opted" system that can support the expression of ToM reasoning, but the possession of grammar does not guarantee successful performance on ToM tasks. Rather, ToM reasoning in young children is triggered, tuned and speeded up by engagement in conversation about mental states contents, such as what speakers want, pretend and believe.

Mental modularity and cultural diversity

Altogether, substantial research to date indicates that grammar and ToM reasoning are the products of mechanisms that are modular to a significant degree, given their unfolding with minimal environment stimulation and their independence from each other during development. The evidence supports the view that there are communalities in the capacity for – and emergence of – grammar and ToM in that both represent the elaboration of innate processes that are achieved automatically and effortlessly by typically developing children. In this sense, grammar and ToM can be seen as parallel modular systems that come together to provide a foundation for the transmission of culture.[31]

Drawing a parallel between the expression of grammar and the expression of ToM creates insight into the nature of culture in relation to universals in cognition. Humans, regardless of culture, acquire a grammar. Culture determines the specific nature of the native grammar to be acquired. Similarly, all humans regardless of culture acquire the concept of a belief that possesses true and false attributes once it is triggered by exposure to conversation about the mental states of others, and in doing so manifest a theory of mind. Culture influences the specific beliefs that people hold about the minds of others and shapes non-core aspects of ToM. In this sense, ToM and grammar emerge as autonomous domain-specific systems that normally come online at set times in development despite wide variations in the environment. These systems interact to support word learning and the acquisition of specific beliefs.

In tandem with cues from the grammar of language, ToM in the form of the ability to interpret others' intentions contributes substantially to how children learn the meaning of words. For example, in one study carried out at the University of Michigan by Susan Gelman and Karen Eberling, children saw aged 2–3 years drawings of various nameable objects (e.g. a man). Each drawing was described as illustrating a shape that was created intentionally (e.g. someone painted a picture) or created accidentally (e.g. someone spilled some paint).

Participants were simply asked to name each picture. Children used shape as the basis for their naming primarily when the shapes were intentional and substance (paint) when the shapes were accidental. In this way, they displayed evidence of sharing the speaker's viewpoint in conversation that is vital for effective communication.[32]

With the support of grammar and ToM, children also acquire the specific vocabulary and beliefs of their community. These words and beliefs are encrypted to be accessible to those within a culture – and function to protect it. As the Rutgers linguist Mark Baker remarks, the parameters of variation in language in particular and in culture more generally have many of the same properties as engineered codes and ciphers (with a secret key) insofar as these properties function to conceal a message, rearrange its parts, and replace its symbols at different levels of structure. More generally, as Baker points out, the factoring of language into a universal grammar available to everyone and parameters encrypted to be accessible to the few suggests that language variation is not an evolutionary accident. Instead, it is part of the inherent design specifications for communication that have the goal of producing messages that are easily understandable by the intended audience but not by those outsiders who may attempt to listen. Modular systems in theory of mind and grammar interact to form the basis of problem-solving resources that children use to acquire words and culture, but their autonomy is reflected in the domain-specific breakdown of function following brain lesions in adulthood.[33]

One of the main functions of human culture is to clarify what people value, what they take seriously in their daily lives, what they will fight for to include or exclude others in their groups.[34] Founded on the capacity for grammar and ToM, enculturation involves specific languages and beliefs that are encrypted to be easily accessible only to those within a culture. The human mind possesses the capacity to marshal a series of autonomous modular systems such as grammar and ToM. These are systems that emerge universally across all cultures. In grammar, there is no conceptual change, just an increasing awareness of when and how words should be used that is part of enrichment in children's knowledge. Similarly, there is no early conceptual deficit – no radical conceptual change required – that marks the core of ToM reasoning.

Does a lamb have a theory of mind?

Where does ToM end? Does it apply only to humans or extend to other species in the animal kingdom? Here is an anecdote that suggests caution in presuming that animals have ToM ability.

After the first few weeks in Australia, I knew things were different. This was a place where leisure was taken very seriously. Just two months after having arrived, we went out to the bush for a country barbi (barbecue). Traveling down a dirt road, we came across a car that had just careened front first into a ditch with its tires still spinning. A lanky disheveled boy no more than 20 was leaning again the side. "Are you alright?" we asked. "No worries, mate!" was the laconic reply. We seemed to have passed into the land without worries.

My wife at the time was feeling lonely so I decided I should get something special for her birthday – a lamb! What could more cute and more Australian? So I set off in my 1970 Ford Falcon station wagon to the Brisbane stockyards. I was able to catch a seller there after an auction. "Good on you," he said, and when I asked him whether he had a spare lamb, he casually offered, "You can have this one for $20." "How do I take him home?" I asked meekly. His curt response was, "There's some rope over there."

I had seen cowboys tie up steers in the movies but I had never come close to doing anything like this. Still I made the effort and looped the rope around the small four legs. I then loaded the lamb with great difficulty through the tailgate of the station wagon. Off I went with the lamb bleating all the way. I started to cross the main bridge that links the north and south sides of Brisbane – a bit of a monster six-lane bridge built to resemble that over Sydney Harbour. Ascending to the middle of the bridge, the lamb got loose and was running amuck in the car. I soon was fighting it off my lap. I was able to stop the car on the other side of the bridge, grapple with the lamb and this time tie it securely around the legs. Then after a further half hour of bleating, I was able to arrive at my destination and deposit the lamb on five fertile acres of grass.

Does a lamb have a theory of mind? *(cont.)*

My wife was enthralled by this unexpected gift that she dubbed Lambchop. However, it soon became apparent that Lambchop was oblivious to everything but the grass underneath his feet. No matter how much I waved the hay and called, Lambchop seemed to be getting further and further away. Before I knew it, Lambchop was over the hill for good. Not like my old horse, Scamp, who was over the hill but then would come back when you held up some hay. I had to face up to it. Lambchop didn't have insight into the mental states of others. She couldn't bring herself to share my belief that staying close to us would provide a guarantee of food and safety. Instead, she became mutton for a fox out there.

The lamb with a ToM?

There is lot of debate today over whether one can attribute a "theory of mind" to animals. Dogs and cats have a sense of expectations and like to rely on the "truthful" nondeceptive behavior of their keepers. Apes and chimpanzees, and even birds, may be reasonably viewed to deceive others over food – though whether this involves a matter of intentional design on their part remains unclear. Sheep seem at least to recognize other sheep.[35] However, could it be in any way said that a lamb has a theory of mind?

Chapter 3

Astronomy and geography

We watched the ocean and sky together
Under the roof of blue Italian weather.
Percy Bysshe Shelley, *Letter to Maria Gisborne*

There is a Mediterranean theme to this chapter. The ancient Greeks and Romans were fascinated with the sky and stars; the Romans devised their calendar and based much of their way of life on the sighting of celestial bodies. Early astronomers such as Ptolemy were Greek and, in recent times (1992 onwards), a Greek psychologist, Stella Vosniadou, first working in the US at the University of Illinois and then later in Athens, has been instrumental in demonstrating the importance of research on what children know about astronomy and geography.

Vosniadou, together with her Illinois colleague Bill Brewer, proposes that young children have a naive theory of astronomy.[1] In their view, children's ideas about the shape of the Earth are founded on two "entrenched presuppositions:" (1) that the Earth is a flat plane (the "flatness" constraint) and (2) that unsupported objects fall "down" (the "support" constraint). These basic presuppositions are said to be constantly confirmed by everyday experience, are resistant to change, and are used by children to generate answers to questions about their astronomical knowledge. Given these suppositions, many children initially seem to believe that the Earth is in some sense flat, consistent with their everyday observation of the Earth as a physically flat plane. They also seem to believe that the Earth has an edge from which people could fall off, consistent with their everyday observation that unsupported objects fall down. Therefore, according to Vosniadou's analysis, children are constrained to confuse appearance with reality. In this sense, they commit phenomenism errors in believing that the outward appearance of a flat Earth is a genuine reflection of the Earth's real shape.

As children grow older, their naive theory of the shape of the Earth is said to come into contact with the culturally received view. In Western countries, of course, this view is based on the accepted scientific case is that the Earth is a spherically-shaped body. When children are told that the Earth is round, they are said to form "synthetic" mental models that guide their reasoning about the Earth's shape. These mental models are an amalgam of the child's naive theory based on entrenched presuppositions and the culturally received view. Such models reflect a coherence of beliefs and assumptions that are wrong or only partly adjusted to the currently accepted scientific information that they may encounter in school. Alternatively, in some instances, children may form incoherent models. These reflect the effects of entrenched presuppositions that they cannot reconcile with the information to which they are exposed.

To support this view on what children know about astronomy, Vosniadou carried out a series of studies. The first one involved 60 American children aged 6–12 years. The children were asked to draw pictures to show the location of where people live in relation to the shape of the Earth. Vosniadou interpreted the children's drawings to correspond to one of six mental models:

1 Spherical Earth model: This model represents the dominant scientifically accepted perspective in the United States and other Western cultures. The child demonstrates an understanding of shape, the force of gravity, and the concept of limitless space. Children are also unlikely to respond that there is an edge to the Earth from which people will fall (38 percent of their sample).

2 Flattened sphere model: This model is characterized by the belief that, although the Earth is basically spherical, it is flattened at the top and bottom, and it is in these places that the people live (6.66 percent).

3 Dual Earth model: Children in this category express a belief in two Earths: one in the sky and one on which we live. The Earth in the sky is the round Earth that has been photographed, and the Earth we live on is the "real" Earth. The round Earth is most

often referred to as the "Earth," whereas the flat Earth is referred to as "ground" (13.33 percent).

4 Hollow or dual sphere model: Beliefs typical of this model as shown in the drawing below include the idea that people live inside the Earth, and that the sky is an upper hemisphere that covers the Earth (20 percent).

5 Disc Earth model: The central concept is of a flat Earth, supported by water or ground, with the sky directly above it. Children holding this model are most likely to respond that the Earth has an edge from which you can fall. However, it is noteworthy that, in Vosniadou's research, the percentage of children holding a "pure" flat Earth initial model is very small (1.66 percent).

6 Rectangular Earth model: This was essentially the same as the disc model, except that the Earth is represented as rectangular rather than circular. The percentage of children holding a rectangular Earth model is again very small (1.66 percent).

A further 18.33 percent of the children were classified as inconsistent or mixed because they did not meet the consistency criteria for being placed in any of the above categories.

Schematically then, Vosniadou proposes that children's mental models of the shape of the Earth can be depicted as follows:

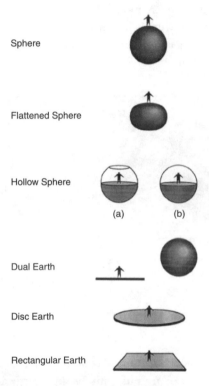

Sphere

Flattened Sphere

Hollow Sphere

(a) (b)

Dual Earth

Disc Earth

Rectangular Earth

Based on this analysis, Vosniadou and Brewer contend that young children typically "assimilate" culturally transmitted information in resorting to synthetic mental models that combine roundness with flatness in partial adjustment to the cultural norm. The support presupposition leads them to deny that people can live at the bottom of the Earth whether flat or spherical.

In follow-up studies, Vosniadou and Brewer asked children questions about the day–night cycle.[2] Again, their answers were interpreted in terms of entrenched presuppositions. The support presupposition is said to lead children to explain the disappearance of the sun and the appearance of the moon in terms of mechanisms related to the appearance and disappearance of objects. They hold one of four geocentric types of synthetic models involving the

Earth (E), Sun (S), and Moon (M), as shown below. Many young children think that the day–night cycle happens because the Earth rotates while the Sun and Moon are fixed in the sky (Type 1), the sun and Moon revolve around the Earth (Type 2), sinks below the horizon at dusk and rises at dawn (Type 3), or the Sun or Moon is occluded by the clouds, mountains or by darkness (Type 4).

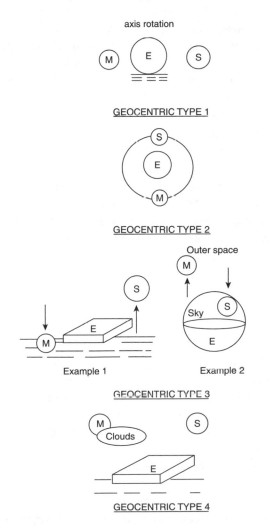

Vosniadou's original work was carried out with children from one of the flattest parts of the world: Urbana-Champaign, Illinois. Naturally the flatness of the terrain where the children lived might have influenced their responses. However, she has proceeded to study children in many other regions, and interprets the results of studies in countries such as Greece, India, and Samoa, as well as the United States, to indicate that children living in different cultures and in various local topographies hold synthetic mental models of the shape of the Earth and the day–night cycle. To be sure, Vosniadou's research shows that the cosmology of children is marked by significant cultural variations. In India, for example, children may appear to embrace a cultural tradition that the Earth resembles a large disc or shallow dish floating on water. When told that the Earth is round, they may recruit intuitions that arise from the flatness constraint to conceptualize its shape as circular or disc-like rather than spherical. In this way, naive cosmologies are not only consistent with phenomenal observations that give rise to the flatness and support constraints proposed by Vosniadou, but they are also consistent with lay culture. Indeed, even in Western countries, adults make reference to the sun rising and setting – terms that could be construed by children with a naive cosmology of the day–night cycle as consistent with a support constraint.

According to Vosniadou, the power of cultural influences on what today's kids know about astronomy has a parallel in the historical conflict between cultural and scientifically advanced conceptions of the cosmos. Before the discoveries of Copernicus and Galileo in the Italy of the sixteenth and seventeenth centuries, Western adults' understanding of the world was based on the theological doctrine of a geocentric universe with the Earth at its center. Heliocentric cosmological theory positing that the Earth is a spherical body that revolves around the sun met with very strong resistance and its acceptance was gradual and hard won.[3] For Vosniadou, children go through a process analogous to that of scientists in coming to accommodate their thinking about aspects of astronomy such as the shape of the Earth and the day–night cycle to the scientifically received view. Vosniadou suggests that conceptual development occurs as a result of making connections between facts with a progressive revision of the child's naïve theory to create more coherent and unified scientific knowledge. On this account, theory revision in children's cosmology is a continuous, gradual process that is often characterized by synthetic models or misconceptions requiring a fundamental conceptual change.

Are naive knowledge and synthetic mental models present in children everywhere in the world?

In considering Vosniadou's approach, some questions seem obvious: Must presuppositions be entrenched to the same degree in children across all cultures? Do all children have misconceptions that inevitably flow from these presuppositions? Could it be that, in some cultures, children may be exposed early to a culturally transmitted view that coincides with the scientifically accepted one? If so, would entrenched presuppositions in children's interpretation of the cosmos be less likely to emerge? For example, young children's apparent belief that is possible to fall off the Earth may reflect the view of those growing up "on top" of the Earth in America, Britain, and other northern hemisphere countries. It may not be typical of children living "down under" in southern hemisphere countries such as Australia, where children often are exposed early to the view that the Earth is a spherical body on which people can live on top or down under.

Another issue concerns the degree to which children actually have any beliefs at all about the shape of the Earth or the day–night cycle before they are given instruction at school. If they do not have prior beliefs and have not yet turned their minds to issues of cosmology, they would hardly be striving to find out if their beliefs are accurate. Once they do encounter relevant information about cosmology, this may be absorbed as fragmented and unsystematized rather than guided by presuppositions along the lines proposed by Vosniadou. Scientifically accepted cosmological knowledge is difficult or impossible for children to acquire through direct experience. They cannot actually see the spherical nature of the Earth that is populated both above and below the equator. For this reason, knowledge about cosmology may be more dependent on culture for its transmission than is knowledge within areas more directly amenable to perception and action such as, for example, their reasoning about the edible–inedible distinction in the domain of biology – an issue that is close to survival and that will be examined in the next chapter. For example, the problem of whether an object can be eaten is a constant source of conversation at home and school. Children can and do enact rudimentary experiments to determine whether substances are edible and, on this basis, they are constrained to seek and receive feedback and advice from parents and others in various forms.[4] No such feedback process may take place to determine the shape of the Earth and the day–night cycle.

Therefore a central issue in what children can know about astronomy is whether there is a universal, stage-like progression in which they intuitively begin with a type of flat Earth model, which is progressively synthesized with, and then replaced in Western cultures, by theories about the spherical shape of the Earth and the heliocentric nature of the universe in which the Earth revolves around the sun. If not, a more significant role in children's development must be accorded to the direct transmission of scientific information by parents, teachers, and the media within Western cultures and also to the transmission of nonscientific beliefs in traditional cultures – a role that may permit even young children to have a form of scientific understanding.

How to ask questions about what children know?

There are of course many ways by which children's cosmological knowledge can be tested. Vosniadou chose to determine the existence of various flat or hemispherical intuitions about the shape of the Earth and the day–night cycle largely from children's drawings, and the extent to which these are consistent with their verbal responses to questions.

However, kids do not draw in the same way as adults. Rather, they often draw "diagrammatic" pictures that show the parts of an object and their interrelationships without regard to characteristics such as depth and information about how some objects or parts of objects hide others from view. As children are unable to draw a sphere well, they may instead produce on paper what seems to be a variant of a flat Earth and geocentric representations of the day–night cycle. So rather than guided by entrenched presuppositions and by flatness and support constraints, children's drawings of people standing on a flat surface may simply reflect a bias toward orienting figures to reference points that are vertical or horizontal.[5]

At any rate, children's drawings may not be a valid basis for making inferences about how they represent aspects of the physical world such as the shape of the Earth. Few kids prefer these drawings in comparison to drawings with a conventional perspective that do include characteristics such as depth and partial occlusion. It is these conventional drawings that they believe best depict objects in the physical world.

Vosniadou has not been unaware of this problem. In follow-up research that she and others carried out in India, the aim was to determine how children reason about the shape of the Earth using "external" representations rather than drawing. Children were asked either in English, Hindi, or Telegu (a regional language used in the city of Hyderabad) to indicate their concepts of the Earth's shape by making models out of clay and by using styrofoam models that took the form of types of spheres as well as a cone, flat disc, and square. Some Indian children appeared to conceptualize the shape of the Earth in terms of flat discs or squares suspended in space or water. This result might seem to confirm the results of earlier research with American children. Nevertheless, to produce clay models might even be a more difficult task than for children than to draw models because children may not necessarily understand that the request is to choose the model that best corresponds with their conception of shape of the Earth. Rather than giving due consideration to the styrofoam sphere as a model of the Earth, children may interpret the request as a more concrete one, that is, to select a styrofoam model as one that requires the best match between what they have produced in clay and the corresponding styrofoam representation. Consistency between making clay models and selecting styrofoam ones would then merely reflect an attempt to match the artwork produced with one of the models provided for selection.

Potentially the most troublesome aspect of Vosniadou's research program concerns her method of questioning. As is the case for the appearance–reality distinction, there may be a gulf between the conversational experience of adults and children such that children encounter difficulties in interpreting the purpose and relevance of questions about what they know in the area of astronomy. Vosniadou's research was conducted mainly in connection with the use of open-ended "generative" questions such as "If you walked in a straight line for many days, would you fall off the Earth?" For Vosniadou, correct answers require children to make an inference from a knowledge base, rather than the mere repetition of culturally received "facts" such as "The Earth is round" in response to "factual" questions such as "Is the Earth round or flat?" Hence, in Vosniadou's studies, children were repeatedly questioned on a theme ("Would you ever reach the edge of the Earth? Say we kept on walking and walking and had plenty of food with us? Could you fall off the edge of the Earth?"). Their responses were then classified according to the mental model suggested by the consistency (or inconsistency) of their response to such generative questions.

All the same, under repeated questioning in the generative style, the child may vary his or her answers simply in an attempt to provide what the experimenter believes is the right answer or in an attempt to rationalize what may seem to the experimenter to be contradictory answers to a line of questioning.[6] Vosniadou astutely observes that in some cases this process might have prompted inconsistent responses in children who would otherwise be classed as "spherical" in their Earth concepts, but maintains that the result would be to underestimate consistency in children's response patterns among a group who were already highly consistent.

Still, the method of using open-ended "generative" questions might have prompted some children to construct a "coherent" though misconceived story. If so, children may base their answers on what they have previously said in order to create the appearance of consistency, rather than simply revealing their authentic preferential views (if any) on the shape of the Earth and the day–night cycle as would be revealed by their simple choices of answer from two alternatives – one correct and one incorrect. In recent research carried out in Sweden, Jan Schoultz and his colleagues have shown that introduction of a globe as a tool for thinking produces radically different responses than those reported by Vosniadou.[7] Young Swedish children can identify countries in both the northern and southern hemispheres and use explanatory concepts relating to gravitational pull to answer questions about why people in the southern hemisphere countries such as Australia and Argentina do not fall off the Earth. If this is the case in Sweden, what should children's understanding of astronomy and geography be in Australia itself? Might Australian children, owing to their continent's distinctive location in the southern hemisphere under dazzling sunny skies, be aware at an early age of properties of shape and motion of the Earth and the location of various countries?

A re-examination of what children can know about astronomy and geography

To investigate this issue, I teamed up with George Butterworth of the University of Sussex in England and Peter Newcombe, at the University of Queensland in Australia. George was long influential in his studies of Piaget's notion of egocentrism in children's thinking and was determined to investigate conceptions of the shape of the Earth and the day–night cycle of children in Australia and England. Peter had been a schoolteacher in Brisbane. His PhD thesis in psychology was on the topic of children's capacity to recognize and recall incidents in stories that they had been told.[8] George and Peter's interests complemented mine concerning the nature of conceptual development and change in young children. Together we set about the task of re-examining the provocative claims that arise from the entrenched presuppositions analysis put forward by Vosniadou and her colleagues. We sought to compare the knowledge of kids who live at opposite ends of the Earth in Australia and England to determine the extent to which Australian children who are exposed to substantial early instruction about cosmology differ from their English counterparts.

One point was clear to us: that even countries that share many cultural features, including a common language, historical and political traditions, have children who differ in their beliefs about the physical world. For example, despite the strong cultural affinity between England and America, cultural differences in religiosity exist. The great majority of Americans, unlike in England and many other countries, believe that humans originated through a form of divine intervention. This religious orientation is compatible with a "teleological" bias in children to treat objects as if they are intentionally-created artifacts. For example, when asked to say why rocks are pointy, American children often reply that the pointy shape was designed so that "animals wouldn't sit on them and smash them" or so that "animals could scratch on them when they got itchy." Given the difference in religiosity between American and English adults, it perhaps is not surprising that American 7- and 8-year-olds significantly more often endorse such purpose-based "intentional" explanations than do their English counterparts – differences that do not occur in older children.[9]

In a similar fashion, despite the strong cultural affinity between England and Australia, there exist differences in exposure to beliefs about geography and astronomy. From an early age, Australian children are aware of their cultural links with the Northern Hemisphere and of Australia's distinctive location as a large landmass below the equator remote from other English-speaking countries. This awareness is reflected in the school curriculum, through which children are given systematic instruction about the essentials of cosmology. In the Australian state of Queensland, for example, the school curriculum syllabus provides that Year 1 (5–6-year-old) students identify and describe changes in the obvious features of the Earth and sky including changes in the appearance of the moon. Also in Year 1, children are instructed in examining and explaining the process of day and night. In Year 2 (6–7-year-olds), children continue by studying the phases of the moon together with special events in the night sky: meteors, comets, daytime eclipses. In Year 3 (7–8-year-olds), children study the solar system, other star systems, the orbit of planets and their major moons, together with advances in space exploration and the possibility of sustainable space stations. Even in preschool (4–5 years), curriculum guidelines are that children should describe aspects of the sky during the day and night and identify the moon and stars. In this respect, it is noteworthy that the Australian flag features the Southern Cross star constellation.[10]

By contrast, it is not until about 8 years of age that children in England are formally exposed to instruction about cosmology.[11] Therefore, compared with their English counterparts, Australian children should have special access to information about the shape of the Earth and the heliocentric nature of the universe through their culture, and should be more likely to advocate the scientific worldview. This worldview may be directly transmitted in home and school and not necessarily through intermediate synthetic models.

In our study, George, Peter and I decided to depart from the principal testing format that Vosniadou used to make sure that we tested children's knowledge about astronomy and geography rather than their ability to draw or to understand the purpose and relevance of questions. For that reason, we used 3D models and forms of questioning in which the children were mainly asked to identify – rather than generate – the correct response in a manner designed to align the child's perception of the purpose and relevance of the questions with that of the interviewer.

The kids that we interviewed were divided into three age groups of 4–5, 6–7, and 8–9 years. The Australian children came from a university preschool playgroup, a suburban preschool, and elementary school groups in Brisbane, Queensland, and the English children from admissions classes and elementary schools in Newhaven, Sussex, England. We asked the children 14 questions in three phases: questions on (i) the shape of the Earth (Qs 1–7, 13–14), (ii) the day–night cycle (Qs 8–10), and (iii) perspective-taking (Qs 11–12). The questions were intended to determine whether children from the two cultures would be different in their general level of reasoning about relations between objects in space as well as in their knowledge about astronomy and geography. For each question, the children could choose between answers that a "scientific" and an "intuitive" response that would reflect adherence to a flatness or support constraint. They were also free to say that they did not know the answer.

In all cases but one where statistically significant differences emerged these favored the Australian children. On Q1 (Is the world round or flat? If it's round/flat, does it look like a circle or a ball?), nearly all Australian children responded that the Earth is round whereas about a fifth of English children claimed it is flat – a result picked up and reported with almost masochistic glee in the English tabloid newspaper *The Sun*, with a commentary from the chief executive of an organization called "Save British Science" maintaining that our results reinforced his position that British science was going

Questions asked of children in Australia and England aged 4–9 years

1. Is the world round or flat? If it's round/flat, does it look like a circle or a ball?
2. How do you know that the world is round/flat?
3. Look at these models. Here is a round ball. Here is a part of a ball with a flat top and a lid. Here is a flat surface. Can you point to the model that shows how the world really is?

4. If you walked for many days in a straight line, would you fall off the edge of the world? Why/why not?
5. This little girl has sticky stuff on her. You can put her here (top), here (side), or here (bottom). Show me using the little girl where people in Australia/England live on the model.
6. Can people live up there/down there? Show me where the people in England/Australia live.
7. Some children think that the sky is all around; other children think that the sky is only on top. Point to where the sky really is.
8. I have another ball here. Let's pretend this is the sun. When the sun shines on this part of the world, is it day or night on the other part?
9. When it shines on the other part of the world, is it day or night on this part?
10. Some children say that day happens because the sun goes down in front of one part of the world and comes up underneath to shine in front of the other part. Some other children say that day happens because the world turns around so that the sun only shines on part of the world at one time. What do you think?
11. Pretend you are standing just where this little girl is standing at the bottom of the moon. She's looking at her friend who lives down here on the world. Does her friend look the right way up or upside down to her?
12. Does her friend look like she is at the top of the world or at the bottom of the world?
13. What is the shape of the Earth? Show me the best model?
14. I have a globe here. Can you show me where Australia is on this globe? Can you show me where London, England, is?

down the drain. At 8–9 years of age nearly all the Australian children responded on Q2 (How do you know that the world is round/flat?) that the Earth was shaped like a ball whereas about half of the English children preferred the circle to the ball. On Q3 (Can you point to the model that shows how the world really is?), nearly all the Australian children regardless of age chose the sphere as the model whereas nearly half the English 4–5 year olds chose the hemisphere or disc – a result confirmed on the retest in Q13. On Q4 (If you walked for many days in a straight line, would you fall off the edge of the world? Why/why not?), there were no differences between the Australian and English kids. However, on Q5 (Show me using the little girl where people in Australia live on the model) as well as on the retest on Q14), Australians of all ages were adept at finding Australia unlike English children who often could not. There were no differences in the children's ability to locate England (though on Q14 English 6–8-year-olds were better than Australian children at locating England on a globe with features). On Q6 (Can people live up there/down there? Show me where the people in England/Australia live), nearly all Australians, including most of the 4- to 5-year-olds, believed that people could live all over the world whereas a third of English children said people could not and many others said that they didn't know the answer.

With regard to the questions concerning the day–night cycle, there were no differences between children in the two countries on Q7–9. In contrast to the young children, most 8-year-olds in both countries responded that the sky was all around the Earth rather than just on top and could accurately identify that when it is dark on one side of the Earth it is light on the other side. However, on the critical Q10 (Some children say that day happens because the sun goes down in front of one part of the world and comes up underneath to shine in front of the other part. Some other children say that day happens because the world turns around so that the sun only shines on part of the world at one time. What do you think?), about two-thirds of the Australian children (and all at 8 years) said that the Earth revolves around the sun whereas less that half of the English children recognized the fact. Even at age 8, about a fifth of English children claimed that the sun moves around the Earth. On Q11 (Pretend you are standing just where this little girl is standing at the bottom of the moon. She's looking at her friend who lives down here on the world. Does her friend look the right way up or upside down to her?), there was again a difference in favor of the Australians, though this did not carry over to Q12 (Does her friend look like she is at the top of the world or at the bottom of the world?). Not until the age of 8–9 years did most children in either country answer this question correctly.

Our cross-cultural comparison showed that many children in both countries, regardless of age, often produced responses consistent with a conception of a round Earth on which people can live all over without falling off. However, as predicted, Australian children were often significantly younger to offer the "scientific" answer and to eschew "intuitive" alternatives than their English counterparts to questions about the shape of the Earth or world. At 4–5 years, they were significantly more likely to indicate that the Earth is spherical, and by 6–7 years they were significantly more likely to express a heliocentric, rather than a geocentric, conception of the day–night cycle in keeping with differences in their respective school curricula. From Q5 onwards, the model of a sphere was used as a basis for questioning the children. However, it is highly unlikely that this procedure served to bias children's answers away from a flat Earth model by implying that the other two models were incorrect as similar numbers of children refrained from choosing the sphere on the retest in Q13 with the same overall cultural advantage to the Australians. Moreover, the Australian advantage appeared on Q1–3 even before the spherical model was used as the focus for questioning.

We carried out a follow-up study to see whether we would find the same pattern of results in Australian children with a different sample of 45 4- and 5-year-olds and to compare our questioning method with that used by Vosniadou. The children's responses using our method of questioning were similar to those in our first study and were unrelated to measures of their general verbal and nonverbal intelligence. However, using Vosniadou's questioning method, it was clear that the children were answering the wrong sort of question.

Here are three examples. First, in response to the simple question used by Vosniadou, "What is the shape of the Earth?" many children responded that it looked round or like a circle and few that it looked

A child on "top of the world" after having indicated that the earth is a rotating spherical body in orbit around the sun. This knowledge forms the basis for understanding the day–night cycle and predicitng that when it is day in Australia, it is night in England.

like a ball. In response to our question, "If the Earth is round, does it look like a circle or ball?" most children said that it looked like a ball. Therefore nearly all children in response to the Vosniadou question generated "round" or some variant ("circle" or "ball"), as their response, but only in with our explicit questioning was there a clear preference shown for the ball over the circle. The term "round" is ambiguous as, of course, it can refer to a ball or a circle. Children's actual preferences for a ball-shaped Earth emerged only through explicit questioning involving two meaningful choices. In response to our next question, "How do you know that the world is round?" they backed up their choice by references to globes, maps, atlases, television, and instruction from parents and teachers.

Second, differences between the children's answers to Vosniadou's questions and ours also emerged on those that concerned whether people could fall off the Earth. In response to Vosniadou's question, "Is there an edge or an end to the Earth?" two-thirds of the children indicated that this was indeed the case. Yet here in referring to their two-dimensional drawings, children may have been answering the question, "Is there an edge to the circle that you have drawn to represent the Earth?" By contrast, in referring to the 3D models that we used to clarify our questioning procedure, most of the children denied that there was an edge from which they could fall and many of the minority who responded that they could fall off nevertheless referred to the Earth's round shape, alluding to the slippery nature of a body that was not flat.

Third, children offered largely geocentric answers on Vosniadou's questions concerning understanding of the day–night cycle, "Where is the sun at night? How does this happen? Does the Earth move? Does the sun move?" Many simply claimed that, at night, the sun is behind clouds. Others just said that the sun goes down below the horizon at night and rises in the morning. They seemed to be answering the question, "Describe what happens when the sun sets and rises." By contrast, when asked explicitly to say whether the day–night cycle occurs because the sun goes down in front of one part of the Earth and come up underneath to shine in front of the other part, or because the Earth turns around so that the sun only shines on part of the Earth at one time, children overwhelmingly endorsed the latter choice.

Conclusion: models and methodology in children's cosmology

Overall, in our re-examination of Vosniadou's entrenched presuppositions hypothesis, we found that understanding the shape of the Earth and the day–night cycle does not inevitably include or proceed from the child's naïve, perceptually driven knowledge of the Earth. We had to look hard for evidence that would provide a basis for Vosniadou's approach. In terms of hypothesized flatness and support constraints, there was consistency only in the responses of a quite small number of the English children. It is possible to a limited extent that synthetic mental models of the Earth and day–night cycle may be held by some children in countries such as America, India, or England – cultures in which children are not provided early with the scientifically-received knowledge that the Earth is a rotating, spherical body that revolves around the sun. Should instruction be delayed about the Earth as a spherical body and the day–night cycle, intuitions may gain time to form and coexist with whatever culturally transmitted knowledge that children do receive. Children's early naive theory of cosmology may indeed reflect presuppositions of flatness and support and give rise to synthetic models of the shape of the Earth and the day–night cycle as proposed by Vosniadou. This theory may then undergo conceptual change.

However, synthetic mental models – as limited as these may be even in children living in countries such as the United States – cannot be universally present in cultures everywhere. Evidence for constraints to the extent that these could be regarded to reflect entrenched presuppositions was completely absent in the Australian group. Insofar as the Australian children answered incorrectly, their responses could be best characterized simply in terms of an inconsistent pattern of answers that reflect the absence of prior theorizing about issues of cosmology rather than the presence of powerful constraints that direct their thinking across questions. On this account, intuition and scientific knowledge occupy separate "mental spaces" in that early knowledge is fragmented and unsystematized.[12] Young children in countries such as England may hold both intuitive and scientific concepts, without knowing clearly when and where each type of concept should apply (but with no indication of synthesis). With development, the child comes increasingly to apply the two sources of knowledge to the relevant mental spaces.

At the same time, there was strong evidence in our investigation for the influence of culture. Although the Australian kids at all ages exhibited expertise compared to their English counterparts in locating Australia "down under" on a 3D model and on the globe without labels, most of the differences between the Australian and English children were eliminated by 8–9 years at the time when English children are introduced to cosmology in school. By contrast, on the questions that pertained to perspective taking there was little difference between the cultures. The only slight cultural advantage was that, at 8 years, the Australians were in advance of English children in inverting their own perspective, whereas English children were more likely to describe a person at the bottom of the world as appearing "upside down." Despite the immersion of the Australian children in an environment that emphasizes the characteristics of "down under" living, they did not identify the sky at the bottom of the world. For both the

Australian and English children, identifying the sky as around the world rather than just on top only clearly occurred at 8–9 years. Further research is necessary to determine the basis for children's responses about the location of the sky in order to clarify whether they interpret the question to refer to the location of the sky above the heads of people wherever they may live or to the location of the sky in relation to different vantage points on Earth.

Overall, the pattern of results in response to explicit questions that focused on 3D representations supports the view that the Australian advantage comes from the early transmission of scientific knowledge about the shape of the Earth and other cosmological information. The proficiency of Australian children in recognizing the location of Australia (and to some extent even England) on a 3D model and a globe testifies to their awareness of this knowledge. By contrast, the English children displayed an inconsistency that reflects this early lack of instruction on cosmology and geography. However, even for English children, the already-noted problems in drawing and in representation using clay models may be circumvented by the use of novel questioning methods. Gavin Nobes and his colleagues at the University of East London recently asked groups of kids in England to indicate cards that show the best representation of the shape of the Earth.[13] Even many young children preferred to choose cards showing a sphere with the people living all over (left) than a disc-shaped Earth (right):

It might be claimed that if children were robust in their under-standing, then differences in responses to the testing format would not exist. This contention assumes that children's awareness of the purpose and relevance of questioning in the testing context is as com-plete as that of adults. However, differences in responses to testing formats may not necessarily be interpreted to indicate a lack of robustness in understanding. Children – though certain of the answer – may not reveal what they know in response to some testing formats. Even adults may not reveal the depth of their understanding in response to questions and contexts that are liable to misinterpretation. Despite their knowledge that the Earth is round, as indicated on a multiple-choice questionnaire, a Greek PhD student of George's, Georgia Panagiotaki, found that some adults in England draw flat, hollow, or dual Earths using Vosniadou's drawing technique and plas-tercine models, for example, as shown below:

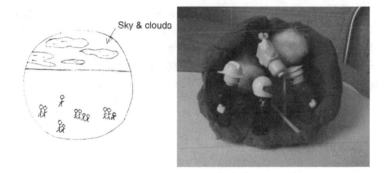

The results of our study stand in contrast to the proposal that chil-dren's knowledge in astronomy and geography needs to undergo a strong conceptual change. These results contradict the view that knowledge in this area necessarily begins with entrenched presuppo-sitions within an overarching framework theory that leads to children to embrace synthetic mental models of the shape of the Earth and the day–night cycle. Instead, our work shows that very young children can and do benefit from scientific information about the shape of the Earth and that some of this information may only be available by direct cultural transmission. However, it may be that the cultural context does not help with other aspects of spatial reasoning, such as knowing whether you are upside down in the southern hemisphere. There may be fragmentation and "compartmentalization" in children's knowledge of different aspects of cosmology that concern space, geography and astronomy. The problem in children's development may be to coordinate these different sources of knowledge into a unified system – a process that continues into adulthood.

Whether incorrect responses are guided by presuppositions or are based on fragmented knowledge, the differences between the Australian and English children were largely eliminated by age eight and coincide with the time that geography is introduced into the curriculum of English school children. Australian children are made aware of cosmology through transmission of factual knowledge by parents, media, and formal schooling at an early age. Just as Aboriginal Australian children who live in the desert have developed superior techniques of visuospatial memory,[15] urban Australian children may be accelerated in the development of cosmological knowledge.

The answers of the children that we interviewed indicate that knowledge in a domain such as cosmology may be transmitted directly through language and other cultural artifacts and need not be very much filtered through intuitive constraints based on entrenched presuppositions. However, the results of our study do not show that young children easily embrace scientific concepts. The internally consistent knowledge of the spherical Earth held by many children in our Australian sample, as shown in our investigation, reflects their ability to use nonobvious properties to conceptualize the cosmos but it cannot be claimed that their knowledge points to the possession of a deep explanatory understanding, for example, in defining concepts of gravity. Though this knowledge may serve well for elementary predictions, it need not entail an underlying causal understanding. Rather, it may simply serve as a "placeholder" for a causal essence that may not be understood until late childhood or even adulthood.[16] Indeed there are many processes that remain subject to misconceptions in adulthood, such as the process of diffusion when dye is dropped into a container of water. Such processes require understanding of randomly occurring simultaneous interactions among many variables.[17]

Each domain of knowledge – whether astronomy and geography, theory of mind, biology, or number – has its own rules and criteria for understanding. On this view, people's knowledge of unobservables, such as the spherical shape of the Earth, is determined by the ability of these beliefs to survive transmission from generation to generation, unlike, for example, aspects of the domain of number such as counting that occur spontaneously.[18] Cosmological knowledge may need a kind of double entry "book-keeping," in which assumptions about causes are based on actual world experience that do not actually overwrite what children hear from their culture but remain in coexistence with this culturally transmitted knowledge. The child may move equally comfortably between these various intuitive and scientific (culturally received) viewpoints whether actual or imagined, visual or verbal. One possibility has been raised by Richard Shweder, a psychological anthropologist at the University of Chicago, and his colleagues. It is that intuitive or modular constraints may be so "skeletal" that they must always be accompanied by sociocultural constraints.[19] In the case of cosmology and astronomy, these constraints are so skeletal that "general-purpose" learning can easily take over. This observation serves to explain how responses that seem to point to the existence of a flatness constraint may in reality be part of a fragmented and incoherent understanding. In essence, the rich knowledge acquired through cultural learning enables intuitive constraints in domains of knowledge such as astronomy and geography to be set aside early in development with the appropriate instruction.

For young children, cultural artifacts such as maps and globes are a means for comprehending those aspects of the world that lie outside direct experience. In the case of Australian children's early exposure to scientific information about cosmology, these artifacts can effectively protect knowledge from intuitions that are sometimes fallible. Recently, a group of Australian researchers who are favorably disposed to Vosniadou's theory have shown that children in Australia can be easily trained to hold a spherical conception of the Earth's shape, though on Vosniadou's measures they would have appeared to have held synthetic mental models constrained by presuppositions that are resistant to alternative points of view.[20] So much for entrenched presuppositions!

Strong words to this effect come from the Swedish interviewers in their article with its nice title, "Heavenly Talk," on conversations with children about astronomy.[21] Their work further dispels the notion that, in studies that have reassessed what children know, the kids were simply prompted to give a pattern of false positive results by making available as a choice the scientific alternatives to which they have most often been exposed, creating the illusion of understanding when they do not. They give the example of Cecilia (a child in grade 2) who is questioned with a globe:

Interviewer: Can people live all over the world?
Cecilia: Not in the sea.
I   Somewhere else where it is difficult to live?
C   Where there is war going on.
I   Do people live in Argentina? (pointing at Argentina on the globe).
C   Yes.
I   In Australia? (pointing at Australia on the globe)
C   Yes they do.
I   Isn't it peculiar that you can live on this side of the Earth?
C   No,'cos there is no up and down on the Earth.

Even if they do not immediately recognize the point of the interview, children may answer questions about Australia that allude to the ludicrous possibility that one could fall off the bottom of the Earth by striving to give a relevant answer. For example, when asked, "Isn't it strange that people can live down there?" Johan (in grade 2) replies, "They talk in a strange way." and Erica (grade 2) replies, "Well,'cos there has been a lot of fires there." Some even suggest "gravity" as the reason for why people do not fall off the Earth (though that does not of course mean that they have a full understanding of the theory of gravity). Given the strength of cultural learning in this respect, it is hardly surprising that some children would find such questions very difficult to answer as intended.

A final note is that George – whose mother was Greek and came from a Greek family with relatives in Melbourne – died tragically in an accident before our results where published. This chapter is a tribute to him.

Tripping across America

Under the rigors of modern travel, any adult – I think – can become easily confused with the day–night cycle. Here is one story.

It seemed simple enough. I had a discount air ticket that let me cross America at what seemed to be almost no cost at all. I had an unexpected opportunity to combine a visit with relatives in Detroit with dropping in to see a friend, a famous child psychologist in Berkeley, California.

I started off from Detroit on the way to San Francisco with a change in Kansas City. The weather in Detroit that December was fine, but once airborne we seemed to have quickly been caught up in a blizzard. We were able to land in Kansas City, but because of bad weather, the connecting flight that apparently had originated in Miami did not land in KC. I was stranded in KC airport for hours (not KFC – or Kentucky Fried Chicken – Airport, though I felt well and truly fried by the end of it). Finally, I was told that I could go to Mile High Airport in Denver and then connect on a flight to San Francisco (SF). I went to Denver and was grateful that after only about an hour there, I was able to last make my way to what at last was the final flight of the day.

Finally I arrived at SF Airport, tired and finding that there was no transportation. The "Airporter" was on strike and a taxi all the way to Berkeley would have cost $100 – a lot of money in 1988. Waiting at the baggage carousel was a young man named Tim (not his real name) who told me that he was a music student at Berkeley. He said that his family was going to pick him up and offered me a lift into town with them. We waited outside the terminal. An old Chevrolet drove up with what seemed to contain Tim's entire family with at least five adults or adult looking persons together with a dog whose head and tongue hung out the right rear window of the car. I squeezed into the back with Tim and the dog and then off we went for the ride into the town. About 40–50 minutes later we were crossing the Bay Bridge that leads from San Francisco to its outlying regions. A sign ahead indicated that Berkeley was to the left and Oakland was to the right. The family headed into Oakland! I had

Tripping across America *(cont.)*

heard that Oakland was a dangerous ghetto of poor, discontented people. Sure enough there were rows upon rows of derelict housing. We seemed to be going deeper and deeper into Oakland but Tim reassured me that it was all right. They were going to let me off on a bus stop where I could get a bus to Berkeley in no time.

The family did finally let me off. I thanked Tim and waited patiently. A bus arrived within 10 minutes. Now darkness had fallen. Yet that didn't bother me until we seemed to be headed deeper and deeper into a hellish part of the area with numerous bars and pawn-brokers. Then all of sudden, the bus driver called out, "Everyone out. There's smoke coming from the back of the bus! It could be on fire." I was left on the street for half an hour (that at the time seemed like a week). The bus kept smoking and I was stranded in front of a pool hall from which all sorts of scary noises seemed to emerge. There seemed to be lots of menacing street people about who would knife me at any moment. Then at last another bus arrived. I got on. Some passengers who crowded in looked at me quizzically, others as if they had seen a ghost. After about 20 minutes, the bus headed north into Berkeley. Gradually, the street people got off. Then a few stops up, a trickle of university people got on. The bus stopped at the Durant Hotel in Berkeley. I called my friend. By prior arrangement, he was going to pick me up there so that I could stay at his house, but it was after 10 p.m. I was supposed to have arrived by 4 that after-noon. His first words were, "Where were you, Mike? I thought you'd be here hours ago."

I couldn't explain until the next day while having breakfast with my host and his family. To this day, I remember especially the particularly Californian habit, I think, in which my host's daughter engaged – carefully brushing the pet dog's teeth with special toothpaste as she did after every one of the dog's meals. While she brushed, I spoke and told the story. But my host seemed most fascinated how I had miscalculated the time. Moving from east to west across the States meant that starting at 12 Detroit time and planning to be in San Francisco by 4 p.m. local SF time would mean a 7-hour trip with the three hour time change. Somehow

Tripping across America *(cont.)*

I had confused the time, thinking that SF time was three hours later than Detroit's. My trip actually had taken 13 hours, given the time change and the fact that I had arrived after 10 p.m. local time. Somehow in disbelief I had compressed this back to 7 hours! My disbelief at what had happened left me dazed and short of time. I had regressed in my astronomical and geographical knowledge.

Aftermath

When the two flights (Detroit–Kansas City, Kansas City–San Francisco) became three flights (Detroit–Kansas City, Kansas City–Denver, Denver–San Francisco), my bags seemed to be lost for good. It was no surprise that they did not arrive for 10 weeks. Still, I was grateful. The moral of the story: do not be taken in by the attractiveness of cheap airline travel unless you wish to risk all sorts of unanticipated adventures that arise from such unexpected travel opportunities.

Chapter 4

Biology, food, and hygiene

Cleanliness and order are not matters of
instinct; they are matters of education,
and like most great things, you must
cultivate a taste for them.
Benjamin Disraeli

Astronomy and geography involve an understanding of the properties
of things that are extremely large, such as the shape and rotation of
the earth and other bodies in the cosmos. Biology and health involve
the understanding of the properties of things that are very small such
as microbes and genes. Knowing about the nature of the biological
world is similar to knowing about the cosmos, in that it requires
knowledge of the distinction between the appearance of objects and
their underlying reality. As even young children have a grasp of this
knowledge, they should have the capacity to have a rudimentary
understanding, at least, of some basic biological processes. In this
chapter, we explore to what extent young children understand food
contamination and purification and the microscopic basis of the
transmission of illness.

From the outset, children's understanding must be placed in context
of what adults know. Over two-thirds of the world's human population
is dreadfully poor and even adults in Third World countries are
unlikely to exhibit much practical knowledge in instances of biology
and health. They may not be adept at disease prevention through
understanding how food and water can become polluted and what
measures can be taken to ensure purification. In terms of sheer numbers, these Third World countries are representative of the human
condition in the twenty-first century. Take Burkina Faso, formerly

called Upper Volta (pop. 13 million), in Africa. Based on 2002 statistics, people in Burkina Faso have a life expectancy of 46 years and a GDP per capita of US$191– a little over 52 cents a day – so that one American has the same GDP as at least 202 citizens of Burkina Faso. However, Burkino Faso's "prosperity" dwarfs that of other African countries such as Ethiopia (population 68 million) with a life expectancy of 44 years and a per capita GDP of $94. In July 2005, there was considerable publicity about the plight of Africa in a "Make Poverty History" Campaign, but poor health and wealth is not confined to that continent. For example, people living in the Asian country of Myanmar, formerly Burma (population 42 million), have a life expectancy of 52 years and a per capita GDP of US$97.[1] Throughout rapidly industrializing China and India, there remain many millions of people whose circumstances are similar to those of Myanmar.

In countries such as Burkina Faso, Ethiopia, and Myanmar, the average education level is poor, life expectancy very low, and knowledge of Western science is uncertain. In such places, there is little research about children's understanding of biology and health – let alone that of their parents.

Conceptual change in children's biological concepts

Published over 20 years ago, Susan Carey's *Conceptual Change in Childhood* remains one of the most significant works on the topic of children's biological understanding so far. In this book, Carey, then based at MIT, makes several strong claims about the nature of children and biology. For one thing, consistent with Piaget and Flavell, she maintains that "young children are notoriously appearance bound." She subscribes, for example, to the view that young children regard gender to be tied to appearances rather than a matter of biology; they believe that boys and girls can change into the opposite sex if they wear opposite sex clothes or play opposite sex games.

However, as Carey recognizes, concepts can change in many ways in that these can be "differentiated, integrated, or reanalyzed" in the course of cognitive development that takes different forms in different areas of knowledge. In this regard, her approach departs from that of Piaget. Her view expressed in 2000[2] is that the "main barrier to learning the curricular materials we so painstakingly developed is not what the student lacks, but what the student *has*, namely, alternative conceptual frameworks for understanding the phenomena covered by the theories we are trying to teach." That is, children's initial concepts in domains of knowledge can act as obstacles toward a mature understanding. The "entrenched presuppositions" view on children's cosmology is one. Another example comes from Carey's position on children's early concepts of biology.

For Carey, young children's ideas about biology – at least in Western countries such as the United States – progress through two phases of development. In the first phase, from the preschool years to approximately age six, children learn facts about the biological world. For instance, preschoolers know that animals are alive and that babies come from inside their mothers and look like their parents. Immersed in family conversation, they recognize that people can get sick from dirty food[3] or from playing with a sick friend, and that medicine makes people better. Though this knowledge is impressive, it is quite different from having a "framework theory" that involves the connecting of facts to create a coherent, unified conceptual structure. Not until the age of 7 years or so are children said to begin to construct a coherent framework theory of biology through a process of "conceptual change."

Carey maintains that such change in the domain of biology is most probably of the nonconservative, strong variety. Children's early concepts are undifferentiated in that these embrace notions that are inconsistent or "incommensurable" and so demand cognitive restructuring in the strong sense. Change consists of differentiation and reanalysis to the extent that it involves strong restructuring and children acquire new causal concepts.

According to this analysis, young children cling to appearances rather than underlying realities that involve true causal mechanisms. In their biological understanding, they think that irritants such as pepper as well as germs transmit appearances that correspond to colds, that traits such as eye color are the result of environmental influence rather than biological inheritance, and that a dead corpse retains certain biological attributes of life. Change in this area does not proceed very rapidly as children have presuppositions of the nature of the world – similar to those that Vosniadou maintains exist in the area of cosmology – and they cling to their initial theories in the face of conflicting evidence. Thus it can be very hard for some young children to concede that death involves the breakdown of the organization and functions of body organs. They often think that the buried still need bodily functions such as eating, breathing, and excretion.[4]

Carey's position on conceptual change in childhood understanding of biology can profitably be seen in relation to the work of the Canadian philosopher and cognitive scientist Paul Thagard. Most notably, Thagard has made a distinction between conservative and nonconservative conceptual changes in relation to how scientists reason about disease.[5] Conservative conceptual changes involve extensions to existing concepts and beliefs – a form of "knowledge enrichment." The expansion during the twentieth century of the causes of diseases to include nutritional, immunological, and metabolic factors does not challenge the standing of germ theory and thus involves conservative conceptual change. By contrast, the humoral theory of disease causation held by the ancient Greeks has made way for germ theory in a process of nonconservative conceptual change.

The Greeks, led by Hipprocrates, proposed that imbalance in the humors or fluids of blood, phlegm, yellow bile, and black bile were associated with heredity, diet, or climate results in illness. It was not until a colleague of Copernicus, the Italian physician, poet, and astronomer Girolamo Fracastoro, published his treatise on contagion

Fracastoro

in 1546 that infection through the transmission of invisible particles was seen to be the cause of some diseases. Yet for many years, this account coexisted with the notion of humoral causation. As Thagard observes, in the nineteenth century, the eventual transition from humoral theory to germ theory involved a conceptual change that may be deemed nonconservative in substantial respects, as new causal concepts and rules replaced the old ones.

Is it possible that children need to begin as adults were in the sixteenth century? Can we yet make conclusive statements about children's biological understanding? Is there good evidence about their knowledge of the biological inheritance of physical traits, the properties of life and the permanence of death, and the nature of germs, microbial contamination, and processes of purification? Although the analysis that children have entrenched presuppositions that impede conceptual change may apply well in some domains, we have seen that it not the case for cosmology. Is it applicable or not to certain key aspects of biology?

Children's understanding of germs and the biological basis for illness

One view, following Piaget, is that children aged 2–6 years of age claim that illnesses such as colds are transmitted through magic or God, or from the sun or trees. In particular, young children may believe that illness is the result of having been punished for naughty behavior. They think that a child who transgresses by lying or stealing or by playing with prohibited objects will be more likely to meet with a mishap and fall ill than a child who behaves well. According to this account, young children believe that illnesses such as colds are the result of punishment for misbehavior (a belief in what Piaget termed "immanent justice") rather than caused by microbial contamination that is not readily visible. Children's concepts of illness need to undergo change to embrace the belief that germs can create illness.[6]

However, we know now that young children in Western countries and Japan generally do not endorse misbehavior as a cause of illnesses that can be readily explained in terms of germ transmission. If asked to consider as a cause of colds either a child's naughtiness or his nearness to another child who coughs and sneezes, they choose the latter alternative. Moreover, young children regard susceptibility to illness, rather than naughtiness, to be a likely cause of colds. For example, two Japanese psychologists, Kayoko Inagaki and Giyoo Hatano, showed children cards illustrating two boys: boy A, who often hits and pinches his friend on the back but eats a lot at meals every day, or boy B, who is a good friend but eats only a little. When asked which boy is more likely catch a cold from a child who has a cold and is coughing a lot, most of the 5-year-olds that they tested chose boy B. They placed more weight on the biological cause (insufficient nutriments) rather than misbehavior.[7]

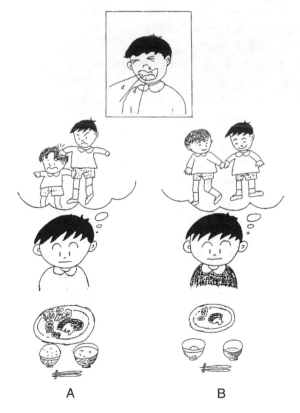

A   B

In this way, children may prove able in at least some circumstances to consider the invisible nature of contaminants in the transmission of illness. Even so, they may still not have a biological conception of disease that involves the notion that germs are living organisms that reproduce. For example, instead of identifying germs as living organisms that multiply, American children aged 4–7 years appear to maintain that germs are not alive and do not eat or die and that colds are equally likely to be transmitted by poisons, or by irritants such as pepper, as by germs. They may also express the view that illness transmission through germs occurs immediately on contact rather than after a period of incubation, and that germs grow like tumors but do not reproduce inside the body.[8]

On this basis, it might be concluded that young children may make judgments about the role of germs in illness without considering biological causality at all. They may regard illness as simply due to contact with noxious substances rather than as the outcome of microscopic infection by germs. If so, they may simply be reproducing a learned fact ("colds come from being close to someone else who is germy with a cold") rather than embedding their knowledge of illness within a biological theory. However, as Chuck Kalish of the University of Wisconsin has observed "Poisons and other chemical/physical entities can be viewed as mechanisms of contagion and contamination. Poison is clearly a contaminant. If one contacts poison one may become ill. Poison may also be a vehicle for contagion. For example, if someone gets a particularly virulent poison on his hand and then touches someone else, that second person may come to show the effects of the poison as well. This transfer of materials (and the effects of the materials) represents a coherent model of physical infection ... Germs function like poisons, as physical agents of contamination."[9]

Moreover, even though children may be overinclusive in labeling irritants and poisons as agents of illness transmission and some may appear to believe that germs do not function as living organisms, their responses on the tasks used to test their knowledge do not necessarily reflect the absence of an understanding that apparently fresh substances may in reality be contaminated.

Some years ago, I collaborated with an educational psychologist, David Share, in attempt to determine what children know about contamination. David and I sought to test the hypothesis that 3-year-olds are sensitive to the invisible nature of contamination in a naturally occurring context and, accordingly, can make evaluations and inferences for others' false responses and choices about contamination. We devised a situation in which Australian 3-year-olds during their snack time viewed some juice that had been contaminated by a cockroach – a situation that can occur naturally in Australia and many countries with a climate conducive to a large and varied insect population.[10] Our experiment consisted of three simple phases in which the children were interviewed individually. Within each phase, the orders of the stories, questions and alternatives were counterbalanced. The actual names of the story characters were the same sex as the children.

In the first phase on contamination labeling, the experimenter told the children in the course of natural conversation during their snack time, "Here's some juice. Oh! It has a cockroach in it." The cockroach *(Periplaneta americana)* floated to the top. The experimenter removed it from sight without a trace and asked, "Is the juice OK or not OK to drink?"

In the second phase, the experimenter gave the children two stories and asked them to evaluate the responses of others. Story A was: "A grown-up poured juice into a glass with a cockroach in it. The cockroach floated on top and then the grown-up threw it away. He asked John, a boy your age, whether the juice would be OK to drink or whether it would make him sick? John said that the juice would be OK to drink. Was John right? Would it make him sick?" Responses to the last question were used as the evaluation measure. Story B was the same except that a child said the juice would make him sick.

In the third phase on inferences for others' false choices, the children were shown two glasses and told, "Here is some chocolate milk and here is some water. A cockroach fell into the chocolate milk. It floated on top. A grown-up pulled it out and threw it away. A boy named Jim came along to ask for a glass of chocolate milk which was his favourite drink. Jim didn't know the cockroach had fallen in. Which glass did Jim want? Which glass should the grown-up give him?" The experimenter displayed two signs and continued, "Jim wanted to tell other children that one of the two drinks would make them sick. He had two signs: "happy face" and "sad face." Which one should he choose to tell the children? You take the "sad face" and put in front of that drink to tell them not to drink it." To see whether children would be consistent in their labeling of contamination, a different interviewer who was unaware of the children's answers re-enacted the first phase about two weeks later using a different drink.

Contrary to the notion that young children lack the capacity to comprehend the nature of contamination, 77 percent consistently responded that the juice was not good, 83 percent correctly evaluated the responses of other children to the incident in both stories, 67 percent correctly inferred that, while a child may want a chocolate drink, he or she should be given an alternative, and 75 percent chose a sad face without prompting as a warning against the drink. Since we wrote up this study, several other students have reported results that are broadly consistent with ours.[11]

How then do kids represent germs? If given limited instruction, children may be inhibited in applying their ability to distinguish between appearance and reality and may not be encouraged to think of germs as the biological organisms that they are. In the absence of such knowledge enrichment, they may seem limited to a "physical theory" of transmission. However, in practice, adults may not be so good at distinguishing between appearance and reality also. Rather, they can conceive of germs as "cute" or "nasty" depending on their origin, and may become convinced that their loved ones are too pure to carry harmful germs and that others who are impure and unloved and are especially prone to transmit germs and infections.[12] In fact, when asked to draw the germs of those who are not among their loved ones, undergraduates at American universities give the examples shown here:

Given that adults themselves often do not possess adequate representations of germs, it is hardly surprising that children also do not. Despite the ability of even young children to understand the difference between appearance and reality, few kids are asked to draw their ideas of a germ and to discuss how germs infect the body in the form of harmful live organisms. Yet when asked to draw a germ, the outcome is similar to that of adults:

Portraying germs in the form of tiny menacing human-like organisms can be used as a strategy toward improving children's knowledge of health and well-being. However, children may not be told as much as they could know about germs. Instead, they are often simply told that germs are to be avoided by keeping one's distance.

Still, it is possible to facilitate children's understanding about germs, particularly as preschoolers can discriminate the basis for movement of animate objects such as animals and inanimate objects such as rocks. They know that, even if a rock looks like an animal, the rock cannot move by itself just as it does not eat or breathe. As shown by work of Christine Massey and Rochel Gelman at the University of

Pennsylvania in Philadelphia, American children aged 3 and 4 years are able to use the distinction between animate and inanimate objects in deciding whether an object can move by itself.[13] They can distinguish between animals – even if unfamiliar – that can initiate their own movements, such as a sloth or a pygmy marmoset, from objects for which movement must depend on an external source, such as statues of animals or vehicles like an electric golf caddy. These representations can serve by analogy as a foundation for learning that germs are like other living things that eat, multiply, and die, though they cannot be seen. In this regard, explicit discussion about the microscopic basis of infection through contact with germs can help young children to understand the microscopic nature of contamination.[14]

Once in contact, always in contact: contagious essence and conceptions of purification in American and Hindu Indian children

So far virtually all research on children's understanding of biology and health has taken place in Western countries and Japan. How are ideas about contamination and purification transmitted to children in the developing world?

We began to address this question in a study in which I was fortunate to team up with Paul Rozin and Ahalya Hejmadi, a postdoctoral fellow from India who had come to work in Paul's laboratory, also at the University of Pennsylvania. Author of over a 150 articles, many of which bear extraordinarily creative titles such as "You can bring a rat to poison but you can't make him think," Paul is indisputably the world's greatest living authority on the psychology of food and cuisine. Ahalya was at Penn to learn from Paul about how culture influences our conceptions of food and cuisine – an issue on which I had corresponded with Paul for many years. Ahalya, Paul, and I reasoned that conceptual change in American children may involve a progressive "tuning in" to the biological nature of invisible contaminants, in which children relinquish the notion that contamination simply reflects an immediate contact or association with noxious substances, in favor of the Western culturally received view that contamination results from infection through the transmission of biological organisms.

During the time when they may be coming to develop a biological understanding of contamination, we hypothesized that children's conceptions are likely to be influenced by the "laws of sympathetic magic" that have been extensively studied by anthropologists.[15] These laws seem to be present among people in both Western and nonWestern cultures.

One of the laws, "the magical law of contagion," states that persons or objects that have come into contact with each other continue to exert an influence on each other even after the physical contact has been severed (once in contact, always in contact). Any kind of properties might be transmitted, whether these are physical, moral or psychological in nature and harmful or beneficial in effect. The "source" and the "recipient" of contagion may come into direct or indirect contact (mediated by a "vehicle") that may be brief or intimate. Transmission of properties occurs through the transmission of "essence" which is believed to contain the essential unchanging properties of the source.

The area of food and eating is particularly appropriate for investigating the magical law of contagion, because in many cultures it is frequently believed that persons receive the properties of a source from ingesting food.[16] The act of eating is a biological necessity embedded in a social framework and, as a result, it has strong social and moral implications for most people. The mouth is the principal incorporative organ. Nothing could be more threatening or intimate than to take something into the self (and allow it to enter the body), and yet this process occurs in every act of ingestion. Biology dictates that ingestion is an absolute and frequent necessity, incorporating benefits such as nutrition, as well as risks such as inadvertently ingesting toxic substances. Consequently, as Rozin notes, ingestion is an act about which people feel strongly, and liking and disliking are terms that naturally apply to food. If a substance is a contaminant, it can prompt individuals to reject an otherwise acceptable food because they perceive the food to have been soiled or made impure by even a trace amount of that substance, whether visible or not. This process can extend to involve associational thinking about contamination, in that persons believe that mere proximity between a contaminant and an object can contaminate a previously neutral object.[17]

In magical contagion, the nature of the relationship between the source and the recipient determines whether contact has an impact upon the recipient's perceived well-being and what type of impact it will be. For example, the Kai of northern New Guinea believe that "everything with which a man comes in contact retains something of his soul stuff." Accordingly, one's enemy's character, or evil intent could be absorbed into his clothing and passed on to the next person who is in contact with the garment. The Dowayo in Cameroon believe that mountain water cannot be safe to drink unless offered by the owners and that uninvited drinking will result in disease.[18] These beliefs are not inconsistent with those that we find in Western countries. At least for American adults, there are three different models of contagion: an association model (mere association in proximity between the contaminant such as a cockroach and the self or the substance to be ingested), a material essence model (transfer of physical properties, e.g., contamination of an edible substance through contact with a contaminant), and spiritual essence (transfer of nonmaterial properties such as through contact with a stranger or "impure person").[19]

In our study, we sought to compare American and Hindu Indian children's responses to situations of potential contamination and purification. In Hindu India, food is the major vehicle for maintaining social distinctions and an important way of enacting basic moral beliefs.[20] The moral status of food derives from notions of purity and pollution that help define the caste structure. On the one hand, sharing of food has a homogenizing function in that it equalizes the status of sharers and promotes intimacy and solidarity. On the other hand, food has a "heterogenizing" function. A refusal to share food with members of lower castes serves to establish rank, distance, and segmentation. The basic rule in Hindu India is that higher caste members can give food to members of a lower caste, although one cannot accept food prepared by members of a lower caste. Rule violations are often viewed as disgusting, a threat to the soul and a danger to the spirit, and hence contribute to forms of contamination sensitivity in Hindu Indian children that differ from children raised in a Western culture.

To examine possible age and cultural differences in contamination and purification, we gave a sample of American and Hindu Indian children a variety of situations in which they had to judge whether juice that had been in contact with a foreign object and then "purified" through a variety of techniques was all right to drink. These were 125 children (boys and girls aged either 4–5 or 8 years) in the eastern Indian state of Orissa, from two schools located in the state capital of Bhubaneswar, and 106 children (boys and girls) in Philadelphia.[21]

We read the children a picture storybook in which they looked at a series of pictures. The story characters in the pictures were identical from one story to another and between the two cultures, except that the complexion of the characters in the Indian story was darker, and the mother in the Indian story wore traditional Indian clothing (a sari). The juice, the contaminants, and purifiers were chosen to be appropriate for both India and the US. The contaminants included a cockroach (in or near the juice), a strand of hair, and a male stranger (dressed in trousers and a shirt, touching or taking a sip from the juice), and a distasteful food (spinach). For each contaminant, the children were first asked to name the contaminant objects in the pictures and to agree with the acceptability of each object to ingest in the words of one or the other twin who offered either a "yes" or "no" choice. Except in the case of the stranger, each object was illustrated to appear separately on a plate in front of the twins. In the case of the "stranger near" condition, the pictures illustrated a stranger who comes in and picks up the glass of lemonade, but does not drink from it. Instead, he merely holds it in his hand. The pictures for the "cockroach near" condition showed a cockroach that remained near the target (a glass of lemonade), but did not get inside the glass.

The objects were depicted in front of two twin boys or girls (matched to the gender of the child who was the story listener) who were offered a glass of lemon squash/lemonade in a number of situations. In all cases, one twin said it was OK to drink the juice, and the other said that it was not. Rather than answer a series of direct questions about whether the juice was good to drink, we asked each child to indicate which one of the twins was right. The purpose of using this type of questioning format was to better enable children to express what they know in the presence of an adult who may appear already to have the correct answer.

In the second part of the procedure, the children were asked to indicate whether the lemonade remained contaminated when each of the contaminants was removed without a trace. Then in the third part, the purifiers were introduced in relation to the specific contaminants of cockroach, stranger, and hair. These took the form of (1) addition of a color to the previously contaminated juice, (2) boiling and cooling of the uncolored, previously contaminated juice, and (3) the mother of the twins taking a sip of the uncolored, unboiled, previously contaminated juice. In addition, the children were asked whether juice that had not been in previous contact with the contaminants would be drinkable following the addition of each of the three purifiers (color change, boiling, or mother sipping).

During the story, the children were asked if it was OK or not to drink the juice after it had been in contact with the contaminants and undergone various forms of "purification." Again, children were asked to agree with one of the twins in the story. In the case of the mother sipping, it was made clear that the mother did not know the juice was contaminated.

Consistent with the emphasis on purity and pollution in Hindu culture, the Indian children – even at 4–5 years – were more often sensitive than the Americans to contaminants. In many cases, this level approached 100 percent rejection of juice with a contaminant, in contrast to about 10–33 percent of American children who indicated that juice would be acceptable even if it had been in contact with one of the contaminants. Contamination sensitivity in the Indian children becomes more indelible with age so that, for contamination though contact with a cockroach or a stranger, Indian 8-year-olds regard boiling as significantly less effective as a purifier than do Indian 4–5-year-olds, and as ineffective as adding coloring and the mother sipping. Indeed, in the Oriya language of Bhubaneswar, there is a particular word, *aintha* (*jhuta* in the Hindi language used in many parts of India), that refers to the food remaining after another person has consumed some. In this context, any contact with the mouth, either direct (through biting or sipping) or indirect (through the hand or saliva) can render the entire amount of food unacceptable. By contrast, many American children in either age group considered boiling to be an effective purifier: about a third indicated that boiling would reverse contamination in the case of juice judged to have been contaminated by the cockroach and about a half in the case juice judged to have been contaminated by the stranger.

Our study is an initial step toward an examination of cultural influences on the development of contamination sensitivity and purification conceptions. More information is needed on the basis of why children perceive objects to be contaminated and purifiers to be effective or ineffective in eliminating contamination. On the basis of a perceived indelible material or spiritual essence, children may reject a drink that has been in contact with a contaminant such as a cockroach and regard it to be impervious to any sort of purification, despite having knowledge of germs and a biological understanding of the microscopic nature of contamination. Alternatively, some young kids may lack a biological understanding that would permit them to acknowledge the effectiveness of boiling in order to purify a contaminated substance. Though this knowledge that boiling is an effective purifier may serve well for elementary predictions, it need not entail an underlying causal understanding in terms of germ theory. Rather, as might be the case for cosmological facts, it may simply serve as a "placeholder" for a causal essence that may not be understood until adolescence or adulthood–if at all.

Even when children do judge that a purifier would be effective, as in the case of the mother sipping the drink, they may be responding to social pressure or influence rather than seeing the drink as imbued with a positive essence. One interpretation of this result is that the children in our study were indeed responding to the spiritual essence of the mother that they regarded as powerful enough to reverse the effects of contamination. Alternatively, children may know that the mother's sipping juice cannot act as a purifier. However, they may be unaware that, in a well-meaning effort to test their conceptions of purification, an adult experimenter could portray a mother as wanting to show that the juice is all right to consume, implying that the juice can be made pure after all. Children's responses that mother sipping can act to purify a contaminated substance may then be based on an expectation that the purpose of the question is to show their willingness to accede to the example shown by the mother. This possibility remains to be examined in further research.

Knowledge of biology, food and hygiene in Third World countries

The high rate of rejection of juice that had been contaminated for the Indian children shown in our study could conceivably stem from contamination being more of a practical daily concern for them than for American children. It might be thought that contaminated food or water is more of a real threat in India, in which case a more conservative approach to contamination might result from practical experience rather than cultural beliefs. In our sample of Hindu Indian children, however, food and water were always safe so cultural differences are consistent with the Indian emphasis on purity. Within Hindu culture, washing is a generally effective way of ridding the self of pollution. In this context, boiling would be the close to this method of purification, and it was generally the most successful procedure for older children.

Nevertheless, many adults as well as children in Third World countries do not appear knowledgeable about the essentials of cleanliness. There is a need to make explicit the range of possibilities by which disease is transmitted from persons lacking hygiene directly to other persons or via contact with animals, as illustrated on the following page. An issue that cries out for further study concerns cultural differences in conceptions of hygiene that are fundamental to disease prevention. For example, in Third World countries, diarrhoea causes the deaths of over three million children a year – deaths that could be prevented through washing with soap and clean water. Moreover, although India is rapidly developing, there is still poor sanitation in regions such as Bihar and Uttar Pradesh, where lack of hygiene in high-density populations alarmingly facilitates transmission of polio in children and jeopardizes the effectiveness of vaccine.[22] An urgent need is to carry out intervention programs in areas of the world that lack hygiene and to ensure that these are effective.

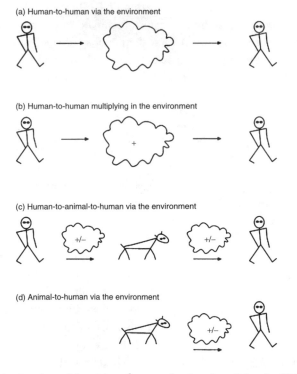

(a) Human-to-human via the environment

(b) Human-to-human multiplying in the environment

(c) Human-to-animal-to-human via the environment

(d) Animal-to-human via the environment

Valerie Curtis and her coworkers at the London School of Hygiene and Tropical Medicine recently carried out an intensive three-year study of hygiene practices in Bobo-Dioulasso, the second largest city in Burkina Faso. The aim was to ensure that mothers' hands were washed with soap after going to the latrine and after cleaning their babies' bottoms. Communication involved house-to-house visits, discussion groups in health centers, hygiene curriculum in primary schools, and a total of 82 street theatre presentations and 2580 radio transmission spots. An observational survey after the intervention ended showed that mothers washed their hands with soap after going to the latrine on 17 percent of occasions that, as opposed to 1 percent before the intervention. The proportion of occasions in which mothers washed with soap after having cleaned their babies' bottoms rose from 13 percent to 31 percent. These effects are highly significant statistically but there still remains the overwhelming proportion of occasions, 69 percent of the time, that mothers did not wash with soap thus rendering their children, themselves, and others liable to infection.

The intervention program was very active and visible. It is difficult to believe that any parent who cared for a child would ignore its vital message, even if it was presented in terms of the social and aesthetic desirability of hygiene rather than in terms of avoiding diarrhoea germs. As shown by a recent study in neighboring Benin, even when parents do want to have a readily available latrine for use, this may be for the expressed purpose of prestige, such as a need to have a latrine to receive guests and to avoid shame or embarrassment. It may also be for convenience and comfort (e.g., avoiding exposure to dew, strong sun and rain) or for safety from personal dangers (e.g., fear of voodoo sorcery, magic, and dead spirits in the night). If anything, prevention of disease is a minor consideration.

The research reports produced by Curtis and her colleagues[23] with provocative titles such as "Is hygiene in our genes?" and "Why the latrines in Benin are so few and far between" lead to this pivotal question: Is it the case that information about contamination and purification needs to be transmitted early in life as it is Western countries and cannot wait for adulthood? The answer to this question is not yet clear, but there is no doubt that understanding of the Western message of germ theory can elude adults, not only in Africa, but in many underdeveloped countries thoughout the world. I remember a visit to a hotel in the Yucatan Peninsula of Mexico in the 1970s in which a cleaner carefully boiled, filtered, and cooled drinking water for guests, and then added ice cubes that were made from straight tap water! Given the lack of understanding of hygiene in many parts of the world, are we expecting too much of children to have this sort of knowledge? Much more remains to be known.

Conclusion: conservative vs nonconservative conceptual change

In the cases of germs and the biological basis for illness, children can be capable at an early age of recognizing the existence of invisible causal processes, though they are not yet able to specify their nature. Certainly there is a strong case for education in general, and education about food and hygiene in particular, that would prolong life and enable children to survive to benefit from education in other areas. Burkina Faso, for example, has been observed to have the highest adult illiteracy rate anywhere with 87.2 percent of adults unable to read – an astounding nearly 9 out of 10! It is small wonder that Burkino Faso and its neighbors do not rate very highly on quality of life indices.

Whether children can have a biological understanding that involves a conception of germs in processes of contamination and purification is uncertain. However, clearly, development in the domain of biology may often involve knowledge enrichment and conservative conceptual change with no strong presuppositions – or no knowledge at all – that holds back their understanding.

Until alternative explanations are eliminated, there is reason to be cautious in embracing the position that children's biological understanding necessarily undergoes a nonconservative conceptual change that requires a strong restructuring in which previous causal concepts that are "incommensurable" with the culturally received scientific view are abandoned. It may be inertia and habit rather than presuppositions that impede understanding, and there is every reason to believe that even very young children in both the developed and developing world have the potential to profit from instruction about biology and health. Here, Inagaki and Hatano again provide valuable insights. They note that children in Japan and elsewhere are often involved in caring for other things and so learn rules for maintaining the health of animals and plants, as well as for themselves.[24] This understanding is adaptive in that it enables them to form predictions about the behavior of familiar natural kinds such as mammals regarding food procurement and reproduction.

Disgust as a weapon

Reactions to food are powerful tools in expressing our feelings. These concern the success of biological processes such as ingestion, and how we perceive our own biological health.

I had just returned from a conference from hell. The papers that people gave were among the most trivial and boring I had ever experienced. A woman insisted that she give me a ride to the airport and for the next two hours she poured out her heart. She had been jilted and abused by family and friends and was about to get the sack at work – the plotting of which she described in minute detail. After this cheery ride, we said goodbye never to see each other again. I waited in line to check in for the flight back home. Finally, I got my boarding pass and then patiently ascended to the packed plane. I thought my troubles were over but then found that the elderly lady sitting next to me was petrified of flying. For the whole of the two hour flight, she kept murmuring, "I've got the heebee jeebees." Then about 10 minutes before the plane was about to land, I heard a rush of vomit hissing into a paper bag with accompanying smell. I couldn't wait to get off the plane and ran into a taxi.

I was so glad to have been dropped off at home. I made some coffee and started to read the newspaper. I thought my troubles for the day were over. But then that woman appeared. All of my neighbors were fine gentle people except for one who was a hypochondriac and liked to complain to me about everything that was wrong with her: the neck, the back, the sensitive stomach, the migraines in the head, the loopy legs, loss of hearing, loss of vision, etc. She was only 46 but could have been 96 in the litany of complaints that prevented her from relating to people properly. She even tried to admit herself to hospital on a number of occasions but had to be escorted off the grounds because doctors never regarded her problems as serious enough to warrant hospitalization. This time she arrived wearing a heart monitor, apparently having been in contact with someone who had told her about the prevalence of heart problems. But I couldn't find a way of politely saying that I wanted to be alone.

Disgust as a weapon *(cont.)*

Just then my cat Minou arrived. Minou and I had come a long way together and somehow she could sense my frustration. She did something she had never done in the 15 years we had been together – coming in through the door with a tasty mouse in her mouth! The sight of the mouse made the dials on the woman's heart monitor go berserk. She ran out of the house disgusted beyond belief. Minou seemed not to enjoy the woman's company. She had frequently threatened to make Minou wear a bell to scare off the birds that Minou, who naturally being a cat and having no relation to Socrates's Meno, liked to chase.

Minou and the mouse in the house

Once the woman had left, Minou simply dropped the now very dead mouse outside and went off to engage in other catlike pursuits. Minou never again brought a mouse or other another animal into the house with her. These days the woman is never seen.

Chapter 5

Life and death

It is impossible to experience one's death
objectively and still carry a tune.
Woody Allen

If children can have insight into the microscopic nature of germs as
a cause of illness and have knowledge of processes of food contamination and purification, what do they do know about the fundamentals
of life and death? Do they have an understanding of properties that
are transmitted by natural birth parents such as physical appearance,
and those that are transmitted by cultural influences by nonbiological,
adoptive parents, such as beliefs about animals? Do they understand
the finality of death in a material sense as the cessation of biological
functioning? Do they understand that things that are no longer alive
stop eating, sleeping, and breathing?

Children's understanding of biological inheritance

In an influential study, Susan Carey and her colleagues (Gregg
Solomon, Susan Johnson, and Deborah Zaitchik) investigated
whether children understand that the family in which a child grows
up does not determine physical characteristics such as eye color.[1]
American children aged 4–7 years heard a story about a little boy who
was born to a shepherd but grew up within the home of a king or,
conversely, a story about a little boy who was born to a king but grew
up within the home of a shepherd. Before the testing began, the children were asked two control questions to ensure their comprehension
of events in the story: "Where was the little boy born? Where did he
grow up?" These were answered correctly. Then the children were
asked several test questions that concerned, for example, pairs of

physical traits and beliefs said to be characteristic of the king or the shepherd, such as, "When the boy grows up, will he have green eyes like the king or brown eyes like the shepherd?" and "When the boy grows up, will he think that skunks can see in the dark like the shepherd or that skunks cannot see in the dark like the king?"

Many of the 4-year-olds answered that both physical traits and beliefs are determined in the environment created by the adoptive parent, whether this was a shepherd or king. Not until 7 years of age did children often report that physical traits are associated with the biological parent and beliefs with the adoptive parent. On this basis, Carey and her colleagues concluded that children undergo conceptual change in their biological understanding in that they start to differentiate biological from environmental influences on physical traits only after the age of 6 years.[2]

Studies in dramatically different cultures support these findings. For example, Rita Astuti, a social anthropologist at the London School of Economics, travelled to the island of Madagascar off the coast of Africa and asked native Vezo children and adults questions similar to those posed by Carey and her colleagues. In Astuti's test of their understanding of the influence of birth and adoptive parents, the Vezo were told a story about a baby born to one set of parents and raised by another.

The birth parents – described in Vezo idiom as "the father and mother who generated the child" – are traveling through the forest; they are attacked by bandits; they have time to hide the baby under a bush; the parents are killed but the baby is found and raised by another set of parents; the adoptive parents – described as "the father and the mother who raised the child" – nurture him with affection and love.

Then the Vezo were asked questions as follows:

The father who generated the child had pointed ears, whereas the father who raised the child had roundish ears. In your opinion, when the child is fully grown up, will he have pointed ears like the father who generated him, or roundish ears like the father who raised him? The father who generated the child believed that chameleons have 30 teeth, whereas the father who raised the child believed that chameleons have 20 teeth. In your opinion, when the child is fully grown up, will he believe that chameleons have

30 teeth like the father who generated him or will he believe that chameleons have 20 teeth like the father who raised him?

As in Carey's study of American children, most young Vezo children, unlike adults, did not give a biological interpretation for physical characteristics (similar to the natural father) and an environmental interpretation for beliefs (similar to the adoptive father). Even many Vezo adolescents either did not differentiate between the two, or reflected a birth or adoptive bias in both cases.[3]

All of this seems in keeping with a story told by Carey on young children's native understanding of babies based on an American mother's report of a conversation that she had with her 4-year-old son. This mother was originally sceptical of Carey's claim that preschoolers' concepts of *animal* and *baby* differ from those of adults in that they do not realize that all animals have babies and that reproduction is a core property of each animal species. To put this claim to a test, she asked her 4-year-old, whether pigeons have baby pigeons. He answered, "Sure, and dogs have baby dogs; cows have baby cows; cats have baby cats ...." At this point, she asked "and what about worms; do worms have baby worms?" He stopped dead in his tracks, thought for a long time, and finally replied, slowly, "No... worms have *short* worms." Being an articulate youngster, he could explain perfectly the difference between baby animals and short ones. The essence of his account was that babies are small, helpless, versions of larger creatures. Because of their limitations in moving about, they require the bigger ones to take care of them. As he explained, baby birds cannot *walk* and need their parents to bring them worms; baby cats and dogs do not have open eyes, and cannot walk; and *baby* people, the archetypical baby creatures, are useless – they can't talk, walk, play, and eat by themselves. His idea seemed to be that, as long adult worms are so limited in what they can do, there is not much difference between the longer and shorter ones. Therefore, you would not want to call short worms "babies." When asked by his mother whether you could think of short worms as baby worms, he replied that you could if you wanted to, but then you might as well think of small rocks as baby rocks.

This incident may be interpreted to illustrate that young children have a concept of animal and baby that departs from biology or even excludes biology. However, another possibility is that the boy's focus of his conversation with the mother has shifted, or was never on the same track in the first place. The 4-year-old is talking about what it takes to ensure that a baby survives, whereas the mother is still talking about the necessity for babies in animal reproduction. Probed further and more specifically, the boy might well have embraced the idea that babies in a biological sense are as necessary for the maintenance of worms as an animal species as they are for cows, dogs, cats and birds. Adults also talk about the relation between adults and babies in nonbiological terms. For example, a man may not be viewed as a father unless he provides food for his babies.

Moreover, the position that young children do not distinguish between heredity and environment seems incompatible with other studies that have shown not an environmental bias for explaining the nature of physical traits but a biological interpretation. For example, American children aged as young as $4^{1}/_{2}$ years are generally able to identify that same-species plants are the sole originator of seeds for new plants of that species. Similarly work carried out by Ken Springer of Southern Methodist University in Dallas has shown that most American 4- and 5-year-olds understand that human babies grow inside their mothers (77 percent of the children that he questioned).[4] According to Springer, they possess a "naive theory of kinship" in that they can use this knowledge to predict the properties of offspring. They can say that a baby who is physically dissimilar to the mother will likely share her stable internal properties (e.g., "grey bones inside her fingers") and lack transitory properties (e.g., "scrapes on her legs through running through some bushes").

Springer has also studied the effects of adoption on children's responses to "phenotypic surprises." He gave both adopted and nonadopted children aged 4–7 years situations such as "There's a red-haired baby. His hair is bright red. But his mom and dad both have black hair. How could that happen? How could two black-haired parents have a red-haired baby?" In contrast to the nonadopted group, most of the younger adopted children generated biological kinship explanations in referring to grandparents or properties running in families. To some extent, adopted children's concepts of kinship may simply be more "accessible" than are those of nonadopted children.

If asked simply to select outcomes, even young nonadopted children may distinguish physical appearance as a trait that is biologically rather socially determined.

What is the basis for the discrepancy between various results? It is likely that it has to do with differences in the method of asking children questions. In the work of Carey and her colleagues, preschoolers may have not easily followed the narratives that were used to evaluate their understanding of biological and adoptive influences; the adoptive mother (who was present at the birth and brought the baby home from hospital) was depicted as loving her very much and immediately calling her "daughter." Loving itself implies a relationship that transcends the limits set by biological functioning. For example, children may interpret questions in the context of loving to imply that the relationship between the child and the adoptive parents is so loving that their answers should convey the strength of this relationship by indicating that it could even transform the appearance of the adopted child to resemble that of his or her adoptive parents. In fact, loving can be seen as such as powerful trait that it is regarded by many American adults as well as children to transcend the termination of life – a cute animal such as a mouse, rabbit or hamster may be judged still capable of loving even after he has been killed by another animal.

Under these circumstances, preschoolers may attach their own notion of relevance to what the interviewer has regarded as incidental features of the stories and assume that some relationship between the birth and adoptive mothers must have existed (e.g., they were sisters or other relatives) to produce resemblance in physical traits and behavior. If so, heritable traits could conceivably be seen as linked between the baby and the adoptive mother, especially as they were pictured as of the same race and no information about the fathers was provided. In fact, in the Vezo study, children may simply have judged on the basis of familiarity as little was familiar to the children about the actual situation of adoptive parenting, unlike the case in Springer's investigation with adopted children in America.

Although studies that appear to support Carey's position on conceptual change in children's biological knowledge supply a valuable source of information, the research to date does fall short of providing decisive evidence on what children can and do know about biological influences on appearance, beliefs, and behavior. Further studies are needed. To this end, Lakshmi Raman and Susan Gelman at the University of Michigan have recently carried out a series of studies on children's knowledge of genetic disorders and contagious illnesses.[5] They asked children aged 5–11 years, as well as adults, to consider scenarios concerning genetic disorders described in terms of a story character who "gets very sick when he or she eats peanuts, cannot see the color yellow, cannot hear well, so he or she can only hear people if they talk loudly, or who gets bad headaches when he or she eats cheese." Other scenarios described contagious illnesses and were described in terms of a story character who "has a runny nose, has a temperature and head that feels hot, has a sore throat, or has a stomach that feels very sick and is throwing up." For each scenario, the child was asked to consider whether an adopted 6-year-old would resemble her biological parents or her adoptive parents. For example:

> Mr. and Mrs. Robinson had a baby girl. That means that the baby came out of Mrs. Robinson's tummy. Right after she came out of Mrs. Robinson's tummy, the baby went to live with Mr. and Mrs. Jones. They named her Elizabeth. Elizabeth lived with them and they took care of her. They fed her, bought her clothes, hugged her, and kissed her when she was sad. Now Elizabeth is about 6 years old. Whose tummy did Elizabeth come out of: Mrs. Robinson's or Mrs. Jones's? Who does she live with now: Mr. and Mrs. Robinson or Mr. and Mrs. Jones? Mr. and Mrs. Jones are allergic to peanuts. So they get very sick when they eat peanuts. Mr. and Mrs. Robinson don't get sick when they eat peanuts. They are okay. One day Elizabeth ate some peanuts. What do you think happened? Do you think she got very sick like Mr. and Mrs. Jones or do you think she was okay like Mr. and Mrs. Robinson?

Contrary to Carey's position that young children do not have a conception of biological processes that differs from the environmental influences, even the 5-year-olds in Raman and Gelman's investigation were able to distinguish genetic disorders such as food allergies from contagious illnesses such as colds. They recognize that genetically transmitted characteristics are often permanent whereas contagious illnesses are transitory. These results are consistent with findings on children's understanding of germs and processes of food contamination and purification, and support the position that young children can be knowledgeable about the role of biological inheritance in illness even before they start school.

Life, death, and conceptions of the afterlife

One of the fundamental issues that children are liable to confront sometime early in their development has to with the death of loved ones and pets. Like adults, children can agonize about the meaning of death. Do they know that the beloved person or animal no longer exists in a material sense in that biological functions such as eating, sleeping and breathing have stopped? At the same time, do they expect that the dead in some sense can live on in spirit?

For one thing, as noted in the previous chapter, it is clear that young children have a concept of "life" in that they are adept at distinguishing between animate and inanimate objects. In fact, even babies by the age of 10 months show patterns of attention that suggest that they differentiate the properties of humans from nonhuman animals such as dogs and objects such as cars. They have expectations about the world such that, even at 6 months, they expect a person's speech to be directed to another person rather than to an object, and a person's reaching with a sweeping movement to be directed at an object rather a person. They stare longer at situations that violate such expectations.[6]

Moreover, young children are adept at distinguishing between biological processes that are controlled voluntarily by the human as distinct from involuntary processes controlled by the body. As shown by Inagaki and Hatano, given the choice of two alternative answers, most 4- and 5-year-olds sampled in Japan understand that bodily characteristics such as eye color are fixed and not under involuntary control. Similarly, children understand that they cannot stop their heartbeat or stop their breathing for a couple of days. By contrast, they recognize that they had control over other bodily characteristics such as the speed of running and mental characteristics such as memory. Even babies seem to conceptualize voluntary and involuntary contract in their reactions to other people. For example, by the age of 16 months, they become angry when a person is unwilling to give them a toy instead of when she is unable to do so.[7]

However, the early ability to discriminate between the properties of humans and nonhumans and sensitivity to biological processes that are under human control does not necessarily mean that young children have an understanding of the biological mechanisms underlying life and death. As is the case of inheritance, Carey has proposed that the preschooler's concepts of life and death are incommensurable with that of older children and that these concepts likely undergo strong restructuring in the course of a conceptual change that occurs in childhood. For Carey, the preschool child has an undifferentiated core concept of "life" in that life is a concept that embraces things as alive, active, real, and existent. By contrast, "death" refers to things are not alive, inactive, unreal, and absent instead of things that do longer eat and breathe. Thus it can be very hard for some young children to concede that death involves the breakdown of the organization and functions of body organs. They often think that the buried still need bodily functions such as eating, breathing, and excretion. Further, Carey maintains that the preschooler's concept of "animal" is incommensurable with a biological understanding of animals. The core of this concept derives from its role in an early intuitive theory of psychology that is in place by age 4, and is essentially a psychological concept involving an entity that behaves. In this sense, Carey's account resembles that of Piaget who maintained that young children assign internal states and motives to inanimate objects and believe that any object may possess consciousness at a particular moment, especially a thing that moves like a bicycle.

According to this analysis, the preschooler's concept of "death" is essentially not biological. Young children should not recognize that death entails the cessation of the biological signs of life. As evidence, Carey and her colleagues (Virginia Slaughter and Rachel Jaakkola) report a study in which kids were classified as life-theorizers or nonlife-theorizers and interviewed about the nature of death. Children aged 4–6 years were probed about the heart, brain, eyes, lungs, blood, stomach and hands. They were asked three questions about each body part: "(1) Where is X? (2) What is X for? and (3) What would happen if somebody didn't have an X?" They were also asked questions about the bodily processes of eating food and breathing air: "Why do we eat food/breathe air? What happens to the food we eat/air we breathe?" Those classified as life-theorizers mentioned staying alive, or not dying, at least twice.

All children were then given a "death interview" designed to measure children's understanding of various subcomponents of the concept of death: recognizing only living things can die, knowing that death is a necessary part of the life cycle and how death ultimately comes about, and understanding that death is a permanent state and involves a cessation of all bodily needs.

Questions in the death interview:

1. Do you know what it means for something to die?
2. Can you name some things that die? If people aren't mentioned: Do people sometimes die?
   (a) Does every person die?
   (b) What happens to a person's body when they die?
3. When a person is dead ...
   (a) do they need food?
   (b) do they need to pee and poop?
   (c) do they need air?
   (d) can they move around?
   (e) do they have dreams?
   (f) do they need water?
   (g) If a dead person had a cut on their hand, would it heal?
4. How can you tell if a person is dead?
5. Can you name some things that don't die?
6. Can you think of something that might cause something to die?
7. Once something dies, is there anything anyone can do to make it live again?
8. Could a doctor make a dead person live again?

As predicted, many of the nonlife-theorizers indicated that the dead would retain biological functions.[8] Their answers may seem to indicate that they genuinely do believe the dead possess biological life attributes. However, in this respect, it is unclear how far children depart from the normative, anthropomorphic view of the outcomes for persons who have died but live on in a form of heaven (or hell) that is held by many adults. In any event, children can be quite easily trained to reason about biological phenomena using a form of inter-mediate causality that has been called "vitalism," involving the transmission of energy by an organism.

According to the Japanese account of vitalism described by Inagaki and Hatano, vitalism (referred to as *ki* in Japanese and translatable in English as life or life force) is not necessarily beyond the grasp of young children. It can be seen as a rational metaphor used to locate some unidentified causal mechanism that is distinct from an organ employing psychological attributes of intentionality to maintain biological functions. For example, both young children and adults are likely to ascribe to the conception of the stomach as taking in energy from food. In this sense, even preschoolers can profitably understand messages about the biological processes such as digestion should they be provided messages such as:[9]

> We need food to keep us alive. Our bodies need food to make them go, just as a car needs petrol to make it go. Food gives your body energy and helps it to grow… When we eat food our teeth cut it up into little pieces and when it gets into our stomach it breaks into even smaller pieces. These pieces are so small they can get into our blood and because blood is always moving around our body the blood takes the food to all the parts of our body that need energy. It is very important that our body gets energy for it to stay alive.

If preschoolers are trained to think vitalistically, they are likely to indicate functions such as needing food, water, and air that cease at death. In this sense, vitalism in biology – like facts about the earth's field of gravity and rotation in cosmology – serves as a form of "placeholder" that dissolves when the causal mechanism is identified.

Moreover, in at least one sense, young children clearly do have an understanding of death as the cessation of biological functioning. This has been demonstrated by Clark Barrett, an anthropologist at UCLA, and Tanya Behne at the Max Planck Institute for Human Development in Berlin. Clark and Behne propose that mechanisms have evolved to ensure that people identify dead animals as incapable of movement and other biological processes whereas sleeping animals are seen to retain these abilities, because there are costs in terms of unnecessarily vigilance and lost food opportunities in failing to make this discrimination. As a consequence, children at an early age should discriminate between live and dead animals. Barrett and Behne asked children aged 3, 4, and 5 years living in two very different cultures to consider whether animals could perform various actions if they were dead or asleep.[10] One group consisted of German children in Berlin, the other Shuar children from the Amazon region of Ecuador. The German children had frequent experience of animals as pets and in zoos, whereas the Shuar children had frequent experience with live animals as well as those about to be killed for food.

The children were given stories about chickens and animals such as lions, as well as stories about humans. For example, in the case of sleeping, the interviewer told them, "This lion (or chicken) has been running around all day. It's night now and the lion/chicken is very tired. It lies down and sleeps." In each instance, the children were asked the test questions, "Is the lion (or chicken) dead or asleep? Can it move? Can it be afraid? Could it hurt you? If you walked by and made a noise, could it know you were there? Could it move if you touched it?"

In the case of death, the interviewer told the children stories such as, "This woman is a cook. She wants to eat this chicken, so she takes a knife and cuts the chicken's neck and the chicken dies. The chicken is now dead. This man is a hunter. He is walking in the forest and he sees a lion. He takes his gun and shoots the lion and the lion dies. The lion is now dead." Again the children were asked the test questions, "Is the lion (or chicken) dead or asleep? Can it move? Can it be afraid? Could it hurt you? If you walked by and made a noise, could it know you were there? Could it move if you touched it?"

At the age of 4 years, children in both cultures answered the questions mostly correctly. They discriminated between instances of sleep where biological functioning was maintained and those of death in which biological functioning ceased. There were no differences in children's answers to stories involving humans or various animals. As Barrett and Behne point out, even the 3-year-olds might have performed well had the stories been simplified further with the use of pretense and story characters that are well within the personal experience of a very young child.

Seen in the light of this particularly graphic illustration, we may consider how children may reason about life after death. In a study carried out recently by Jesse Bering and David Bjorklund, two psychologists at Florida Atlantic University, children aged 5–12 years and adults in south Florida were given stories using puppets about the death of a mouse. They were then interviewed to see whether the mouse could still function biologically as well as still smell, see, feel, hope, want, know, and believe. Here is one example of what the participants in the study were told:[11]

> Hi, I'm going to do a puppet show for you today, and the first thing I'm going to do is introduce you to the two characters. Do you know what kind of animal this is? That's right! It's a mouse. And this mouse is a baby mouse. One day he's going to grow up to become an old mouse. Do you know what kind of animal this is? Right again! It's an alligator. And this alligator's favorite food is baby mice. Now, we both know that these animals aren't real, they're just puppets, but for today let's just pretend that they are real.
>
> One day, Baby Mouse decides to take a walk in the woods. There are flowers, and Baby Mouse loves how the flowers smell. The flowers smell very nice. While he's walking, he's thinking about a lot of things. He's thinking about his mom, and how much he loves her. He believes his mom is the nicest grown-up mouse in the whole world. Baby Mouse wonders where his mom is right now. Baby Mouse is also thinking about numbers. He likes numbers, but he's not very good at using them. He doesn't even understand how to add numbers together. He hopes that one day he'll be better at using numbers. Baby Mouse's feet are very tired, and he wants to go home now. But he realizes that he's lost and he doesn't know how to get back to his house. He's very sleepy and really wants to go to bed. Baby Mouse has a sore throat and he feels sick. Maybe if he drinks some water he'll feel better. He goes to drink some water from the pond but before he gets there he notices something funny. The bushes are moving! An alligator jumps out of the bushes and gobbles him all up. Baby Mouse is not alive anymore.

Then an interviewer asked each of the participants in the study a number of questions prefaced with the conditional "Now that Baby Mouse is not alive anymore…" These questions were biological ("Do you think that Baby Mouse will *grow* up to be a grown-up mouse? Do you think that Baby Mouse will ever need to *drink* water again?"), psychobiological ("Do you think that Baby Mouse still feels *sleepy*? Do you think that Baby Mouse still feels *sick*?"), perceptual ("Do you think that Baby Mouse can still *smell* the flowers? Do you think that Baby Mouse can *see* where he is now?"), emotional ("Do you think that Baby Mouse still *loves* his mom? Do you think that Baby Mouse is still *scared* of the alligator?"), desire ("Do you think that Baby Mouse still *hopes* he gets better at math? Do you think that Baby Mouse still *wants* to go home?") and epistemic about the mouse's knowledge and beliefs ("Do you think that Baby Mouse *knows* he's not alive? Do you think that Baby Mouse still *believes* his mom is the nicest grown-up?").

Both children and adults in the study generally accepted that the dead mouse will not grow up to a grown-up mouse, will never drink water again, does not feel sleepy or sick, or can smell and see, although the kindergarten-aged children were less likely to answer that this would happen. With regard to the questions about emotions, desires, and knowledge and beliefs, even many older children and adults responded that the dead mouse could still love his mom, be scared of the alligator, hope to do better at math, want to go home, know he's not alive and believe his mom is the nicest grown-up, although again such answers were more prevalent in the younger kindergarten aged children.

Bering and Bjorklund suggest that the younger children's deficient knowledge about the cessation about biological functioning following death can explain age differences between their answers and those of older children and adults. Notice, however, that yes answers to all questions indicate a consistent belief in life after death in all respects, even biological and psychobiological, whereas no answers to all questions indicate a rejection of the continuation of life after death in any respect. Although study participants were asked to justify their answers, having a bias toward giving all yes or all no answers might have contributed to the pattern of results. A positive yes bias may result from wishful thinking, especially on the part of young children, that the cute mouse in the puppet show does live on even if the alligator swallows him up.

Moreover, consistent with kids' wishful thinking, many – if not most – adults in cultures everywhere do profess certain afterlife beliefs. Death that admits of a spiritual afterlife is of course a hallmark of religion in both Western and tribal cultures. In New Guinea, for example, survivors of the deceased eat parts of their fingernails and toenails so that their loved ones may continue to live on.[12] In many cultures, there those who continue to believe that the departed who have led a just life will receive heavenly rewards and even may return one day. As Noam Chomsky, the MIT linguist and political activist, has been quoted to say provocatively:[13]

> Three quarters of the American population literally believe in religious miracles. The numbers who believe in the devil, in resurrection, in God doing this and that – it's astonishing. These numbers aren't duplicated anywhere else in the industrial world. You'd have to maybe go to mosques in Iran or do a poll among old ladies in Sicily to get numbers like this. Yet this is the American population.

This kind of statement does seem reckless in that it does not do justice to the power of religious beliefs in overcoming tyranny, war and disease. Indeed it can be argued that beliefs such as those about the afterlife have arisen in response to a harsh social environment.[14]

Moreover, we often say in the modern secular world that a person continues to lives on in the form of his or her children or in the form of a cultural legacy – an "afterlife" has been bequeathed to later generations. Shakespeare has been described as "not for an age but for all time" and Jane Austen regarded *Pride and Prejudice* as her own little child. Shakespeare and Austen are culturally alive – they are part of the living heart of humanity – even though materially they have long departed. In this sense, the notion of an afterlife is not necessarily confined to the spiritual, although for some adults, the contribution of dead writers, poets, artists, and musicians does in fact amount to a form of spiritual afterlife.

So beliefs in some sort of afterlife cannot be easily dismissed. Their pervasive existence in adults makes it difficult to argue that there exists that a radical restructuring in children's understanding of life and death – one amounts to a strong conceptual change in their development in which the young necessarily have naive conceptions of life and death accompanied by beliefs in an afterlife that give way to sophisticated and highly differentiated conceptions in adulthood that are exclusively biologically based.

Packed in the plane

Many countries are so crowded today with commuters and tourists that there is gridlock on the roads and elsewhere. The United Kingdom, for example, is without any doubt in a perpetual transportation crisis, though the locals do not like to complain. Once in August 2004, while on a bus completely paralyzed in traffic, I saw a sign on a British motorway that read "Expect delays until Christmas 2005," and I thought that I would be trapped for more than a year, so this might be my final journey and that I might even eventually have an afterlife experience of some sort where I was. The trains are no better. Many have had their schedules "retimed" so that they can no longer be called late and their operators fined. I've heard it said that the trains between Manchester and Liverpool – a distance of only 30 miles that now takes 50–60 minutes to complete – ran faster in 1900. Although the train was invented in England, it seems that the very same trains still run through my village. The symbol for train services in the UK is officially described as consisting of "two-way traffic arrows on parallel lines representing tracks with the top arrow therefore always pointing to the right" (because trains in the UK keep to the left). But I tend to see this as a symbol of going nowhere in that the arrows seem to be canceling each other out.

Part of the problem is that there are actually not enough roads and train tracks to go around. The UK has 371,603 kilometres of surfaced roads including 3303 kilometres of freeways (known locally as motorways) and 16,878 kilometres of railways of which 4928 are electrified. Comparable figures for Italy with a similar

Packed in the plane *(cont.)*

population and similar area are 654,676 kilometres of surfaced roads of which 6460 kilometres are freeways and 19,394 kilometres of railways of which 11,434 kilometres are electrified. So compared to the UK, Italy has almost twice as many kilometres of freeways and more than twice as many kilometres of electrified railways.

However, this is not to say that all is well with Italian transportation. The Italians have their own legendary traffic jams. While leaving Britain by air seems to be relatively simple and organized these days, in Italy there may be another set of problems, as represented by the experience of flying the Italian way on Alitalia. Although it can't be true, I've heard that the name actually means, "Always Late In Takeoff, Always Late In Arriving."

I took a flight from Rome to Sydney when Alitalia used to fly between Italy and Australia. I knew something was up when we were on the tarmac at Rome. A series of incidents occurred one after another. A passenger on the plane with me was drunk and another had either refused or could not put on his seat belt. The rapid response was to allow so many soldiers on the plane to intervene that it seemed the whole Italian army was on manoeuvres. It seemed like an overreaction to send hundreds in to trample the sober passengers in order to eject the inebriated. After this incident had passed, it was noticed that the person in the seat behind me kept falling into the lap of the passenger behind him. To secure the seatback required homemade repairs from the crew. Then we had a late arriving passenger. She was an exceptionally plump lady who really should have flown business class. The plane was packed except for one middle seat that was occupied on the window side by another very plump lady and on the aisle by her tiny Italian husband. The late arriving lady was then told to sit on the aisle with the tiny man instructed to move to the middle. This meant that the man would be squashed on either side. Realizing what had happened, he grumbled and screamed for the next 11 hours until the plane arrived in Singapore.

Packed in the plane *(cont.)*

The flight was finally on its way. True to the motto, it was late in take-off and late in arrival. A further delay occurred when the flight stopped to change crew in Mumbai (Bombay) to change crew. It was like an Italian movie with the air attendants and hostesses in their scarves and designer outfits greeting each other as if they hadn't met for years. There were lots of kisses, hugs, and excited chattering that seemed to go on for several hours.

Once in the air again, I tried to find out what time we would land. The attendant I asked didn't seem to have a good command of English so I pointed to my watch and gestured about landing. He then wound his watch forward to show me what time it would when we arrived.

Since I took that flight, I have not been so keen to get back on board with Alitalia though I have visited Italy many times since and Italy is one of my favorite countries anywhere.

Chapter 6

Number and arithmetic

For the things of this world cannot be made known without a knowledge of mathematics. Roger Bacon, *Opus Majus part 4 Distinctia Prima cap 1, 1267.*

Given the studies discussed so far, is children's understanding necessarily held back by alternative conceptual frameworks or entrenched presuppositions? Do they need to go through a long period of non-conservative conceptual change? The evidence suggests that they do not – at least in the case of appearance–reality (AR) knowledge, language grammar, ToM reasoning, certain aspects of cosmology or biology such as knowing about the shape of the earth, the nature of contamination and transmission of contagious illness, and processes of life and death. The ability of even young children to grasp knowledge of the distinction between appearance and reality is compatible with their abilities to indicate that, though the earth looks flat, it is in reality round like a ball and, though a food looks fresh, in reality it may be contaminated. In all instances, it is difficult to make the case for a radical or nonconservative conceptual change during development.

Of course the fact that children can grasp this knowledge does not mean that they do. In their early years, no one may talk to them about cosmology or biology and children themselves may not put their minds to knowing. In the case of cosmology, their thinking is not typically channelled or constrained along lines that would lead them to ask about the shape of the earth or the day–night cycle. These issues are not close to survival and so an awareness of cosmology is far from being present in all cultures. Why would children want to find out about the planet Earth, the sun and moon, when there are so many other topics that they have not yet explored?

Knowledge of contamination and purification is different. Children can't help but talk about what is good to eat and drink. At home and school, they are continually immersed in conversations about whether food that has been dropped on the floor is too dirty to eat. They speak about food in terms of amusement and disgust. Nevertheless, in many cultures, children do not receive information that leads them to adopt the Western scientifically accepted view of food that is uncontaminated and pure. So an awareness of contamination and purification is not a cultural universal. All the same, there are very substantial conceptions of purification and contamination sensitivity in young children who have been exposed early to Western cultural experiences that underscore the clash between appearance and reality in relation to food, health, and hygiene.

Regardless of their culture, kids normally do not have a well developed understanding of either cosmology and biology to the extent that they can explain the theory of gravity or germ theory. Still they can have knowledge of key scientific facts that serve as placeholders until this knowledge is enriched in adolescence or adulthood by explanatory theories such as the theory of gravity or germ theory. Persons in Western cultures are liable to encounter such theories, but even here many adults may fall short of a full understanding. The travel and science writer Bill Bryson describes the situation neatly, as he does so often, in *A Short History of Nearly Everything*. Commenting on the fact given to him while at school that the center of the earth is a red hot mass of iron and nickel, Bryson remarks,[1]

> I didn't doubt the correctness of the information for an instant – I still tend to trust the pronouncements of scientists in the way that I trust those of surgeons, plumbers, and other possessor of arcane and privileged information – but I couldn't for the life of me conceive how any human mind could work out what spaces thousands of miles below us, that no eye had ever seen and no X-ray could penetrate, could look like and be made of. To me it was just a miracle. That has been my position with science ever since.

It took Bryson until adulthood to develop a considerably deeper understanding through his very exceptional motivation for reading about science and talking to scientists. In non-Western cultures, there may be no contact with Western cosmology and biology and theories in these areas may be nonexistent, even among adults.

Luckily, however, cosmology and biology do not encompass all that humans can know. In contrast to cosmology and biology, children everywhere appear to have a sense of number and arithmetic. Yet ask any group of children what is the most difficult subject to study and you will find at least one, if not all, who say that arithmetic is the hardest. Why is this so? Is it that unlike reasoning about astronomy or biology or ToM, proficiency in arithmetic demands more from children – an understanding that from the start requires a unique type of abstract reasoning? Does children's arithmetic typically require a conceptual change in reasoning that goes beyond enrichment and requires that a previous theory is overturned and abandoned?

Everyone counts, don't they?

Proficiency in arithmetic is based on an understanding of "numerosity," the term used to describe the number of things in a set.[2] These things can be bricks, apples, toys, thoughts, dreams, or aims. In fact, members of a set can be of any type, guaranteeing that numerosity requires an abstract representation on the part of whoever is counting, whether this is a child or nonhuman primates such as monkeys.

An understanding of the concept of numerosity requires the fundamental knowledge that two sets must have the same numerosity if each member can be put into one-to-one correspondence with none left over. Related to this knowledge is the recognition that the numerosities of such sets are no longer the same if a member is added or taken away from one of the two sets without a corresponding operation performed on the other. Also related to this knowledge is the recognition that sets of things to be counted can be tangible or intangible based on, for example, the numbers of sights (e.g., dogs), sounds (drum beats), flavors (ice cream), things to do, likes and dislikes.

To arrive at the numerosity of a set involves counting. This process is complex in that we need to honor five criteria that Rochel Gelman and C. R. Gallistel, two psychologists at Rutgers University, have deemed "principles." First, there is the "one–one principle" that involves separating the things to be counted and counting each thing without omission or repetition. Second, the "stable order principle" involves the consistent use of an arbitrary list of words or gestures such that we use words such as *one*, *two*, and *three* in counting three things. Third, the "cardinal principle" involves the ability to use the last word in the count to indicate the numerosity of the set (e.g., as *one*, *two*, and *three* – three dogs'). Then there are the "abstraction" and "order-irrelevance principles." The child must recognize that anything can be counted and that counting can start and end with any member in the set.

A long-standing matter for debate concerns the origins of the concept of numerosity. Can numerosity be innate in that it is present in everyone, everywhere, in all human cultures and at all ages, even in early human infancy or, alternatively, is numerosity a concept that is not innate but is acquired gradually in childhood and only by those children who are exposed to a culture that has established a system for counting large quantities?

Verbal counting – using words for the whole numbers 1, 2, 3, 4, 5, etc. – does come gradually to children. In industrialized cultures, preschoolers at the age of about 2½ years start out by handing over one of the members of a set if asked for one, but grab any number when asked for two or more. Then they give out one or two if asked for one or two respectively, but grab any number when asked for two or more. Then they give out one, two, or three if asked for one or two or three respectively, but grab any number when asked for four or more. Although by the age of 3 years, children have skill at predicting and checking numerosities and detecting others' inaccurate counts, it is not until about the age of about 4 or 5 years that they can use spontaneously use numbers larger than three in their verbal counting.

Piaget in fact claimed that a good measure of young children's number abilities is found in their performance on certain critical tests of their logical abilities designed to see whether they use number words consistently to refer to members of a set.[3] In considering two rows of counters in one-to-one correspondence, children need to (in Piaget's terms) "construct" the notion that number remains the same and is "conserved" if one row of counters is lengthened and the other is bunched together when no counter is added or taken away from either row. But young children commonly tell an interviewer that one row now has more! As noted in Chapter 1, on the basis of what children say when asked to make judgments of number in studies of conservation, Piaget reported that conversation is not achieved until the age of 6 to 7 years – a conclusion that remains controversial to this day. Piaget maintained that the correct use of number words in conversation tasks heralds a conceptual change in children's reasoning about number in that before then they have no little or no understanding of the concept of numerosity.

Another piece of evidence that would seem to argue against the innateness of a concept of numerosity comes from studies of people who speak language with an impoverished vocabulary of words for counting. Among recent developments in the psychology of number is the discovery that there are cultures in which adults have limited number word vocabularies. Peter Gordon at Columbia University in New York journeyed to Brazil to study the Pirahã people, who live on the banks of the Maici River in the Lowland Amazonia region.[4] The Pirahã, with a total population of less than 200, live in small villages of 10 or 20 people. They have only limited exchanges with outsiders and are monolingual in their own language, using primitive pidgin systems for communicating in trading goods without monetary exchange and without the use of Portuguese count words. The Pirahã use a "one-two-many" system of counting. This system contains just the words: *hoy* (said with a falling tone for one), *hóy* (said with a rising tone for two) and *baagi* or *aibai* (for many or large quantities).

Gordon sought to establish whether the innumerate language spoken by the Pirahã prevents them from appreciating numerosities without the benefit of words to represent such quantities. He asked Pirahã adults to match sticks with quantities of nuts with the instruction to "make it the same," and found that performance was poor for quantities above three. The great difficulty that the Pirahã had with such tasks led Gordon to claim support for the "linguistic determinism" hypothesis originally proposed by the American linguists Edward Sapir and Benjamin Lee Whorf that language determines thought. According to the strong version of the Whorfian hypothesis, language allows us to "dissect" the physical and mental world in a meaningful way. It dictates our thinking and problem-solving abilities. For example, Whorfians have contended that because the Inuit people (Eskimos) have many words in their language for types of snow (wrongly, it turns out!), they are good at problem-solving in a snowy landscape, whereas people who have an impoverished snow vocabulary are handicapped.[5] Similarly, according to Gordon's interpretation, having a language that that is rich in counting words enables numerical reasoning whereas having a language that lacks counting words gives rise to severe impairment in numerical reasoning. In this connection, Gordon is quick to rule out the possibility that the Pirahā have a general level of intellectual development that precludes both the use of counting words and having a concept of numerosity. He notes that the Pirahā have "remarkable" hunting, spatial, and categorization skills, and that they show no clinical signs of retardation.

Owing to children's protracted difficulties in counting and in comparing and conserving sets of objects, as well as the apparent absence of a concept of numerosity in some cultures such as that of the Pirahā, it might be concluded that numerosity is not innate. Rather it might be inferred that numerosity as the basis for number needs to be acquired. Accordingly, young children might achieve counting, as characterized by Gelman and Gallistel's counting principles, through learning that follows reinforcement and imitation for correct performance from adults in a culture with a numerate language. In this connection, one possibility that has been proposed is that the child first has a system to attend and track up to three or four objects. They then acquire, through a bootstrapping process that is based on the object tracking system, a continuous number system that allows them to go beyond three or four. This number system is dependent on learning words for counting. After the counting words have been acquired, the object tracking system may be discarded much as a ladder used for arriving at a new place can be kicked away once that place has been reached.[6]

Independence of language from number

Clearly, the complexity of counting does not mean that the concept of numerosity is limited to children who have acquired the meaning of the appropriate words for counting. There are studies showing that numerosity is within the grasp of human infants and children and even monkeys. For example, Prentice Starkey, now at University of California, Berkeley, and his colleagues showed that infants stare significantly longer ("dishabituate") when there is a lack of correspondence between the number of dots that they see and the number of sounds that they hear in contrast to when this correspondence exists. They are also sensitive to changes in the size of objects such that the larger the difference in ratio between objects, the more they dishabituate. This type of work suggests that infants have an early perception of number that permits counting. In another ingenious experiment, Starkey tested children aged 18–48 months of age who had not yet attained the ability to count. He gave the children a task in which they placed a set of 1 to 5 objects sequentially into an opaque searchbox. They then observed an experimenter add, subtract, or perform no operation on the set in the box. For the most part, even the youngest children could correctly search and remove all the objects in the box when the numerosity to be found was 1, 2, or 3. Thus children display a concept of numerosity even before they know the number words for counting or cultural experience with number.[7]

The case has been made that even babies aged 5 months, who are certainly without number words for counting or cultural experience with number, add and subtract. Karen Wynn, now at Yale University, compared the responses of infants to possible and impossible events in which objects are placed behind screens. For the possible event, the number of objects revealed when the screen is lifted corresponded to the number that the infant had seen to be placed or removed from behind the screen (e.g., $1 + 1 = 2, 2 - 1 = 2$). In the impossible event, the number was different. There was now more or less ($1 + 1 = 1, 2 - 1 = 2$). Wynn reported that infants stared longer in the impossible events when objects unaccountably disappear or when extra ones appear, implying that the impossible event violated their expectancies of addition and subtraction. Consistent with the notion that a concept of numerosity is innate, Wynn claims that these results support the existence of arithmetic in babies.

Wynn's research, like that of Piaget's, remains controversial. Critics have described what infants are doing in her experiments in terms of how they "process addition and subtraction events" rather than as performing actual addition and subtraction. One claim is that the

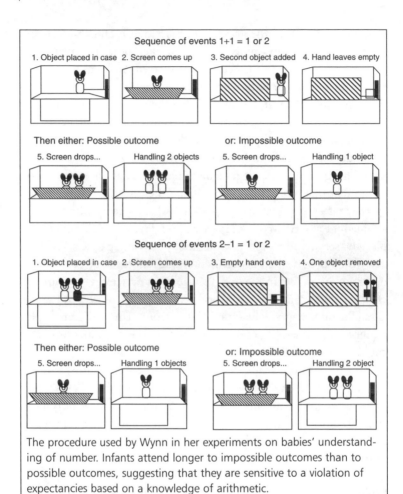

Sequence of events 1+1 = 1 or 2

1. Object placed in case   2. Screen comes up   3. Second object added   4. Hand leaves empty

Then either: Possible outcome   or: Impossible outcome

5. Screen drops...   Handling 2 objects   5. Screen drops...   Handling 1 object

Sequence of events 2–1 = 1 or 2

1. Object placed in case   2. Screen comes up   3. Empty hand overs   4. One object removed

Then either: Possible outcome   or: Impossible outcome

5. Screen drops...   Handling 1 objects   5. Screen drops...   Handling 2 object

The procedure used by Wynn in her experiments on babies' understanding of number. Infants attend longer to impossible outcomes than to possible outcomes, suggesting that they are sensitive to a violation of expectancies based on a knowledge of arithmetic.

infants in her experiments as illustrated above do not show addition and subtraction abilities but instead have a preference for familiarity, along with a tendency to look longer when more items are on the stage revealed when the screen is raised. Another claim is that infants are not counting at all and are not doing at any kind of arithmetic in Wynn's studies. Instead, they are simply responding to changes in mass or density rather than number.[8]

However, quite apart from debates over the interpretation of babies' performance in studies of their understanding of number, it has been established that monkeys have a concept of numerosity. Elizabeth Brannon, now at Duke University in North Carolina, and Herbert Terrace at Columbia University in New York have reported that two rhesus monkeys, named Rosenkrantz and Macduff, could be training to respond to 1 to 4 members of a set of 4 in an ascending number order (1→2→3→4). They could then order pairs of numerosities from 5 to 9 without any training, ignoring the fact that at times the numbers of the pair with the smaller numerosity had the greater mass showing that monkeys represent the numerosities 1 to 9 on an ordinal scale.[9]

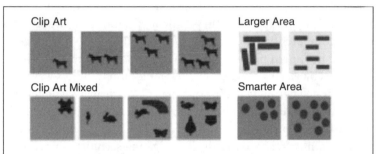

The procedure used by Brannon and Terrace in their experiments on monkeys' understanding of number. Monkeys were trained to order by number members of sets taken, such as a set of 1–4 horses taken from clip art or a set consisting of a mixture of items also taken from clip art. They could then order 5 as less than 6–9, even when the 5 items in a set took up a larger surface area than the items in the comparison set.

Since monkeys are capable of a concept of numerosity as shown in these sorts of studies, it would not seem too far-fetched after all to agree with Wynn's contention that there is a concept of numerosity in human infants, despite their lack of language and ability to count verbally.

Moreover, infants are not the only humans without language. Many older adults have unfortunately suffered strokes resulting in brain damage in the left hemisphere areas associated with language. Although some still can comprehend and express individual words within the lexicon of their language, they still can have a severe form of aphasia in which they no longer have the ability to speak grammatically and to understand the meaning of sentences. However, the patients, though agrammatic, remain numerate. As part of a research team in England involving Rosemary Varley, a neuroscientist dedicated to uncovering the extent to which reasoning is spared in persons with brain damage resulting in aphasia, I became involved in an intensive study of the mathematical abilities of three men in their 50s known as SA, SO, PR.[10] All three suffered from very severe grammatical impairment brought on by damage to their left hemisphere language areas. The patients had great difficulty in indicating whether a sentence was grammatical or not and could not show that they understood sentences, whether written or spoken, such as "The man killed the lion" and the "The lion killed the man" by pointing to appropriate pictures. Yet paradoxically, they could add, subtract, multiply, and divide competently. They could show that they had knowledge of infinity and could provide more than one solution to ambiguous equations by placing brackets in different locations. In this way, they demonstrated flexibility in the expression of "mathematical sentences" using Arabic numerals. They even went home and spontaneously invented more problems to solve in order to demonstrate to everyone, including Rosemary as the investigating scientist, how satisfyingly competent they were in math.

a. SA   b. SO   c. PR

Answers of patients SA, SO, and PR on the bracket equation problems. All three could correctly insert brackets in equations to demonstrate how these would change or retain the solution.

Another look at children's understanding of number

Still, children do have difficulties in verbal counting and in conservation of number, and adults in cultures with an innumerate language have difficulties in mathematical calculations. Don't these types of difficulties suggest that a concept of numerosity hangs upon the acquisition of language and numeracy and that, contrary to the nativist thesis, a concept of numerosity is absent in young children and in some human cultures? A closer inspection indicates that these do not.

Consider the words of Teddy (age 2½ years) in reaction to having received too few M&Ms: "I like *plenty*! I like *too much*! I like some *lot*! I like some *eight*!" This example from an article by psychologists at the University of Michigan, Barbara Sarnecka and Susan Gelman, illustrates the ambiguity in children's early use of number words. Do children such as Teddy use *eight* to mean *plenty* or *a lot* or do they use *eight* to refer to a specific numerosity that is more than they now have in their hand?

Sarnecka and Gelman sought to determine whether children use number words whose exact meanings they have not learned are used indiscriminately to refer to *a lot* or whether they recognize that adding quantities to a set of six means that the set no longer has a numerosity of six. They very simply showed 2- and 3-year-olds some pennies (as well as batteries, beads, beans, buttons, and other items) and placed these in two bowls. For example, each child was told when tested for their understanding of *six*:

> I'm going to put *six* pennies in here (experimenter places six pennies in a bowl) ... and *six* pennies in here (experimenter places six pennies in the other bowl). All right so this bowl has six pennies, and this bowl has six pennies. And here are some more pennies (experimenter pours all remaining pennies – about 80 – into one of the bowls). OK, now I'm going to ask you a question about six pennies. Which bowl has *six* pennies?

When tested for their understanding of *a lot,* each child was told:

> I'm going to put *a lot of* pennies in here (experimenter places six pennies in a bowl)... and *a lot of* pennies in here (experimenter places six pennies in the other bowl). All right so this bowl has six pennies, and this bowl has six pennies. And here are some more pennies (experimenter pours all remaining pennies – about 80 – into one of the bowls). OK, now I'm going to ask you a question about *a lot of* pennies. Which bowl has *a lot of* pennies?

Even 2-year-olds who could not give an adult correct quantities in response to the number three could still indicate that the bowl described as having six pennies and without any more pennies added was the bowl with six pennies. By contrast they did not choose the bowl described as having six pennies and without any more pennies added as containing *a lot of* pennies. The children's performance demonstrated that they had a concept of numerosity even though they had not yet learned the meaning of the number words such as *six*. According to this analysis, learning number words to bootstrap children's concept of numerosity is unnecessary.

Similarly, children may appear in Piaget's conservation of number studies to lack the understanding that number remains the same if two rows of six counters that were once in one-to-one correspondence are thrown out of alignment with one row now longer and less dense than the other. However, in this situation, children are normally asked the test questions (e.g., "Are there the same number in both rows or does one row have more?") twice – once when the rows are in one-to-one correspondence and once after the rows have been transformed. As shown in the example on the opposite page, children may not necessarily understand that the purpose of the questioning is to determine whether they know that number remains the same if no quantities are added or taken away. Instead, repeating the test question may mislead children to change their answers and respond incorrectly, usually by saying that the longer row now has more.[12] This is similar to the effect we see in adult conversations where repeated questioning (for example, "How are you?" Response: "OK." Repeated question, "How are you?") results in response switching or, perhaps in some cases, annoyance at having to repeat the answer.

Children are very sensitive to the contexts under which questions are asked. They themselves may appear not to be able to conserve number. However, even at the age of 4 years, they can show in their reactions to puppets' attempts at solving conservation tasks, that nonconservation answers are prompted by repeated questioning and are the result of a listener attempting to conform to the expectations of the questioner rather than an authentic lack of conversation skills based on the absence of a concept of numerosity.

This sort of evidence does not completely account for why young children often do poorly in tests of number conservation. As the French neuroscientist Stanislas Dehaene concisely puts it, children may also be taken in by an illusion that the longer row of counters has more, as it usually should do, and children may not able to "inhibit" a habitual response based on the usual state of affairs.[13] This lack of inhibition or other aspects of executive functioning on the part of children is in keeping with the role of conversational factors that undeniably play a powerful role here. These can mask an early concept of numerosity in preschoolers that have been demonstrated so vividly in studies of toddlers using searchboxes, in studies of monkeys, and arguably in experiments with babies.

How about the absence of number words in certain cultures, such as the Pirahã culture in the Amazon? Here an innumerate language may not be the root cause of the absence of the expression of the concept of numerosity in counting. Instead, number may not be of central relevance to Pirahã culture, and it is for this reason that the Pirahã have few number words. Should teaching be embedded in an everyday task such as stringing beads, it is not difficult to instruct children in cultures with an innumerate language how to count, just as it is not difficult to show that under such conditions they can solve problems that require applications of formal logic.

Altogether, the weight of studies so far demonstrates that all children in all cultures do count – a pattern consistent with the proposal that a concept of numerosity is innate and is independent of language. In this aspect of mathematics, there is no great divide, no conceptual change required in the reasoning of toddlers, preschoolers and schoolchildren. Vagueness or complexity in the numerical language of a culture may impair the expression of mathematical calculations but these "costs" can be overcome through thinking and reasoning about number that is language independent. In French, for example, there is ambiguity between the indefinite pronoun *un* (a) and *un* as the word for the number one. This ambiguity may temporarily influence children's performance on addition and subtraction problems involving *un*, but it is only a cost in calculation, not a bar on thinking about number. Similarly, Western languages have irregular numerical language systems. In English, the words for 11 and 12 are eleven and twelve, rather than "oneteen" and "twoteen", that are inconsistent with thirteen to nineteen that in turn are inconsistent with the numbers 20 and above described in terms of tens and units. In Italian, there is a reversal between 16 and 17 so that 16 is *sedici* (6 and 10) whereas 17 is *diciassette* (10 and 7). In French, 80 is expressed as *quatre-vingt* (4 × 20) and 90 as *quatre-vingt dix* (4 × 20 + 10). These irregularities in Western language are absent from languages such as Japanese, leading some to propose that children who learn to calculate in such languages are initially more efficient because of the regularity of their number system.[14] Even so, counting and calculations can begin everywhere regardless of the language that they speak.

Moreover, once children explicitly demonstrate their verbal mathematical ability, it is often seen to be independent of language in that, for example, 8-year-olds with dyscalculia – an impairment in the ability to perform mathematical calculations such as addition, subtraction, and division – typically do not show impairments in their verbal language or language related areas such as reading. As shown by the work of Brian Butterworth at University College London, dyscalculia in 8-year-olds, as well as in adults who have suffered brain damage, appears to be the result of specific disabilities in basic numerical processing.[15] These may reflect number-specific memory ability, but dyscalculia cannot be seen as the consequence of deficits in language or other cognitive abilities.

Understanding parts and wholes: fractions and infinity

At the heart of a conceptual understanding of mathematics are representations of the relations between parts and wholes. At a very young age, children are skilled at judgments of part–whole relations that do not refer to numbers. For example, Dean Sharpe and his colleagues at McGill University in Montreal provided a group of English-speaking 3-year-olds with a story about George, a stuffed monkey and Teddy, a stuffed monkey, who ate their breakfast together. The experimenter for their study described George, for example, as liking his apples and as disliking his bananas. Then the experimenter gave George a "love question" and a "hate question" ("George, do you love your whole breakfast? George do you hate your whole breakfast?"), and turned to the children after each question asking them "What does George say?" A large majority answered that George did not wholly like or wholly dislike his breakfast, showing that they appreciated that the whole breakfast consisted of liked and disliked parts.[16]

Once children have a grasp for the words used for counting, calculations involving numbers that represent parts and wholes of sets are speeded along by number facts such as simple addition $(1 + 2 = 3)$, subtraction $(4 - 2 = 2)$, and multiplication tables. It is also facilitated by a conceptual knowledge of principles such as commutativity (e.g., 2 apples + 3 apples = 3 apples + 2 apples) and composition (6 apples + 3 apples = 4 apples + 2 apples + 3 apples). This knowledge may originally be tied to sets of objects such as apples and then to numbers $(2 + 3 = 3 + 2; 6 + 3 = 4 + 2 + 3)$ and finally in a general algebraic form (e.g., $a + b = b + a$). Although there are variations in the rate at which children achieve this knowledge and employ it in their calculations, they generally do achieve competence in this area of mathematics during the first few years after they enter school.

One simple way to help children add and subtract involves "counting-on" strategies using fingers. For example, to prompt children to solve $5 - 2$, they can be shown pictures of five birds and two worms. If asked how many birds won't get a worm, even very young children will often respond with the correct answer. Using fingers, they can compare the number of birds (5) as represented by fingers on one hand with the number of worms (2) on the other. To arrive at the solution, they then count up the number of fingers (1-2-3) on the hand representing birds that will be "without a worm."

Another strategy can be used to convey to children the notion of borrowing in subtraction. This involves using toy blocks. The blocks can be arranged so that they represent "tens" and "units" columns – bars consisting of blocks placed in a line of 10 in the tens column and 1 to 9 individual cubes placed in the units column.

For example, to subtract 47 from 85, the 85 is first represented as 8 ten-bars in the tens column for 8 10s or 80 and 5 ones-cubes in the units column. To the find the answer (38), the instructor tells the child to notice that there are only 5 ones-cubes in the units column – not enough to remove 7. The child is prompted to "borrow" a ten-bar from the tens column to the units column and to separate the bar into ones-cubes. They can then remove 7 of the cubes as part of subtracting 47, write down 8 as the remaining number of cubes in the units column, then remove four more ten-bars from the tens column and count and write down the number of bars remaining to solve the problem.[17]

In this way, children of 4 and 5 years are adept at identifying parts of wholes, as well as fractions and proportions, when they use shapes and objects. They can show that the addition of half of a circle to one quarter of a circle equals three-quarters of a circle. They also know how many pieces of string will result when a whole piece is cut once, twice, or three times. However, problems arise when children encounter fractions as numbers that fill in the gaps between the whole numbers used for counting. Explanations for difficulties with fractions have often been attributed to the entrenched presupposition that numbers consist of the consecutive integers (1, 2, 3, 4, 5, etc.) that are used for counting. Unlike the counting numbers, there is no natural successor. Whereas 2 follows 1 and 3 follows 2, 1/2 does not have a successor that naturally follows. Moreover, the notation for fractions is problematic and places strong demands on executive functioning (EF) abilities. Whereas 4 is greater than 2, 1/2 is greater than 1/4. If asked to order 1, 2, 1/2, 1/4, they will often reply with the sequence 1, 1/2, 2, 1/4. In this sense, children often do not inhibit the knowledge of integers that 4 is greater than 2, and do not connect the idea of a fraction as part of a whole with the operation of division. They do not recognize how it is possible that a small number can be divided by a larger one, and that numbers are infinitely divisible. Despite considerable training on fraction problems, many children regard fractions as if these were whole numbers. In the absence of a "mental model" of fractions as located in amongst a number line of integers (1, 2, 3, etc.), children may overgeneralize their use of counting numbers and treat fractions as whole numbers in a manner that provides a formidable obstacle to accommodating their theory of number to accept fractions as those numbers that fill in the gaps between the integers. Such difficulties require teachers to make a detailed, ongoing assessment of children's developing understanding to ensure that teachers know what students do know or do not know.[18]

In a highly original study, Carol Smith at the University of Massachusetts-Boston, together with Gregg Solomon at the National Science Foundation in Washington and Susan Carey at Harvard, sought to document children's difficulties with fractions.[19] They asked children in Grades 3 to 6 questions about number and physical quantity to determine whether the understanding that number is infinitely divisible is related to the understanding that physical matter is infinitely divisible and still exists in mass and weight no matter how many times it is divided in half (leaving aside the notion of atomic particles). They reported that children's spontaneous acknowledgement of the existence of numbers between 0 and 1 was strongly related to their understanding that numbers are infinitely divisible in the sense that they can be repeatedly divided without ever getting to zero. Children who held a concept of number as infinitely divisible also had achieved the understanding of physical quantities as infinitely divisible. They possessed a model of fraction notation based on successful judgment of the relative magnitudes of fractions and decimals and an understanding of number as infinitely divisible.

To illustrate, some children did not appear to conceive of fractions as numbers that are indefinitely divisible. One example comes from the answers of a child in Grade 3 to questions about fractions:

(*Any numbers between 0 and 1?*) No.

(*How about one half?*) Yes, I think so.

(*About how many numbers are there between 0 and 1?*) A little, just 0 and half, because it is halfway to one.

(*Suppose you divided 2 in half and got 1; and then divided that number in half...Could you keep dividing forever?*) No because if you just took that half a number, that would be zero and you can't divide zero.

(*Are the numbers getting bigger or smaller?*) Smaller.

(*Would you ever get to zero?*) Yes.

The same child responded that matter was also not infinite divisible:

(*Is there a lot, tiny bit, or no amount of matter in this [medium] styrofoam piece?*) A tiny bit. (*Is there a lot, tiny bit, or no amount of matter in this [smaller] styrofoam piece?*) Nothing at all because if you have something small and it's a part of it, the small piece would have no amount because the big piece would take up all the matter.

(*Can there be a piece of styrofoam too small to see?*) No. (*Well, actually some pieces are so small we can't see them with our eyes, which is why we need microscopes and other special instruments.*)

(*Matter Thought Experiment: Imagine it is possible to divide this tiny piece in half and in half again. If we kept dividing the tiny pieces in half and in half, would the styrofoam matter ever disappear completely?*) Yes you could go forever and ever, but after a year, it would stop, there wouldn't be anything left.

(*Does this piece [medium size] of styrofoam weigh a lot, a tiny bit, or nothing at all?*) A tiny bit. (*Does this [smaller] piece of styrofoam weigh a lot, a tiny bit, or nothing at all?*) Nothing at all. [0 g?] Yes, because if you took a tiny piece off, it would just feel like your own skin because it doesn't weigh anything.

(*Now imagine a tiny piece of styrofoam, so tiny that you couldn't see it. Would that tiny piece take up any space at all?*) No, because if you have really big things on a table and kept it in the corner, it wouldn't take up any space.

(*Would that tiny piece weigh anything at all?*) No.

By contrast, other children did recognize the indefinite divisibility of number and matter. Here is an example from a the responses of a fifth and sixth grader respectively:

(*Any numbers between 0 and 1?*) Yes.

(*Can you give an example?*) 1/2 or 0.5.

(*About how many numbers are there between 0 and 1?*) A lot.

(*Suppose you divided 2 in half and got 1; and then divided that number in half.*

Could you keep dividing forever?) Yes, there always has to be something left when you divide it.

(Are the numbers getting bigger or smaller?) Smaller.

(*Would you ever get to zero?*) No because there is an infinite number of numbers below 1 and above 0

(*Is there a lot, tiny bit, or no amount of matter in this styrofoam piece?*) A little bit, it's something, not nothing.

(*Can there be a piece of styrofoam too small to see?*) Yes, microscopic, human eye can't see because the way we focus our eye.

(*Matter Thought Experiment: Imagine it is possible to divide this tiny piece in half and in half again. If we kept dividing the tiny pieces in half and in half, would the styrofoam matter ever disappear completely?*) Half of that is still something and half of that is very very tiny but it's still something. There's nothing that half of it is nothing. There's no one object that half of it is nothing.

(*Does this piece of styrofoam weigh a lot, a tiny bit, or nothing at all?*) A very, very, very, very little bit. Like a trillionth of an ounce. It is some-thing… it is matter.

(*Now imagine a tiny piece of styrofoam, so tiny that you couldn't see it. Would that tiny piece take up any space at all?*) Yes, it is something taking up a certain amount of space.

(*Would that tiny piece weigh anything at all?*) Probably but I don't think there is a machine or scale that can weigh stuff that small.

(*Space Thought Experiment: Now imagine we kept cutting that tiny piece in half, and in half again. If we kept dividing the tiny pieces in half and in half again, would we ever get to a piece that does not take up any space?*) No, no matter how tiny, as long as it's matter it takes up space because it's there.

(*Weight Thought Experiment: Would we ever get to a piece that has no weight?*)… It would be unmeasurable, but it would have weight. If a tiny person tried to pick it up, it would have weight to him.

These results would seem to reflect a conceptual change account of knowledge acquisition in the domain of number that goes beyond enrichment. Children need to cast off their previous theory of number in order to now accept concepts of fractions and infinity. According to Smith and her colleagues, the realization that matter is infinitely indivisible may form the basis for conceptualizing fractions and infinity. In their study, the recognition of the infinite divisibility of matter appeared to precede that of number in that no child had achieved the latter without the former.

It is this appreciation of fractions and infinity that may lead to greater understanding in other areas of knowledge, leading to a grasp of gravity and a concept of the universe, of the magnitude of the biological nature of contamination, and of the myriad possibilities in the expression of language, time and space as found in literature.[20] For example, in his story *The Secret Miracle,* the Argentine writer Jorge Luis Borges graphically depicts how a second could be almost infinitely stretched into a year through the will of a condemned man facing execution in Czechoslovakia during the Second World War. In his *A Portrait of the Artist as a Young Man,* James Joyce demonstrates that his hero Stephen Dedalus has an understanding of part–whole relations in situating himself in infinite space. In his Irish college classroom, Dedalus writes his address in his geography textbook as:

Class of Elements
Clongowes Wood College
Sallins
County Kildare
Ireland Europe
The World
The Universe

So in the case of mathematics, there is the very real possibility of children needing to achieve a conceptual change in order to advance in their numerical understanding – an understanding that may influence the depth of their knowledge in other areas as well. According to this view, once children run up against fractions, decimals, proportions, and ratios, they need to alter their reasoning about number radically or to stagnate in their progress toward achieving numeracy.

There is no easy solution to this issue. Unlike counting of discrete quantities such as candies and wishes that occur in all cultures and appear inherently enjoyable to children, an understanding of part–whole relations involve the use of spatial representations that need to be explicitly taught and practiced. It is of course desirable that this process be made enjoyable, though enjoyment may not be compatible with practice and drill.

However, one inventive approach that has been advocated as effective by Japanese educators is worthy of note.[21] In the Japanese classroom, children are implored to ensure that members of the group learn together and to be attentive and listen to the ideas of group members. In this setting, typically the instructor asks the students to consider a hypothesis and to carry out experiments together. Then the instructor actually provides instruction to the group as a whole. In this way, there is "collective comprehension activity" that facilities filling in the vital gap (advocated by the Russian psychologist and educator L. S. Vygotsky[22]) between what children can accomplish on their own and what they can accomplish collectively through practical activity and formal instruction.

Therefore in a lesson on fractions, the instructor may first focus on continuous quantity in which the unit and numeral value has not been determined a priori in contrast to discrete quantities that possess countable units. To convey the critical notion that she is referring to continuous rather than discrete quantities, the instructor commonly uses a water supply metaphor in which children are shown litre containers of water that are partly filled, completely filled, or overfilled. This acts a powerful metaphor for the measurement of continuous quantity. Having witnessed the relation between water supply and measurement, the children are told to construct their own rulers out of tiles. First, they use the rulers to make comparisons of quantity using their own particular unit of constructed tiles. Then they use these as a means for measurement using the metric system in a process that prompts them to conceive of part–whole relations that demands a representation of fractions. To consolidate and enrich their understanding of the fractional and decimal relations between whole numbers as represented by the litres of water, each individual child in the class provides the others with a verbal demonstration of their knowledge and its point.

Whether through knowledge enrichment or conceptual change, children need to realize that the reality underlying the phenomenal world of appearances may not only be invisible but may also be decomposed into an infinite number of units. Japanese researchers report that their methods are largely successful. However, overall, we have very little understanding of what children can know about representing infinity and fractions – an issue that again cries out for further research. What is clear is that, for many, number and arithmetic are the hardest of all to grasp. Do some children meet up eventually in this area with the need for a conceptual change that is so challenging that it becomes overpowering? Or is there means by which virtually all children can be taken to a high level of numeracy that includes an understanding of fractions and infinity?

However, instead of recognizing this as a central problem, adults as well as children are often defiant in demeaning the importance of number and arithmetic next to that of language. For example, in the preface to his autobiography, the novelist Joseph Conrad remarked,[23] "Don't talk to me of your Archimedes" lever. He was an absentminded person with a mathematical imagination. Mathematics commands all my respect, but I have no use for engines. Give me the right word and the right accent and I will move the world."

Conrad wrote like an angel in English, his third language after Polish and French, but we can't all be like Conrad and it's a good thing too. It would be very hard for words to move the world without the numerical calculations that allow manufacturing, commerce, industry, transport, communication – and indeed all the overwhelming important aspects of human civilization – to develop and flourish.

Council of Small Nations

Everywhere you go today there seems to a class of travel that seems to be out of the reach of the ordinary mortal and yet so commonly on display. The joy of first class and business class relaxation on long arduous plane flights, coupled with the proliferation of five star hotels on the horizon, is there on view for everyone. However, it is beyond the grasp of all but those in the elite stratosphere of society. How many top executives and government officials could there possibly be to maintain these luxurious facilities?

Council of Small Nations *(cont.)*

An answer to this question arose unexpectedly at a wedding that I attended some years ago. Somehow I came to share a table at the reception with an official in the government of a small country in the European Union. He told me about an organization that I had never heard about before: the Council of Small Nations. This organization consists of four very small countries in Europe: Andorra, Liechtenstein, Monaco, and San Marino. There are two observers, Luxembourg and Malta that, although small, are not small enough to warrant full membership and to rub shoulders among the exceptionally small. The purpose of the CSN organization is to discuss the problems of smallness in a world of much bigger countries. The delegates are blessed with an especially fine concept of numerosity that leads to a desire to control numbers. Obviously small countries need an especially detailed scrutiny of the numbers of dollars spent on social programs, health and justice and care. The organization is dedicated to a minute review of budgetary issues with a view toward minimizing costs for each member nation.

However, in today's Europe, there is equality in the sense that big European powers such as Britain, France, Germany, and Italy need to listen attentively to their very small counterparts and to ring fence time and resources to ensure their fair treatment even though the combined population of the four small countries together is less than that of Slovenia (population 1.9 million) or, for that matter, cities such as Strasbourg (population approximately 300,000). In order to safeguard the effectiveness of CSN meetings and to ensure that delegates arrive in the best condition possible, a travel system has been established. All delegates fly first or business class with the airline of the their choice. If they like, they can take Air France instead of Alitalia, wait and drink in the first class lounge, stay at the poshest hotels, and become patrons of the best restaurants in each of the small member countries. In this way, we have a brigade that maintains international diplomatic status regardless of local origin and can enjoy Andorra and Liechtenstein in the ski season and the delights

Council of Small Nations *(cont.)*

of Monaco and San Marino in the summer, although I am assured that all four destinations have attractions to treasure in each of the four seasons.

It seems too scandalous to be true. Indeed for all I know, my friend at the dinner table may have simply been out to shock and tease. I can find no record on Google, for example, that the Council actually does exist with all its privileges of membership. The mystery remains. There must be some reason why there is so much unattainable luxury around today in the midst of the poverty that is endemic to humanity.

Chapter 7

Autism and disorders of development

Sons of the thief, sons of the saint
Who is the child with no complaint?
Sons of the great or sons unknown
All were children like your own.
Jacques Brel, *Fils de* (Translation:
Mort Shuman and Eric Blau)

Thus far, I have discussed studies concerning, for the most part, healthy, typically developing children. These range from all-rounders who do equally well in nearly everything to others who clearly excel in some areas more than others. But not all children who do especially well in some areas can be seen as typically developing. Among the exception are certain children who have been diagnosed with autism. The development of these children is relevant to issues of conceptual change in that there are specific areas of knowledge in which change does not ever seem to occur.

Classically, autism has been defined in terms of a "triad of impairments." First, children with autism typically do not engage in activities that require them to attend jointly to social activities. They are not interested in the characteristics of other people and do not reciprocate when others seek to initiate and capture their attention. Second, children with autism appear to have little imagination. They engage in restricted solitary activities and prefer to pay attention to objects rather then people. Third, children with autism are impaired in the rate in which they acquire language, particularly in their ability to use language in communicating with other people and in understanding the intentions that underpin a speaker's messages.

The exact number of children with autism or some aspect of autism that falls within what has been termed "autistic spectrum disorders" (ASD) remains unclear. Until quite recently, autism was once thought to be a condition that affects a very small minority of children: 4 or 5 in every 10,000, leaving 9,994 or 9,995 in every 10,000 children unaffected, though of course some of those without autism may have some other disorder. However, a claim commonly made in both the media and in medical journals is that we are now facing an autism epidemic. A recent estimate is that the prevalence of autism and ASD[1] – broadly defined – is as great as 116 in every 10,000 or slightly more than 1 in a 100. This newer estimate is a staggering 25 times more than was previously assumed! How can this be? Is there actually an explosion in the numbers of children who can be classified as having autism or ASD?

Obviously, the numbers of persons classified in any category such as for height and weight depend on the criteria for classification. Even an apparently minor loosening of criteria for classification in a particular category can result in a large increase in the number of cases over time. For example, suppose the definition for a tall man was set in 1980 at 6 foot 2. If the criterion was then lowered in 1994 by just 2 inches to 6 feet, there would have been a very significant increase in the numbers of men who met the definition for tallness without an actual change in the numbers of tall men. In these circumstances, we would face nothing less than an "epidemic" in tallness.

Similarly, in recent years there has been a massive broadening of the criteria used to define ASD.[1] For example, in 1980, a person needed to show "a pervasive lack of responsiveness to other people" to meet a criterion for autism. By contrast, in 1994, a person needed only to show "a lack of spontaneous seeking to share ... achievements with other people." There has been a similar broadening of criteria for designating as autistic an individual's degree of interest in objects and patterns of language, along with an acceptance that autism can occur in individuals regardless of their scores on measures of intelligence and alongside other conditions such as deafness, Down's syndrome, and cerebral palsy. Indeed the criteria for ASD have been broadened to the extent of raising speculation that figures such as Isaac Newton, Thomas Jefferson and even Bill Gates can be included in the diagnosis. By this definition, there might be a bit of autism in a great many children and adults, at least to the extent that they display a lack of interest in others.

It is easy to be cynical over the claim of an autism epidemic, but even a conservative estimate of 4 or 5 out of 10,000 based on a "narrow" definition of autism does amount to 120,000 to 150,000 out of a population of 300 million – approximately that of the United States. For the parents of children with autism, the degree of rareness doesn't make the condition any less bearable. It is terribly clear that autism in its extreme form is one of the most severe childhood disorders.

Numerical and artistic obsessions in autism

Sometimes autism is shown in bizarre ways, with profound impairments in certain areas of development and fascinating expertise in others. A few individuals with autism are not only very lopsided in their attentiveness to the nonsocial features of the world around them but also show very exceptional performance in areas such as number calculation and drawing. These people are known as savants. It is estimated that savants make up only 10 percent of those children who have been diagnosed as autistic (about 1 out of 10,000 of all children and possibly fewer). Still, the study of savants has provided remarkable insights into the understanding of autism and the conditions that give rise to its unevenness across domains of knowledge. Here are two examples.[2]

At the Medical Research Council in London, researchers have studied a young man named Michael who had been diagnosed with autism by the age of 3 years. He did seem to be a normal baby but, at the age of 10 months, he suffered convulsions and again repeatedly between 2 and 4 years of age. He was assumed to have suffered brain damage, though this was not substantiated by the results of brain scans.

Michael's development has been extremely lopsided. On the one hand, Michael does not speak and, as shown on a test of verbal intelligence (the Peabody Picture Vocabulary Test), he has very little in the way of vocabulary comprehension. On the other hand, his nonverbal intelligence (as shown on Raven's Progressive Matrices) is outstanding. In keeping with his remarkable expertise in solving complex jigsaw puzzles, even with the pieces face down, he is in the top percentile of adult nonverbal intelligence with an IQ equivalent of about 140.

Michael also has exceptional ability with number. He is able to add, subtract, multiply, divide and factorize numbers and is incredibly quick and adept in determining whether numbers, even greater than 500, are primes or nonprimes. His performance conforms to the use of the computational algorithm invented by the Greek astronomer and mathematician Eratosthenes in the 3rd century BC: to determine whether a number is a prime, it should be divided by all the prime numbers less than, or equal to, the square root of that number. If the number cannot be so divided without a remainder, then it is a prime. For example, if the number in question were 79, then one should try to divide it by the primes 2, 3, 5, and 7. Since none of these divides without a remainder, 79 is a prime number.

On the other side of the Atlantic, in Montreal, is the case of E.C., another adult with autism. Like Michael, E.C. seemed normal at first as a baby but, at 10 weeks of age, he contacted whooping cough and subsequently had two seizures. By the age of 2, he was clearly autistic. He remained mute until the age of 6. Although he was able to attend school, his performance deteriorated until the age of 15 when he had reached a primary school level. E.C. then went on to engage in work as a dishwasher and housepainter in a pilot psychiatric project.

E.C. has occasional tantrums and pathological feeding behaviors. His language is far from normal. It consists of repetitive stereotypes phrases marked by anomalous syntactic constructions. When he is angry, he occasionally reverses pronouns. He does not adjust his speech to engage in a meaningful conversation with others. Instead, he repeats his own topics and interests, and has great difficulty in understanding expressions, including jokes and puns, that rely on understanding the implications of conversation. Unlike Michael, E.C. has very little expertise with number and cannot count. His talent is in another area. He has a special skill at drawing inanimate objects, though not people and animals.

Two psychologists at the University of Montreal, Laurent Mottron and Sylvie Belleville, have studied E.C.'s graphic abilities. They note that, from an early age, E.C. exhibited an amazing ability objects to draw in detail and from memory from unusual points of view.

He repeatedly drew specific types of trucks and central-heating boilers that were his favorite models.

An example of E.C.'s drawing of a kitchen is shown below. As an adult artist, he looks at his model every 10 seconds. He rarely uses color and never erases or crosses out a line. E.C. adjusts the paper to draw straight lines of an object with the result that it may be represented in an unusual orientation on the paper, or only part of the object appears as is permitted by the edge of the paper. He had once enrolled in an art school briefly at the 11 years but was expelled owing to rigidity in his drawing style – a rigidity that his parents maintained was present before he entered.

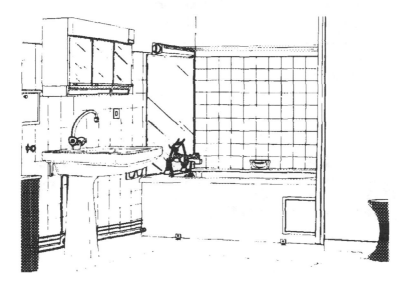

In testing E.C., Mottron and Belleville were interested to see whether his skill at drawing objects might be underpinned by a special focus on local detail. For example, E.C. and a group of healthy adult controls were shown stimuli that are incongruent in global (large) and local (small) aspects: a large C made up of small Os and a large O made up of small C's. These stimuli, together with other congruent stimuli, were presented very rapidly on a screen. E.C. and the group of controls were asked to report what they saw in terms such as "a large… made of a small…." For the control group, there were no differences in local and global errors between the congruent and incongruent stimuli. By contrast, compared to the congruent stimuli, E.C. made significantly more errors in mistaking global characteristics for local ones on the incongruent stimuli.

Mottron and Belleville concluded that E.C. was preoccupied with local, part detail to the extent that it interfered with his perception of the global nature of a scene. One interpretation of this result is that E.C. has "weak central coherence" in processing the local and global characteristics of a situation to construct an accurate over-all representation. However, Mottron and his colleagues prefer an "enhanced perceptual functioning" explanation.[3] They maintain that children with autism such as E.C. do not have problems in taking in the global aspects of information, but that they have a local bias in processing information that reflects a superior performance in low-level perception, that is, in perceiving the simple visual or auditory details of a scene.

As savants with autism, Michael and E.C. are very different. Michael is a case of a mute savant with skill in calculation and E.C. is a case of an individual with high-functioning autism, sometimes termed Asperger's syndrome, who has skill in drawing. What unites the two is their preference to focus on objects rather than people and their poor spontaneous language in conversing with others.

Theory of Mind in autism

It has long been suggested that ToM is often not present in autism and that this deficit accounts for the nonsocial nature of autism. The basis for the ToM explanation was the finding that many children with autism do not seem to understand how the behavior of others can be guided by a false belief, as shown by their incorrect answers on the Sally-Anne task that was described in Chapter 2. Unlike the case for typically developing 3-year-olds, their poor ToM performance appears to be resistant to efforts to change the test question so that it is more specific in referring to Sally's initial searching behavior. Indeed children with autism do display a host of difficulties that would seem to be associated with difficulties in ToM reasoning. For example, they may not recognize that there is a critical difference between knowing and believing. They often do not see that the sentence "He knows that *there are cookies in the cupboard*" implies the truth of the proposition that there really are cookies in the cupboard and that the sentence "He believes that *there are cookies in the cupboard*" does not imply that this proposition is either truth or false. In sharp contrast with the performance of mental age-matched children with language disorders but without autism, children with autism also find it hard to define the word *friend*.[4] Not to have insight into the intentions, beliefs, and feelings of others must be a terrifying prospect – one that might well seem to capture and explain the stark isolation and sadness of autism. In a sense, children with autism might seem to lack a module in engage in ToM reasoning.

However, appealing though it may seem, this form of a ToM explanation cannot provide a full account. For one thing, it is now apparent that failure on the tasks used to test typically developing 3- and 4-year-olds such as Sally-Anne is neither universal in autism nor specific to the disorder. Some children diagnosed with autism pass the tasks whereas many other children without autism do not, including late-signing deaf children, as described in Chapter 2. In fact, some children with autism have been repeatedly tested on ToM tasks to the extent that, when first shown a Smarties box and asked to say what they think is inside, they say pencils instead of Smarties! They know that they are about to experience a test of their understanding of false beliefs. Furthermore, children often display the symptoms of autism, especially a failure to respond to voices, before the age at which they could be ordinarily tested with a view toward determining whether they display ToM understanding, at least as shown on Sally-Anne type tests. Above all, the range of children termed as autistic are certainly varied and heterogenous. Children who have difficulties in one area such as ToM may not have difficulties in others such as on one or more aspects of executive functioning, leading some to advocate that a single explanation for autism is not possible.[5]

The importance of language in autism

In view of these shortcomings, many recent studies have focused directly on the range of language and communication disorders shown by children with autism. The underlying rationale is that knowing more about the language and communication of children with autism may provide a key for understanding many of the difficulties of children with autism in making sense of the information conveyed by others. Indeed, classic autism as defined in 1943 by Leo Kanner, an early pioneer of autism research and the first professor of child psychiatry in the United States, is only diagnosed when serious language and communication problems coincide with the other impairments in social relatedness and imagination. In ASD, the distribution of autistic symptoms in the population is often viewed as a continuum ranging from conditions such as Asperger's syndrome and high-functioning autism to classic (or Kanner-type) autism. However, although classic autism is distinguished by more severe language impairments than are present in Asperger's syndrome, most individuals on the autism spectrum, including those with Asperger's syndrome or high-functioning autism, do experience language delays and communication problems at least to some degree compared to typically developing children.[6]

What exactly are these problems? At 18–24 months of age, typically developing infants are skilled at using a speaker's gaze at objects to interpret novel words. For example, they can see that a speaker is looking at a banana when she says the word "banana" and so infer that this thing is called a banana. However, there is little doubt that many language-delayed children with autism fail to use this strategy to learn new words. This finding parallels work on the neural basis of gaze showing that brain activation accompanying the eye direction of typically developing children occurs in the right hemisphere, whereas it occurs bilaterally and is not specialized in either hemisphere in individuals with autism.[7]

Once children with autism do acquire a vocabulary, the phonology and grammar of their language may also be impaired compared to that of typically developing children. However, the degree to which these formal aspects of language are disordered in autism remains controversial, as such impairments may be seen to be due to general retardation in development rather than to a condition that is specific to autism.[8]

It is in the area of pragmatics that virtually unanimous agreement has emerged on the pervasive language problems faced by children with autism. In contrast to knowledge of word meaning and grammar, pragmatics concerns knowledge of how language is used in communication. It involves the ability to follow the implications of a conversation based on the social context and so helps typically developing children to appreciate jokes, irony and sarcasm.

A central issue in research on pragmatics concerns how listeners derive meaning from the relevant properties of a speaker's message. For example, suppose you hear that the Italian judicial system has launched prosecutions against the Prime Minister and his associates. You ask your Italian colleague "How did the trials end up?" The reply "the associates were convicted" implies that the Prime Minister was not. Consider another example from the Marx brothers. Suppose a speaker asks a new acquaintance, "Where can get a hold of you?" The response, "I don't know. I'm ticklish all over" is humorous – but only to those who understand the double meaning of the question that the speaker did not intend. As yet another example, suppose a messy little boy hears his mother exclaim, "Thank you for putting away your toys again neatly like you always do." To understand the intended meaning of this remark, the boy is required to recognize that his mother is making a sarcastic comment since he has done precisely the opposite.

When adults interpret language, they go well beyond what is said, enriching, and sometimes even reversing, what is conveyed in the literal meaning of language. They commonly add a wealth of implicit information that, when all goes well, enables the speaker's intended meaning to be retrieved – a special challenge for young, typically developing children who are inexperienced in conversation, let alone children with autism.

For these children, just to get pragmatics and meaning in communication off the ground may be a considerable obstacle. For example, children with autism often misuse the singular pronouns for the first and second person ("I" and "you"), but not the pronouns for corresponding to the third person. These specific difficulties may reflect the need to adjust to the referential meaning of "I" and "you" that changes constantly over the course of conversational turns, whereas the meaning of the third person pronouns does not depend so strictly on who is speaking at a certain point of a conversation.

Although children with autism do use proper nouns correctly, they tend to use them later in development when other children without autism would use pronouns instead. They may also show problems with deictic terms such as "this" and "that," or words like "come" and "go," "here" and "there" that require the speaker to assume that the personal perspective of the listener for these terms to be understood correctly.[9]

In a comprehensive investigation that looked at the pragmatic ability of children with autism to recognize coherent exchanges in conversation, the Italian psychologist Luca Surian teamed up with British researchers Simon Baron-Cohen and Heather van der Lely.[10] They sought to test systematically whether children with autism would be more impaired in their pragmatic development than typically developing children or even children with a persistent deficit in syntax and morphology who had been classified as having a form of Specific Language Impairment (SLI). The mean ages of the children with autism and SLI were about 12 years compared to that of the 6-year-old typically developing children. All three groups had a mean verbal mental age of 67–69 months.

The children were given a test of pragmatic understanding that was devised according the highly influential framework proposed by the philosopher Paul Grice. According to Grice, speakers in conversation implicitly follow a Cooperative Principle: they cooperate towards an accepted purpose. To do that they conform to nine conversational maxims, divided into four groups, labeled (after Kant) *Quantity, Quality, Relation*, and *Manner*:

Maxims of Quantity:

1. Make your contribution as informative as is required.

2. Do not make your contribution more informative than is required.

Maxims of *Quality*:

1. Do not say what you believe to be false.

2. Do not say that for which you lack adequate evidence.

Maxim of *Relation*:

1. Be relevant.

Maxims of *Manner*:

1. Avoid obscurity of expression.

2. Avoid ambiguity.

3. Be brief (avoid unnecessary prolixity).

4. Be orderly.

The children heard 27 short conversational exchanges that involved a case where a speaker violated a maxim. These were tape-recorded by three speakers, one male and two female, to correspond to three dolls: Lucy, Tom, and Sally. The children in the three groups tested by Surian and his colleagues were shown the dolls and told that one of them, Lucy, was going to ask questions to the other two, Tom and Jane. They were then told that Tom and Jane would always answer Lucy, but that each time one of them would say something funny or silly. It was added that sometimes Tom would say something silly, and sometimes it would be Jane who said something silly.

The children were asked to listen carefully to the tape recordings. After each episode, the tape was stopped and the child was asked to "point to the doll that said something silly." In each case, one of the answers violated a conversational maxim. The utterances violated the first or the second maxim of Quantity, the first maxim of Quality, and the maxim of Relation. Examples with the silly answers starred are as follows:

> First Maxim of Quantity (be informative):
> Lucy: What did you eat for lunch? Tom: Some food* Jane: A pizza.
> Second Maxim of Quantity (avoid redundant information):
> Lucy: Who is your best friend? Tom: My best friend is Peter. He wears clothes.* Jane: My best friend is John. He goes to my school.
> First Maxim of Quality (be truthful):
> Lucy: Why don't you play with me? Tom: Because I have to go home for tea.* Jane: Because I am playing in the sky.
> Maxim of Relation (be relevant):
> Lucy: What did you do on holiday? Tom: I cycled everyday. Jane: My trousers were blue.*

In addition, the children were given episodes that corresponded to Grice's Maxim of Politeness ("Be polite") that was not in his original list but was suggested by him for possible later inclusion. For example, Lucy: Do you like my dress? Tom: It's pretty. Jane: I hate it.*

Compared to the typically developing children and the children with SLI, the children with autism showed severe and persistent pragmatic problems. Quite amazingly, though many were 12-year-olds, they had considerable difficulty in identifying silly, maxim-violating answers that typically developing 6-year-olds could easily point out.

They did not display an awareness of the fundamental conversational maxims or rules that, according to Grice, enjoin speakers to provide sufficient, relevant and true information in a clear, orderly and unambiguous way. This result is in keeping with the inabilities of children with autism to use language to establish and maintain a focus of joint attention, to talk about topics that are of interest to others, to make smooth transitions to new topics, and to determine the amount of background information to provide others in order to ensure effective communication. Difficulties in the pragmatic understanding of children with autism appear to be related to their lack of success on ToM reasoning and extend to difficulties in comprehension of ironic, sarcastic, and metaphorical speech that require a nonliteral interpretation.

Also related to pragmatics is the use of prosodic information in language – the stress and resonance on words and phases that in normal speech facilitates communication. Prosody is important in the interpretation of ironic remarks as these are often marked by a characteristic prosodic contour that helps the listener to interpret such remarks correctly. Abnormal prosody in autism was first reported in clinical studies and, more recently, in experimental investigations. Many individuals with autism have a flat intonation in their speech that in this respect resembles the vocal announcements assembled automatically by computer programs. They perform poorly on tasks in which they have to make inferences about the mental states of a speaker from his or her vocalizations, such as surprise and irritation. Even adults with the high-functioning autism that is sometimes termed Asperger's syndrome can have difficulty making inferences about the mental states of a speaker, for example surprise and irritation, from his or her vocalizations. Evidence from both behavioral and brain imagining studies show that children with autism often need to try much harder than typically developing children to understand the use prosody in irony.[11]

How do the language disorders of children with autism provide clues for explaining their failure to tune into the social world?

According to research to date, children who have poor language skills are perhaps most likely to show the extreme interest in objects and neglect of interest in persons that is symptomatic of autism. An important possibility is that such children may have difficulties attending to speech and voices. They may not take in information that is vital for participating in conversations and for considering the thinking and behaviour of other persons. Under these conditions, many children with autism or ASD may develop compensating abilities in nonsocial spheres of functioning, such as in mathematics or in drawing objects.

From early infancy, hearing is a fundamental basis for the orientation of attention. In the first week of life, healthy infants turn their heads towards the source of a speaker's voice. This was documented in a classic series of experiments by Morton Mendelson, now at McGill University, and Marshall Haith, now at the University of Denver. For example, in these studies, babies aged 1 to 4 days were placed on their backs facing up to a television camera. They then heard 10 messages such as:

> Hello Baby. It's really nice to see you here today. Believe it or not, you're on television right now. If the folks back home could only see you, wouldn't they be surprised? I hope that you'll keep your eyes open nice and wide and please, Baby, try not to move your head around too much. That's the only way we'll get a good videotape of you. If you cooperate really well you'll have the satisfaction of knowing that you've helped Science find truth and understanding. And remember, Baby, "Truth is beauty, beauty truth." Thank you for trying so hard, Baby. Have a nice day.

In reaction to this type of message, infants turned their heads and looked towards the location of the sound. In doing so, they showed that they could use sound to guide their looking.

Given the early maturity of the auditory system compared to the visual system, it is not surprising that before the age of 5 years, stimuli in the auditory modality dominate children's attention whereas adult attention is dominated by a visual preference. In experiments involving healthy children and adults, Vladmir Sloutsky and his coworkers at Ohio State University found that, unlike adults, children ranging in age from 8 months to 4 years do not pay more attention to new pictures than familiar pictures when they are paired with familiar sounds. However, infants and 4-year-olds do attend significantly longer to pictures – whether these have been previously seen or not – when these pictures are paired with new sounds. This auditory preference is particularly marked for infants and appears to be "automatic" in that it does not need be carried out with deliberation and foresight. An early auditory dominance is adaptive for language learning and is essential to engage in conversation with others. Whereas objects that we see are often stationary and do not disappear, the sounds in speech are fleeting and need to be processed rapidly for effective communication.[13]

In contrast to healthy individuals, individuals with autism have difficulties in dealing with the auditory world, especially speech and voices, such that they are unable to engage jointly in attention with speakers – a skill that can be regarded as "pivotal" in discriminating between healthy children and those with autism. For example, many individuals with autism have difficulty in detecting speech from noise. A wider discrepancy between the frequencies of a signal and a masking sound is required for those with autism than those without autism to hear the signal.[14]

Much of the work carried out here is impressively transcontinental. For example, a study carried out by researchers in Helsinki, San Diego, and Kokuryo, Japan, including the Finnish cognitive neuroscientist Rita Ceponiene, used event-related brain potentials to study the brain activation of school-aged children with autism to sounds. The children had an attentional deficit in orienting to the "speechness" quality of vowel sounds.[15] Moreover, in a brain imaging study using fMRI, a team working in Paris and Montreal that included the French researchers Hélène Gervais and Mônica Zilbovicius studied the brain activation of five adult males diagnosed with autism in response to vocal sounds.[16]

As illustrated on the opposite page, a healthy control group clearly showed activation to vocal sounds in the superior temporal sulcus region in the right and left hemispheres whereas the autistic group did not, although both groups displayed a normal activation pattern in response to nonvocal sounds. This pattern of results fits the claim by Mottron and with autism may be overwhelmed by the complexity of voices as well as his colleagues that the attention of children sounds, such as those in cafeterias or made by vacuum cleaners. By contrast, they are as adequately prepared as healthy children to attend nonvocal sounds such at a single frequency such as pure tones.

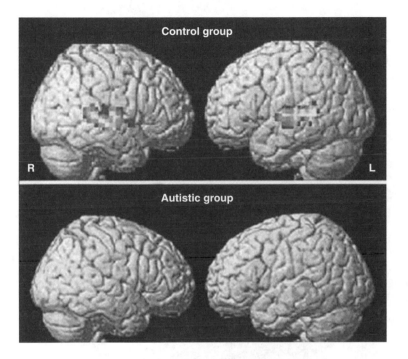

The identification of a voice-selective brain area would seem to have crucial implications for the study of autism, particularly if the next step followed involves the use of transcranial magnetic stimulation or TMS. This is a technique that uses magnetic stimulation to allow a virtual brain lesion to be created. Through TMS, neuroscientists can isolate the area of the brain that may be specialized for a particular function such as for working with numbers, identifying faces, or certain aspects of memory, language, perception, thinking and reasoning.

I was once at a conference in Kyoto, Japan, where a distinguished researcher became ecstatic at the prospects of using TMS to help stroke patients regain the ability to articulate speech clearly. The talk was so memorable that I mentioned it to a colleague who pointed out that it had been invented at my own university – a fact that I did not know and is probably not known generally in the more than 3,000 laboratories worldwide where TMS is used.[17] Armed with this knowledge, I confronted Sheffield medical physicist and engineer Anthony T. Barker to own up to the discovery that he and colleagues had made in 1985. With exceptional modesty, Tony simply said, "If we hadn't done it, then someone else would have." But for the record, here is Tony using the first clinical TMS stimulator on an experimental subject. He used the same coil on me directed at my motor cortex and I duly twitched.

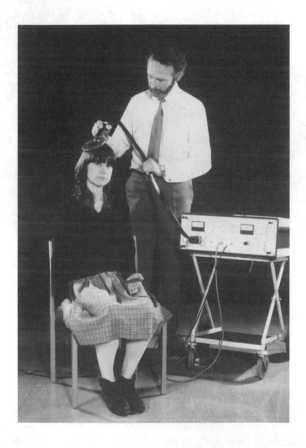

Not every brain area is equally accessible to TMS and there may be difficulties in locating the precise brain site to which TMS is to be directed. However, neuroscientists have welcomed TMS as an ethically safe technique that permits the testing of hypotheses about vital cause-and-effect relationships. Although brain imaging techniques involving functional magnetic resonance or event-related potentials demonstrate what brain areas are activated when a person carries out a task, all this shows is that activation in a particular area is correlated with the task. It does not show that activation in this area is necessary to perform it. Here is where TMS comes in. In suppressing brain activity in a specific area of interest, TMS can serve to establish a causal relationship. If the person does worse on the task during TMS, we now have stronger support for the hypothesis that this brain area is actually used for carrying the task out and is necessary for success.

This type of research has been carried out on the ability to discriminate faces. For instance, persons asked to discriminate photographs as similar to their own faces rather those of the familiar faces of friends and colleagues might show using fMRI activation in the right inferior parietal lobule (IPL). If an experimenter then interferes with the right IPL using TMS, their ability to discriminate faces declines, whereas interfering with the left IPL has no effect. From this work has come support for the hypothesis that the right IPL is important for face discrimination because inferring with right IPL capability contributes to reduced accuracy in face discrimination.

No such research has yet been carried out in the cases of ToM reasoning or on mathematical calculation, though the rationale would be the same. For example, if the left temporo–parietal junction is essential for ToM reasoning, as some have claimed, then "zapping" the left TPJ with TMS while a person is reasoning on ToM tasks should mean that his ToM performance should decline. (This has always struck me as the ideal title of a fantasy article: for example, "Using TMS to assess the impact of the TPJ on ToM.") Similarly it has been claimed that the left horizontal interparietal sulcus (the HIPS) is a left hemisphere language area that is central to carrying out exact mathematical calculations involving operations such as addition and subtraction. If so, then zapping the left HIPS with TMS while a person is engaged in calculating should mean that their calculation performance should decline.[18] Given that STS has been shown to be inactive in response to vocal sounds in adults with autism, would it then be possible to create autistic symptoms involving a lack of response to voices temporarily in healthy individuals by zapping voice-selective STS regions using TMS?

Autism and attention to voices and speech: in search of a causal pathway

All of this is in the future. TMS aside, there remain stubborn issues of cause and effect that need to be sorted out. Critically, since the symptoms of autism are often apparent in some preschool children and even in children less than 2 years of age,[19] it might be argued that auditory processing difficulties in school-aged children and adolescents and adults may be a consequence, rather than an antecedent, of autism. In other words, since causes have to come before their effects, problems in attending to voices and speech could well be an effect of some other cause of autism that happens earlier in development rather than a cause in itself.

In fact, fMRI studies have shown that there are a host of differences in the brain activation of healthy school-aged children and adolescents and those with autism. For example, a group of 10 high-functioning children with ASD and a mean age of 12 years has been reported to have no "mirror neuron" activity in a specific brain region, the inferior frontal gyrus, while imitating and observing emotional responses. Such activity has been proposed as a mechanism for imitation in healthy controls and possibly also the understanding of intentions. Other groups of teen-aged males with autism have been observed to show a strong relation between the time that they gaze at faces in face discrimination tasks and the activation of the amygdala, a brain structure associated with emotional responses such as anger. This relation is thought to indicate a heightened emotional response, compared to that shown by healthy controls, in individuals with autism who characteristically show a weaker fixation, and greater aversion, to faces.[20]

These brain–behavior relationships in late childhood and adolescence could simply be coincidences in that they do not necessarily illuminate a causal effect. They could be a consequence rather than an antecedent of autism that is evident in early childhood and even infancy. However, consistent with a causal account that is specifically based on auditory attention, we now have evidence that autism is marked by a lack of appropriate attention to speech even at a young age. A team led by Patricia Kuhl of the Department of Speech and Hearing Sciences at the University of Washington in Seattle has recently reported a study of 29 children aged 32 to 52 months diagnosed with ASD.[21] Compared to a healthy control group, the children with ASD did not show preference for "motherese" speech with exaggerated prosody that is commonly used by mothers in their communication with children and is thought to facilitate language acquisition over nonspeech analogs. Moreover, event-related potentials as a measure of brain activity indicated that the children with ASD, unlike healthy children of the same age, did not show a significant response to syllable changes in speech. These results are in keeping with the long-standing observation that preschool children with autism have difficulty orienting toward human voices and using this information to recognize faces and to attend to speakers in conversation – a finding not necessarily characteristic of older children and dependent on the nature of the measures used to examine voice processing.

Such studies still do not necessarily rule out auditory attention as consequent rather than an antecedent – and hence a possible cause – of autism. It may be that some other factor in the first year or two of life may give rise to the lack of attention shown by many children with autism to voices and speech. For example, advances in the study of ToM described in Chapter 2 based on visual attention have pointed to the presence of an incipient understanding of false beliefs even in healthy 13-month-old infants. It is possible that future research may show that this type of understanding is absent in autism. Another quite different example is that, in very early development, children who are later diagnosed for autism often have been observed to have an enlarged head size. Again both factors may ultimately not add up to a causal explanation of autism and the same may prove to be the case for auditory attention. Nevertheless, the results reported by Kuhl and her coworkers are consistent with the position that an early attentional speech–voice problem indeed may be a causal factor in autism. If this proposal turns out to be right, a number of other issues in autism fall into place. It could serve as an example of how a specific impairment can give rise to a number of cascading developmental effects that may appear downstream as more general deficits.

First, having impairment in auditory attention, children with autism may be blocked from opportunities for conversation with others that are enjoyed by typically developing children. In fact, unlike healthy kids, many children who are diagnosed with ASD do not respond when their name is called – a pattern that is present even in infancy. While some do speak and have mastered the grammar of their native language, they still do not have access to the experience that allows insight into the implications of conversation, involving understanding speakers' intentions and accompanying humor, sarcasm, and irony. As a consequence, they may not attend to – and may not remember – events involving interactions with others. Instead, they attend to nonsocial aspects of their environment and show the excessive interest in objects that is one of the hallmarks of autism.[22]

For many individuals with autism, the result may involve a well-developed, or even an over-developed, visuospatial faculty. Compared to healthy controls, they may show equal or superior visual search and resistance to visual illusions. They may also perform well on measures tasks requiring pattern matching and spatial orientation. Their success on these tasks requires close attention to the details of objects and is consistent with the weak central coherence and enhanced perceptual functioning accounts of autism proposed to explain the behavior of cases such as E.C.

Second, impairments in attention to voices and speech may also contribute to difficulties shown by many children with autism on Sally-Anne type ToM tasks even after the age of 4 years that are similar to those of late-signing deaf children that were noted in Chapter 2. It is likely that children with autism and those with deafness fail the tasks for different reasons. However, these reasons in turn may be related to language impairment insofar as this impairment limits children's ability to attend to information in conversations about how the mental states of others may be different from one's own – information that is key to success on ToM tasks.[23]

Third, if auditory attention does make a causal contribution to autism, a useful step would be to train children with autism to attend to voices and speech. This is an issue that has been examined extensively in the area of dyslexia or backwardness in reading. At least in alphabet languages such as English, though possibly not in logographic languages such as Chinese, reading has been often been linked to children's ability to analyze speech sounds in correspondence to written letters and syllables. If an impairment in matching sounds to letters is causal to dyslexia, training children to attend to differences in speech sounds should result better preparedness for reading. However, the same problem underlies this proposed link as that described above for autism. Because neither reading nor awareness of differences in sounds are usually tested until children are older (typically 5+ years), it is unknown whether one precedes the other and whether to determine whether improvement in one comes before the other and whether training on sounds helps in the process of learning to read. Still there are training programs such as one initiated by a Elise Temple, a Cornell University neuroscientist, that appear to be effective both in the improvement of reading and even in yielding brain activity that is thought to underscore reading success.[24]

Methods designed to assess and to train children as young as 3 years in discriminating sounds are presently under development.[25] These may involve a computer game in which a sound is heard and then the child needs to report which of the three following sounds differs from the original target. This situation can be portrayed in

terms of a mother cat uttering a sound that can be reproduced by two of her three kittens. The child's task is to point out which kitten of the three has not reproduced the sound. These methods may not only help children at risk of dyslexia to read better but also help children with autism to attend better to voices and speech, thus improving their ability to follow messages in conversation.

Lack of attention to voices and speech may create serious difficulties for children in a wide variety of areas. One of these involves knowing that the appearance of an object can lead to the false belief that it is edible whereas in reality it is contaminated. As discussed in Chapter 4, a rudimentary knowledge of contamination and the edible–inedible distinction is present in typically developing young children by the age of 3 years when they have been engaged continually in conversations about whether substances can be safely eaten. Since gastrointestinal illness (GI) can occur as a consequence of barriers to communication about contaminated substances, children with autism who are impaired in language may be at special risk. This is a matter of heated controversy. Some researchers claim to have found a strong relationship between GI and autism, whereas others have claimed that there is no more GI in autism than there is in the general population. The latter view, expressed in a 2002 article in the *British Medical Journal*, has met with a furious reaction.[26] For example, one doctor in California writes:

> I have yet to see an autistic child WITHOUT gastrointestinal problems (even if no particular diagnosis has been attached to the child by a gastroenterologist) clearly reported by the parents. As a clinician and specialist in autism, I have yet to see a child with this diagnosis without GI problems.... I now find it difficult to believe that researchers could blind themselves to the many excellent studies showing the almost ubiquitous bowel problems in autistic children. Nonverbal children with high pain threshold as part of their illness cannot tell us what hurts, yet when they are evaluated for their autism, we find their guts are teeming with pathogens, food hypersensitivities and nutritional deficiencies are extremely common, and they often suffer nighttime awakening by what excellent researchers have discovered is caused by stomach pain, gas, bloating, and reflux gastritis.

Indeed, the prevalence of GI in their children seems to be one of the very biggest complaints of parents who have children with autism, When I went to a forum on autism organized in London by the Medical Research Council, parent after parent emotionally testified to the feeding difficulties and stomach pains in their child, and that many in the scientific community do not take these seriously. The sad reality of the situation is soberly summed up in a recent comprehensive review from researchers at the Indiana University School of Medicine:[27]

> Parents wondering if their autistic child may be prone to symptoms such as diarrhea, constipation or food intolerance are left with little to read that truly gives them reliable information about whether or not autism itself predisposes a child to increased GI abnormalities.

Toward a coherent, integrative account of autism

Current research on autism needs to be considered with caveats. The ages of those in the studies are variable, the measures given differ, and the sample sizes are often small. Bearing these considerations in mind, evidence is accumulating that those children whose language is severely impaired, especially relative to their nonverbal intelligence, are at risk of displaying severe symptoms of autism. At the same time, other research suggests that at least some children with autism have deficits in auditory processing which preclude participation in conversation with others, possibly resulting in downstream impairments on ToM tasks and excessive interest in objects at the expense of people. This diminishes the child's early opportunities to share at a very young age in spontaneous family conversation at home and in everyday interactive contexts. Deaf children of hearing parents are limited by their sensory problems from full participation in many of these early experiences. Children with autism may also often be cut off from many of these experiences by their inattention to voices and speech. The diagnosis of barriers to auditory processing promises to identify the nature of the social isolation of children with autism. Although there is much more to be done in terms of the search for causal pathways, research in this area holds out the eventual prospect of gaining a deeper insight into the mystery of autism and developmental disorders more generally, with a focus on remediation through improving children's attention to voices and sounds.

Paying attention

These days it is fashionable to speculate on the presence of autistic symptoms in the general population. When we look around, it is easy to find persons who seem not to talk much or not even to understand, or attend to, as much language as they should. There are people who seem obsessed with landmarks and places to the extent that they neglect others around them. There are also persons who prefer repetition to novelty and show a lack of imagination. My own predilection for cereal (confession – Special K) and coffee for breakfast every morning, regardless of my conscious attempts to drop this repetitive habit, has attracted interest from others in terms of a possible autistic side to my personality. Since my earliest recollections, I have been obsessed with street maps of cities, road maps of American and Australian states and Canadian provinces, British road maps, detailed road maps of Europe that have become even more interesting with the break-up of the Soviet Union, Czechoslovakia, and Yugoslavia with the creation of more countries with their own language, culture, traditions, and national capitals. Yet this obsession with landmarks and places has not helped me in finding my way when a tourist. Really, it would be better to process information rapidly about where one should be a particular point in time rather than to be overwhelmed by the physical world.

Some years ago, I visited Florence during a hot Italian summer when there are tremendous crowds of tourists and chaos seems to reign at the railway station. Aside from the unrivalled art, there is the food. In a sense, Italian cuisine is like the English language. English has swept around the world to be the international language. It is the language of business, science, and entertainment and is overwhelmingly the second language for people who are native speakers of another language. But English food – or the food indigenous to English speaking countries – is not the international cuisine. Although fast food names such McDonald's, KFC, and Coca-Cola are global institutions that come from America, the crown for international cuisine backed by a long cultural tradition

Paying attention *(cont.)*

arguably must go to Italy. No other cuisine is so universally popular with Italian restaurants and pizzerias represented in every corner of the world. This achievement is even more impressive when we consider that Italian food, with its regional variations, emanates from a country of fewer than 60 million people – less than 1 percent of the world's population.

However, with any visit and food expedition to Italy, there is the task of finding the *uscita* or way out back home. The main airport for Florence is at Pisa and there is a train that links Florence with Pisa and then a bus from Pisa train station to the airport. It would seem simple then to catch my flight back to England – except that I kept missing signs: try as I may I couldn't follow the advice about where to go and when.

First, I missed the first train to Pisa. I couldn't follow the signs for the right platform and couldn't take in fast enough the muffled sounds in Italian announcing where to go. Then finally having found the next train, I arrived at Pisa station and was not able to find the bus to the airport. After some frantic running around, I was able to locate the bus that was just about to pull out. Then I discovered that you have to buy tickets beforehand and I had to beg for mine from a kindly passenger who took pity on me and lent me a 1,000 lire note. Finally the airport was in sight but I didn't know how close it would actually get to the terminal as I seemed to have got on a local bus rather than the proper airport coach that would take me right there and didn't know enough Italian to ask. So I took a chance and got out at about 500 metres before the terminal. This was unwise as the bus did go right up to the terminal, and though it had been the usual sunny warm weather up to now, the heavens opened up with a massive thunderstorm. I got drenched during the 10-minute walk to the terminal. Upon entry into the building the rain promptly stopped and the sun came out again.

By that time I was frantic, since with all the delays in catching the right train and bus, I thought that I would be late for my flight.

Paying attention *(cont.)*

On the contrary, I discovered that the flight would take off three hours late! It was a Sunday and only a couple of cafés were open at the small Pisa airport. There were no banks open and no foreign exchange booths but there was a foreign exchange machine on the wall. These have always seemed suspicious to me but I was tired, hungry, and wet so I decided that I should use it as I had no more Italian money but did have a smattering of currencies from other places that I had been. The machine took bank notes from about 10 different countries and I had four different currencies left. I tried American dollars. The machine replied that it couldn't change these. I tried Canadian dollars. Again the machine replied that it couldn't change these. I tried British pounds. Once again, the machine replied that it couldn't change these. It was my last chance. I had some Japanese yen and put the yen notes into the machine. It was if I had won the jackpot. The machine duly pumped out a supply of thousands of Italian lire (about US$30 worth). I was able to get something to eat, wait around, and eventually catch my plane.

Looking at my travel attempts retrospectively, maybe it would have been easier not to be so taken in by roadmaps, and instead to be more observant to the spoken environment in which there are people's voices that give good advice as to where to go and when. In the process, wouldn't it be wonderful if during a long plane ride, there would be clear representations of the tastiest and healthiest food that could await travellers when they reach their destination? Today airports are often named after politicians (George H. Bush in Houston, Ronald Reagan in Washington, Charles de Gaulle in Paris) but what better way to look forward to reaching a destination than to name airports after food? The possibilities seem endless. For example, Boston Logan would become Boston (Logan) Clam Chowder Airport, Newark Liberty Newark NJ Diner Airport, and Montreal Trudeau Montreal Smoked Meat. In Europe, Venice Marco Polo would become Venice Pollo (Chicken), Toulouse Blagnac Toulouse Magret de Canard, and Milan Malpensa Milan

Paying attention *(cont.)*

Osso Buco. Beijing Airport could become Beijing Tasty Duck. In Australia, Brisbane could be Brisbane Aussie Beef.

Surely, names could also be sorted out for vegetarians so that airports could have two names – one for carnivores and the other for vegetarians. Travellers themselves could vote on the appropriate names. Once adapted, these could help counteract the increasingly abrasive and tedious process of flying and to prompt travellers to engage in healthy and rewarding eating in a new culture. What better way to pay attention to where one is going!

Chapter 8

Culture, communication, and what children know

The weight of this sad time we must obey,
Speak what we feel, not what we ought to say.
Shakespeare, *King Lear*

A major goal for children is to show how grown up they are, both physically and intellectually. For example, to demonstrate their physical maturity, children strive for achievement in sports. To this end, children in America, Cuba, and Japan often become fine baseball players. Canadian, Russian, Finnish, and Swedish children excel at skating and ice hockey. Chinese children do well at ping-pong and gymnastics. Children in Australia, Fiji, New Zealand, Samoa, South Africa, and Tonga become stars at rugby. In Ethiopia and Kenya, children often turn into fine long distance runners whereas, for example, in Argentina, Brazil, France, Spain, Portugal, and Italy, they often become outstanding at soccer. In each instance, children's achievements lie in the specialized sports that are promoted by different cultures – so much so that success on a world scale can have little to do with a country's actual population.[1]

Similarly, the culture in which children grow up provides specialized opportunities for demonstrating their intellectual maturity. For instance, in Singapore, China, Korea, and Japan, attainment in mathematics – and the display of proficiency with mathematical tools such as the abacus – is one major measure. In countries such as The Netherlands, Denmark, Switzerland, and Slovenia, maturity can be demonstrated by the mastery of three or more languages. In countries such as Russia, maturity may be shown, for example, through proficiency in chess. As I have described in Chapter 3, Australian children seem to score particularly well in astronomy and geography. In each instance, the culture is supportive, encouraging children to explore, to innovate, and to participate in conversations with its more mature members. In this sense, the intelligence of children reflects an "adaptive specialization" that responds to cultural challenges.

Nevertheless, although the cultures of the world provide huge variations in opportunities for children to shine, these also carry restrictions in that some pursuits go unrewarded. It would be peculiar for American children to take up cricket or for British children to take up baseball in the absence of a cultural tradition to play these sports. Similarly, in certain cultures, there are many intellectual pursuits – including knowledge of geography or mathematics – that go unrewarded, or at least are not as strongly encouraged as they could be. As a result, children and even many adults in places such as America or Britain, for example, cannot not identify the difference between Togo and Tonga, between Gambia and Guyana, between Bolivia and Botswana, or even between Iran and Iraq. Moreover, many in America and Britain have difficulty in basic number calculations and cannot do simple fraction problems. In fact, it could be said that there is "freedom" granted through cultural disincentives to choose not to know much about anything except the specialized knowledge that is eventually needed to get a job, together with the basics of literacy and numeracy – and sometimes even these can be escaped by persons who still do well in specialized school and work environments! So today many adults in Western countries can escape knowing, not only about geography, but also about key aspects of mathematics. When we are at a distance with our computers in isolation from others, we may even fall out of practice in applying our ToM.

Under these conditions, it is perhaps not surprising that, outside of the specialized knowledge that is valued by a particular culture, there is so little concern and support for children to measure up to what they broadly can know, and that there is so little conversation and mutual understanding between people from different cultures. If knowledge in areas such as geography and mathematics comes to be seen as optional in a culture, adults may not care whether children try hard or not in these areas. They may not place much weight on children's efforts that result in success or even go all out to discourage such efforts. Yet without effort, children's skills are liable to decline. Why would children strive to learn about other countries, to know more about number, or to acquire more than one language if these abilities are not valued and praised? Sadly, in these circumstances, their abilities in one or more of these areas may never be realized. For many children in industrialized countries such as America and Britain, their knowledge of geography remains sketchy, their mathematics often leaves a lot to be desired, and they remain stubbornly monolingual. Moreover, especially for many children in developing countries such as Benin and Upper Volta but even in the industrialized world as well, knowledge of biology and health and the microbial nature of contamination may be next to nonexistent.

Nevertheless, it is undeniable that children do have the potential to achieve in a much wider range of areas than their own cultures often support. According to a modular account of child development, mechanisms exist that permit children to demonstrate what they know in areas such as ToM, number, and food preferences shortly after they learn to talk and sometimes even before then. To be sure, in some cases of autism, particularly those of autistic savants, an adaptive specialization in knowledge may have come about that is accompanied by the near total absence of skills in an area such as ToM. However, for typically developing children, specialization in one area does not necessarily mean that skills in another area must be pushed out.

The reality is that typically developing children come equipped with a strategy to acquire language and to search for truth in communication in virtually everything they try. Even at the age of 3 years, they prefer to learn new words from a person who is truthful rather than one who is not. They prefer to learn from a truthful child than from an untruthful adult though they recognize that the adult generally knows more. As shown in Chapter 1, under optimal conditions, even 3-year-olds can make distinctions between lies and mistakes. Preschoolers can also indicate that certain behaviors such as hitting and fighting would be wrong even if there were no rules that prohibited such behaviors and even if no punishment that would follow. They can show the same moral side effect as adults in claiming that a person who inadvertently created a bad outcome is guilty in his negligence and should have had the foresight to avoid this outcome in the first place.[2]

If young children have skills as linguists and moralists, why then is their learning in areas such as cosmology, biology, and mathematics not faster? Why is their performance on measures of their knowledge so erratic? Why do they seem to stagnate in a situation in which their knowledge remains so long in a transitional form rather than rapidly taking on a mature form?

Two views have been recently put forward.[3] One is that transitional knowledge in areas such as biology is incomplete or partial or piecemeal – that some component of full knowledge is missing. For example, one interpretation from studies of children's knowledge of biology, health and hygiene is that children see illnesses such as colds as transmitted by invisible microbes but are unable or unwilling to recognize that these microbes are organisms that reproduce and multiply and that microbial infection requires an incubation period. Alternatively, transitional knowledge may be regarded as full knowledge, but knowledge that is inflexible and of limited generalizability outside of particular contexts or contexts. For example, concerning processes of life and death, children may know that a dead mouse no longer breathes, sees, or eats, and will never move on its own again, but they may be unable or unwilling to grasp that the same applies to humans once they have died. For both accounts, the context of the situation in which children are questioned is rightly regarded as important to their expressions of what they know. However, either account is based on two fundamental assumptions that are reminiscent of Piaget. These are that what children say seems to indicate what they can and do know, and that their development toward maturity in many respects seems to require a strong conceptual change.

Nevertheless, there is a third way – one that is compatible with the fundamental proposition that typically developing children everywhere have abilities that, despite their modular intuitions, are not supported by the specialized priorities of the culture in which they grow up. This is that children do have, or can have, a knowledge in many key areas that is reasonably fulsome and flexible but they are operating on a different theory, or even the lack of a theory, of the relevance and purpose of questions in relation to the contexts in which these are asked. This model of development does not assume that what children say does necessarily indicate what they can and do know, and that the acquisition of knowledge in many areas necessarily requires a strong conceptual change. Rather, it proposes that children may have, or can have, knowledge that is full and flexible but that such knowledge needs to be drawn out and enriched through early conversational experience. In this process, children's developing executive functioning abilities serve as a "co-opted" system that enables them to identify – and attend to – the correct interpretation of interviewers' questions and statements.

Finding appropriate questions and contexts to determine what children know

Over the past thirty years, there have been many studies about how we come to understand the meaning of a speaker.[4] Most of these have looked at adults, but some have involved children. Central to this work is Grice's account that I introduced in the last chapter in connection with the difficulties of communication in autism. To reiterate, Grice proposed that a "cooperative principle" governs conversation by which speakers and listeners will cooperate in communication in following certain expectations. These are characterized by maxims which enjoin speakers to say no more or no less than is required for the purpose of the exchange (maxims of *quantity*), to tell the truth and avoid statements for which there is insufficient evidence (maxims of *quality*), be relevant (maxim of *relation*), and avoid ambiguity, confusion and obscurity (maxims of *manner*).

According to the Gricean account, violations of these maxims necessarily occur in that, for example, to follow one maxim may mean that another is violated. This process creates a "logic in conversation" that allows listeners to follow the implications contained in natural language. For example, if a person complains that she has a headache, a friend may respond that there is a drugstore around the corner. The implications are that the walk to the drugstore is short, that the drugstore is open at the time, that it sells tablets to alleviate headaches, and that these tablets are publicly available to be sold to the sufferer. To state all this explicitly would be to violate the maxims of quantity since the implications are likely to be mutually understood among conversationally experienced speakers. If the speaker appears to violate one or more of these maxims but the listener has reason to believe that the speaker is cooperative, then he or she needs to generate pragmatic inferences (termed by Grice "conversational implicatures") to ensure that the speaker's contribution to the conversation is adequate in that the listener can grasp the speaker's intended meaning. To take one of Grice's own examples, if a professor violates the quantity rule by stating in a letter of recommendation only that "This student speaks English well and has been present all the time," the inference to be generated would be that the student is not particularly brilliant since, if he was, the professor would have written much more.

Limitations in children's understanding of how language is used in terms of a Gricean analysis are of particular interest as these may mask the nature of conceptual knowledge in a number of ways, apparently providing support for the Piagetian view that children's early knowledge can be characterized by a conceptual deficit in the ways that they view the world. In particular, young children who are unaware as to why, when, and how conversational maxims are violated often fail to interpret questions as these are intended by parents, teachers, and other interviewers and reveal the nature of what they know. Here there may be a gulf – even a huge chasm – between what a parent or teacher believes they are asking the child and the question that the child is trying to answer. Instead of interpreting questions in the same way that an interviewer intends, a child may be uncertain of the motivation of the interviewer in asking questions in the first place. Under these conditions, children may answer a different question than the one that has been asked. They may vary their answers in an attempt to furnish the right answer or provide cute, provocative or curt answers rather than ones that are accurate and reflect the depth of their understanding.

For example, an interviewer may inadvertently depart from the maxims of relation and manner to see whether, as described in Chapter 1, a child has knowledge of the distinction between appearance and reality. In such instances, 3-year-olds may be asked questions that they do not interpret as distinct and new. Thus they may repeat their answer and wrongly provide the impression that they believe appearance and reality is one and the same thing. Alternatively, children may not follow why an interviewer in studies of conceptual development departs from the maxims of quantity and seems to say more than is required, using repeated questioning, for the purpose of determining the certainty of what they know. This concern has arisen, for example as mentioned in Chapter 6, in characterizing children's performance on Piagetian conservation of number tasks, where they are asked to indicate whether the number of objects in front of them remains the same or changes after these undergo a perceptual transformation. In the face of such repeated questioning, it has often been maintained that children, particularly those aged 4, 5, and 6 years, may inappropriately abandon their original correct answer for a different one in the hope of finding the answer that is intended by the interviewer. Some children may engage in answer-switching if they are uncertain of the correctness of their original answer. However, even if they are certain, children may switch should they come to believe that an interviewer expects them to offer a different reply – an issue that often arises in situations involving eyewitness testimony where children are required to resist suggestive questions in reporting accurately on the characteristics of persons, objects, and events that they have previously witnessed. Children in fact can remember both the actual details of an event and another person's later distorted account of these details. Explicit questioning is necessary (for example, "Can you tell me about the accident just like the first time you saw and heard what happened?") to ensure that they understand which version they should report.[5]

Even when the gulf in communication between children and adults is acknowledged, it may be claimed that a strong conceptual change is needed even to overcome a deficit in understanding the nature of contradictions and tautologies in language.[6] According to one account, children's increasing accuracy in interpreting questions in the way intended by interviewers itself requires conceptual development. It is made possible by the acquisition of a distinction between literal meaning and speaker's meaning. According to this view, young children have yet to understand that the literal meaning of a message may differ from that intended by the speaker and that such messages may be ambiguous. For example, they do not recognize the inadequacy of a description of one of two red balls as "the red one" and that the literal meaning in such instances is not sufficient to convey the speaker's meaning. By contrast, older children recognize that messages can be ambiguous and have more than one meaning that differs from that intended by the speaker.

However, recent findings show that whether children display an understanding of the meaning of speakers involves an increasing sensitivity with age to conversational conventions as described by Grice as well as to extra-linguistic contexts. An important study here has been carried out Kang Lee, now at the Institute of Child Study at the University of Toronto, in collaboration with his PhD student Heather Fritzley.[7] To see whether young children discriminate in their answers to questions or answer questions all the same way, they asked 2- to 5-year-olds comprehensible and incomprehensible questions about familiar and unfamiliar objects that require a yes or no answer. Examples of comprehensible questions about familiar object such as a cup and a book are, "Is the cup red? Is the book about bears?" Examples of comprehensible question about unfamiliar objects such as a fuse and a pressure gage are, "Is the fuse round?" and "Is the pressure gage square?" Incomprehensible questions about familiar and unfamiliar objects involved nonsense words and took the form of "Is the cup nirking?" and "Is the fuse doow?" The 2-year-olds displayed a consistent yes bias on all four types of questions whereas 4- and 5-year-olds varied their answers and showed no response bias toward comprehensible questions and a negative response bias toward incomprehensible questions. Results for 3-year-olds were mixed, suggesting that the age of 3 years is a period of developmental transition in their response tendencies toward answering yes–no questions. Fritzley and Lee concluded that yes–no questions are suitable for older children, providing these are made to be comprehensible (and do not involve meaningless terms). However, when used with younger children, questioning that requires yes or no answers may simply produce a biased pattern in which children answer all the questions in the same way. If the questioning is incomprehensible, even the answers of older children can be biased.

In general, as shown by the results of such studies, young children can be reluctant to say that they don't know the answer to closed-ended questions even when they are explicitly told that such a response is acceptable. This is particularly the case when children are asked closed-ended questions that require either a yes or no answer than open-ended questions that require children to generate their own responses. At least for children in Western cultures, there may be a norm to strive toward providing an answer in line with Grice's co-operative principle rather than admitting ignorance.

Scalar implicatures and the development of conversational understanding

Knowledge in a particular area, as shown for example on tasks designed to examine children's understanding of the appearance–reality distinction or certain scientific concepts, reflects a broad development in conversational competence that continues throughout childhood. Of particular interest to many psychologists and linguists is the ability to draw "scalar implicatures" (SIs). These arise when a speaker uses a weak member of a scale (e.g., *some, or, might*) to imply that the stronger term of the scale (*all, and, must*) does not hold. For example, the statement:

(1) Some of the dwarfs loved Snow White
    implies
(2) Not every dwarf loved Snow White.

The significance of SIs in conversation can be traced back to the nineteenth-century English philosopher John Stuart Mill who noticed that if we say to someone "I saw some of your children today" the person listening is infers that I did not see them all, "not because the words mean it, but because, if I had seen them all, it is most likely that I should have said so". According to Grice, SIs violate the quantity maxim to make one's contribution to the conversation as informative as possible, because the speaker could have chosen the more powerful term *all* yet chose the weaker term *some*. In recognizing that the speaker declined the option to use *all*, the listener draws the implication that the stronger statement (for example, "All of the dwarfs love Snow White" does not hold).

Following Mill and Grice, investigations have now been carried out on children's understanding of SIs in tasks involving the quantifiers *some* and *all*. Some studies have suggested that young children do not distinguish between *some* and *all* (or between *might* and *must*). They believe instead that an action such as a teddy bear shown as having put all available hoops on a pole can be described well as "The bear put some of the hoops on the pole." This answer is compatible with the interpretation that *some* is logically compatible with *all*.[8]

However, when the goal is made more salient, even 5-year-olds can be prompted to choose a pragmatic rather than a logical interpretation and display knowledge of SIs. In a series of clever studies with her colleagues, Anna Papafragou, now at the University of Delaware, has examined how 5-year-olds and adults judge the appropriateness of statements that include the terms *start*, *some*, or *two* when used in contexts that would have justified the use of stronger terms (i.e., *finish*, *all*, and *three*, respectively).[9] The study participants first saw three toy horses on a table and then all three of them were shown to jump over a toy fence. Then a puppet who had "watched" what had happened said "Some horses jumped over the fence" and each child or adult was asked to say whether "the puppet answered well." Adults overwhelmingly rejected such infelicitous, pragmatically deviant statements. By contrast, children performed less well in that they often accepted such statements, but their answers depended on the type of statements and the clarity of the instructions. Their success improved in a follow-up study when the instructions and the procedure made it clear that they were expected to evaluate the felicity of utterances, rather than their truth – a change that would seem to reduce the amount of effort needed on the part of the children to compute the correct answer. In this study, 5-year-olds were shown situations such as one involving an elephant described as having been told to color a set of four paper stars. When asked about what he had colored, the elephant replied, "I colored some." Having heard this answer, 5-year-olds often said that the elephant should not be given a prize. In demonstrating their understanding of SIs, they chose the pragmatic interpretation that *some* was an inappropriate description of a situation in which the task was to color all.

Attention to the context of what a speaker says

The gulf between the conversational understanding of 5-year-olds and adults also appears in how they attend to the context of language. In studies carried out at the University of Pennsylvania by John Trueswell and his team, participants were shown two toy frogs, one resting on a napkin and one on a tray. Next to the frogs there was another napkin with nothing resting on it. An interviewer asked 5-year-olds

and adults to "Put the frog on the napkin in the box." This request was processed far less efficiently by 5-year-olds than by adults. The adults moved the frog on the napkin directly into the box but many children moved the frog that was on the tray onto the blank napkin and then put it into the box.

One interpretation of the different answers of children and adults is that kids are more easily led down the garden path in their use of extra-linguistic context to process sentences. The context may provide a distraction that leads them to believe, following Grice's maxim of relation or relevance, that the presence of an empty napkin implies that it should be used in interpreting the experimenter's request or else it would be absent. However, children are capable of acknowledging ambiguity in the meaning of utterances that accompany such extra-linguistic contexts, as shown by the pattern of their eye gaze. The nature of the communicative setting can be such that even adults may not avoid distractions that preclude taking of account the listener's perspective, whereas if these distractions are reduced even young children can communicate effectively.[10]

Two linguists, Luisa Meroni, now at McGill University in Montreal, and Stephen Crain, now at Macquarie University in Sydney, have proposed that, for adults, the process of acting out instructions like "Put the frog on the napkin into the box" is based on a plan that is completely formed and compiled before it is executed.[11] By contrast, a child listener might start to plan and even act before the instructions are completed. According to Meroni and Crain, should children's planning be less compiled or "automated" than adults, they may act out the meanings of sentences such as "Put the frog on the napkin into the box" in an order-of-mention fashion, whereas adults act them out in the order that is conceptually correct (e.g., using the "given" information first). As children interleave planning and execution, they may to act out parts of the plan before all the planning has been completed that is necessary to interpret the sentence as intended. For example, children aged 4–6 years and adults can be asked to consider a row of six balls in an array where the second, third, and fifth balls from the left are striped:

When asked, "Point to the second striped ball" adults point to the third ball from the left that is the second striped one. Children are unlike adults. They often point to the second ball from the left that happens to be striped. Yet they are able to compile a plan that enables them to respond like adults do if their attention is drawn to the need to hear the whole sentence before they acting out the request.

To support the interpretation that children start to plan and act before they hear the full instructions, Meroni and Crain report an experiment designed to enable children to respond as adults in frog garden path situations. The methodology involved two innovations. First, to prompt children to "inhibit" the pragmatic inference that the empty napkin was present in order so that it should accommodate a frog, children aged 4–5 years were shown both frogs already sitting on a napkin. One frog sat on a blue napkin and the other on a red napkin. Second, to allow the children to formulate a plan without being overly distracted by salient features of the frogs, napkins, and box, the children were asked to turn away from the display while they listened to the target sentence, "Put the frog on the red napkin into the box." Under these conditions, the children had a 93 percent correct performance rate. Meroni and Crain suggest that a failure to use referential information in the research of Trueswell and his colleagues was due to children's tendency to make a reasonable pragmatic inference and to execute action plans on the fly. When steps are taken to block this inference and to prevent a premature execution of a plan for action, children demonstrate that they can parse sentences in the same way as adults by using referential information.

It is noteworthy that children's persistent difficulties on problems in which they are required to identify tautological and contradictory statements as illogical also have been viewed to reflect at least in part an incomplete problem solving strategy that is confined to the first part of a statement – an "order-of-mention" reaction that overlooks logical connectives and the second part of the statement. For example, they may react to a tautological statement such as "It will rain today or it will not rain today" by responding only to the first part of the statement and commenting on today's weather conditions. Similarly, they may react to tautological statement that refers to the outcome of a ball dropping game such as "The ball will land on red or will not land on red" by claiming that the ball has to be dropped on red to show that this statement is true. Rather than remarking that contradictory statements are simply nonsensical, preschoolers will often use local conversational concerns in an attempt to extract meaning.For example, they will interpret a statement such as "The dinner was good and wasn't good" as "The salad was good but the dessert was not."[12] The extent to which young children can be trained to interpret tautological and contradictory statements in terms of logic rather than in terms of empirical verification remains in need of further study, but is likely to be influenced strongly by formal schooling that breaks with the conversational experiences and habits of children before they reach school age.[13]

Characterizing children's conceptual knowledge and conversational competence

Studies of children's ability to understand the implications of statements that include quantifiers or logical connectives, and their ability to process sentences as intended by interpreting extra-linguistic contexts appropriately, illustrate the complex relationship between conversational understanding and conceptual competence. Children's lack of proficiency in appropriately interpreting the contexts of speakers' messages can undermine their performance on measures of their conceptual competence. This is evident, for example, in their answers to test questions that concern their knowledge of the distinction between reality and the phenomenal world of appearances in Chapter 1, their ToM reasoning in Chapter 2, and their knowledge of certain scientific concepts such as those used in cosmology as described in Chapter 3.

Moreover, age differences that have been found in performance on SI and garden path sentence processing tasks illustrate how young children who are fluent conversationalists in their native language are yet to be proficient conversationalists. As shown by research on SIs, children at 5–6 years of age are sometimes not very adept at detecting violations of conversational maxims. They may not follow conversational conventions that require pragmatic, rather than logical, interpretations of speakers' assertions and requests. Even in attempting a pragmatic interpretation, as shown in garden path tasks, they may process sentences by interpreting the extra-linguistic contexts of questions in a manner differently than those that speakers intend.

By comparison, older children and adults are proficient conversationalists who are sensitive to conventions and contexts – both linguistic and extra-linguistic – that serve to guide the interpretation of speakers' meanings. They are experienced in working toward detecting the implications of questions and statements as these are intended. Nevertheless, in certain contexts, young children are still able to display their knowledge of a speaker's meaning and to draw the appropriate pragmatic inferences following violations of Gricean maxims. This occurs particularly when they are aware of the goal of the task and when task demands – and hence the demands for computational effort – are reduced. Under such conditions, if children are led to attend to the relevance and purpose of questions and contexts, they are more likely to demonstrate what they are capable of knowing.

A very old idea in psychology is that children's performance on many measures of their knowledge can be enhanced through prompting them to attend to the relevant features of the tasks at hand. In this connection, there have often been calls for parents and teachers to promote "distancing behaviors" in separating themselves from what they immediately see and hear so that they can develop skills in acting on the basis of fully compiled plans. These skills have been linked to mechanisms of learning and attention that lead to academic success.[14] A modern view is that understanding this process involves, in part, mechanisms of executive functioning that underlie forms of conceptual change.[15]

For example, conversational understanding based on accuracy in identifying the beliefs, intentions, and feelings that underlie speakers' messages can be seen as an outgrowth of the application of ToM reasoning. In this sense, one mechanism that underpins improvements in conversational understanding with age can be seen as similar to Leslie's Selection Processor (SP) – a mechanism of attention that enables children to express ToM accurately. Recall that, according to Leslie, the advantage of 4-year-olds over 3-year-olds on standard Sally-Anne ToM tasks does not occur because children are undergoing a conceptual change that leads to accurate reasoning based on an understanding that others have false beliefs that do not accord with reality. Rather it occurs because the SP comes online as an "executive functioning" process that permits children to compute the true or false contents of others' beliefs correctly. This enables 4-year-olds to recognize that the question refers not to the issue of where Sally will have to look, or must look, for the ball that she wants to find but instead carries that implication that it refers to where Sally will look first. As pointed out in Chapter 2, asking the more explicit question "Where will Sally look first for her ball?" enables most 3-year-olds children to "inhibit" the straightforward interpretation that the question refers to where Sally will have to look or must look for the ball and instead to interpret the question as intended to refer to the consequences of Sally holding an initial false belief about the location of an object. Put somewhat differently, the standard test question "Where will Sally look for her ball?" conveys less information than is needed for effective communication and hence departs from Grice's quality maxim, whereas the simple addition of "first" to the question now enables the child to interpret the test question as intended – a result consistent with the pattern of attention shown by preverbal infants on ToM tasks.

EF mechanisms, similar to that of a ToM-SP, may serve in part to underpin the development of conversational understanding. As Akira Miyake and his coworkers at the University of Colorado have shown, there are three subcomponents of EF that can be delineated.[16] First, there is the process of "shifting" between tasks involving the ability to perform another operation without distraction. Second is the "updating" subcomponent that requires monitoring and coding incoming information for relevance to the task at hand and then revising working memory by replacing older irrelevant information with new relevant information. Then there is a third subcomponent that involves the inhibition of prepotent responses. Clearly, proficiency in conversational understanding in which children come to interpret the intended relevance and purpose of a speaker's meaning requires skill in all three subcomponents. Children need to shift back and forth between alternative interpretations of speakers' messages, to update representations of the linguistic and extra-linguistic contexts of these messages, and to inhibit prepotent responses. In the latter case, for example, children need to recognize the possibility that speakers who, according to a Gricean framework, can be assumed usually to abide by the quality maxim and not to deceive can still be sarcastic or utter falsehoods.

What can speed along children's proficiency in conversation so that they may be more likely show what they know? One possibility is the richness of exposure to language itself, in that bilingual children who are exposed early to more than one language may develop EF skills that in turn influence their expertise in interpreting the implications of conversation.[17] For example, compared to monolingual children, there is evidence that children who acquire two languages early perform better on appearance–reality and ToM tasks, possibly because they are adept at inhibiting incorrect answers by switching appropriately from one dimension of an object to another. Recent work with adults also appears to confer an advantage to bilinguals in mechanisms of attention.

However, this line of reasoning is based on the premise that there is an accepted definition of bilingualism. In fact, this definition is elusive as the degree and quality of proficiency in language can vary enormously. Speakers can vary in their understanding and production of a language. Some children (and adults) have native-like general proficiency in one language and simply a proficiency in the other that is specific to certain contexts such as food. Moreover, bilingualism in languages that share a similar structure and vocabulary such as Italian and Spanish is liable to place different demands on a speaker's performance and EF than is bilingualism in languages such as English and Japanese. For this reason, there are a great many terms that have been used to describe the nature of bilingualism in a particular group of people, such as:[18]

> Achieved bilingual, additive bilingual, ambilingual; ascendent bilingual; ascribed bilingual; asymmetrical bilingual, balanced bilingual; compound bilingual, consecutive bilingual; coordinate bilingual; covert bilingual, diagonal bilingual, dominant bilingual, dormant bilingual, early bilingual, equilingual; functional bilingual, horizontal bilingual, incipient bilingual, late bilingual, maximal bilingual, minimal bilingual, natural bilingual, passive bilingual, primary bilingual, productive bilingual, receptive bilingual, recessive bilingual, secondary bilingual, semibilingual, simultaneous bilingual, subordinate bilingual, subtractive bilingual, successive bilingual, symmetrical bilingual, vertical bilingual.

Even if we could move toward an accepted categorization of forms of bilingualism, the hypothesis that bilingualism confers an EF advantage would seem to point to a situation in which cultures characterized by extensive early bilingualism, such as Switzerland, have children with better EF and hence generally better performance on measures of AR, ToM, and even the ability to draw implications in conversation in appreciating humor, irony, and sarcasm than in places where children are mainly monolingual, such as Britain or Japan. This seems quite unlikely. Might it be the case instead that any sort of pressure to switch back and forth in an area of specialized knowledge would lead to sophistication in EF? If so, for example, might monolingual children who are skilled in the language of mathematics based on their expertise in expressing quantities and equations in various ways be able to shift, update, and focus as well as their bilingual peers? The answer to this question is unclear.

In any event, EF by itself cannot be the whole story for why some children succeed on cognitive tasks and others do not. In the case of ToM, for example, as shown by studies carried out with American and Chinese children who both can be assumed to be mainly monolingual, there do seem to be significant correlations between EF and the expression of ToM within both cultures. But causality cannot be inferred on the basis of a pattern of correlations. Although Chinese children do outperform American children on EF, they paradoxically show no advantage on ToM. Might it be that EF plays a direct role in the expression of ToM in Chinese children whereas, for American children, ToM and possibly conversational understanding more generally is more strongly based on exposure to opportunities for discussions with parents and siblings about beliefs and other mental states? Studies of deaf children emphasize the importance for ToM of early opportunities for conversation about mental states within a close sibling relationship. These studies support the notion that advanced EF abilities, though important, are not the only ingredient in ToM. Whereas EF in hard-to-manage children with behavior problems has been linked to ToM, this has not always been the case for typically developing children without such problems.[19] In fact, there may be a bidirectional relation between EF and children's exposure to, and fluency in, conversation that includes the expression of ToM.

So also may EF development facilitate children's success on tasks that require them to follow the implications of conversation, but proficiency in following conversational implications might contribute to how well children focus, shift, and inhibit responses when devoting attention to reasoning and problem-solving. This process may be fundamental, not only for performance in the ToM domain, but for others as well.

Conclusion

Evidence from cultures around the world reveals the presence of marvelous minds, even in very young children. If the potential of children is considered from a global viewpoint, there is so much more that they do and can know than what they have traditionally been credited. Links between children's conversational understanding, their cultural context, and opportunities to display what they know are clearly evident. The gap between the conversational experience of adults and children require we consider developmental processes that characterize children's conversational understanding, together with the important methodological problem of how to question children with the aim of determining their conceptual competence. Research on children's knowledge of the appearance–reality distinction, ToM reasoning, and their appreciation of basic cosmological concepts provides illustrations of how children may misinterpret the linguistic and extra-linguistic contexts of questions designed to determine what they know. Studies of children's responses to scalar implicature and sentence processing tasks demonstrate the extent to which task success demands sophistication in planning and attending to the relevant criteria for interpreting what people say. Based on the research reviewed here, it can be seen that tasks and test questions can often be framed in a way that circumvents the gap between the conversational experience of children and adults in order to draw out more clearly the nature of children's knowledge.

In the light of recent studies, the need for children to acquire a conceptual distinction between literal meaning and speaker's meaning that was viewed as central to conversational understanding more than 20 years ago can be now seen in terms of another explanation that involves an emphasis on access to language and attentional development rather than conceptual change. When a mother says to her messy child, "you are really tidy now and your toys are put away nicely," the child – who already knows that messages can have more than one interpretation – needs to attend to the intended sarcastic meaning that, in fact, is the opposite of its literal interpretation. All of this points to new directions in conversing with children in discovering how they develop. Systematically taking issues of conversational understanding into account promises to lead to a richer, more complete account of what children know.

Notes

Chapter 1: Kids, appearance and reality

1. Word learning in dogs: Kaminski *et al.* (2004). Joy in dogs, rats, and other animals: Panksepp (2005).

2. Generalization statements ("Birds fly") in young children: Goldin-Meadow *et al.* (2005).

3. Indeed, the Latin motto for one of the two universities where I divide my time, Sheffield in England, is *Rerum Cognoscere Causas* – "Know the cause of things." Sheffield is where the first cure using penicillin was recorded in 1930. A culture of penicillin-producing mold was grown on meat broth and then used to treat two babies with serious eye infections, both of whom made a complete recovery. It was also where the Krebs Cycle for food digestion was discovered, as well as where the movie *The Full Monty* was filmed. The cultural and scientific heritage of the location of my other university, Trieste in Italy, can be found at http://triestenet.tripod.com/indexeng.htm. It has been described in the *Daily Telegraph* (12 February 2005) as "Arias and Aromas by the Adriatic." It is there in the sunny Dog and Cat (Can e Gato) restaurant that you can have an incredible lunch while it is raining cats and dogs in England.

4. For Piaget's analysis: Piaget (1929, 1930, 1962). My comments are not meant to join a chorus of "Piaget-bashing." Piaget's methods of assessing what children are ingenious – so much so that studies of researchers and educators for generations have been based on Piaget's work. Above all, Piaget demonstrated that it is possible to do simple, elegant experiments with young children (Siegal 1999).

5. The conceptual change position: Gopnik (1996), Gopnik and Wellman (1994), Perner (1991).

6. Innate devices or modules: Gelman & Williams (1998), Premack & Premack (2003), Rozin (1976, 2006). According to Barrett & Kurzban (2006), modularity can be best conceptualized in terms of a functional specialization that permits effective problem-solving. This is in contrast to an earlier, and perhaps more complex, view (Fodor 1983) that saw modules as "encapsulated" and "automatic" in that their information-processing properties that are mandatory and are not influenced by outside information apart from their relevant "bottom-up" inputs. Nativist views on cognition and development can be found in a collection of essays edited by Carruthers *et al.* (2005, 2006). Other sources on nativism can be found in Fodor (2000), and in popular books by Pinker (2002) and Marcus (2004) that have been written, at least partly, in response to Elman *et al.* (1996) and Cowie (1998). A perspective on innateness in psychology from a philosophical and historical viewpoint is contained in an extraordinary book by Macnamara (1999).

7. Incommensurable with a mature scientific understanding: Carey (1999). Fractions and conceptual change: Gelman (2000).

8. Example of Maynard the cat, De Vries (1969); also Siegler (1986: 3).

9. Questions and counterquestions in the gender constancy interview: Slaby and Frey (1975).

10. Theoretical significance of the gender constancy interview: Kohlberg (1966), Martin *et al.* (2002).

11. Flavell's research on children's appearance–reality knowledge: Flavell *et al.* (1983, 1986), Flavell (1999).

12. Children's fantasy and imagination: Dias and Harris (1988), Richards and Sanderson (1999).

13. Appearance–reality knowledge in a show and tell game: Gauvain and Greene (1994).

14. Appearance–reality knowledge in natural conversation: Sapp *et al.* (2000); flexibility in object naming: Clark (1997).

Infants' categorization of objects: Ellis and Oakes (2006), Mandler (2004), Mareschal and Tan (2007).

15. Deák's studies: Deák (2006), Deák et al. (2003), Deák and Enright (2006).

16. Children's responses to questions about the constancy of gender: Siegal and Robinson (1987); distinguishing reality from pretending in 2- and 3-year-olds: Ma and Lillard (2006).

17. Distinguishing lies from mistakes: Siegal and Peterson (1996, 1998).

18. Earlier book: Siegal (1997).

19. The tale of the twins in Ireland is from Simon Hoggart's column in the *Guardian*, 14 February 2004, adapted from *Beyond Coincidence* by Martin Plimmer and Brian King.

Chapter 2: Language, conversation, and theory of mind

1. Shakespeare's deception of Burbage: Bate (1997).

2. Newborns learning sounds for language while sleeping: Cheour et al. (2002); babies' preference for speech to non-speech sounds: Vouloumanos and Werker (2004). Babies' responses to language: left hemisphere specialization for babbling as shown by more right mouth rather than left mouth activity: Holowska and Petitto (2002). As in adults, neuroimaging studies point to left hemisphere dominance for speech perception and production in the first year of life (Dehaene-Lambertz et al. 2002), though greater plasticity in the maturing brains of infants may allow for more right hemisphere substitution than in adults following left hemisphere damage (Dehaene-Lambertz et al. 2004).

3. "Poverty of the stimulus" account: Chomsky (1980), Laurence and Margolis (2001), Lidz et al. (2003), Newport (1990), Stromswold (1990). Predictability of children's errors in language acquisition: Crain and Pietroski (2001). Children not corrected for the grammaticality of their language: Brown and Hanlon (1970).

4. Babbling of profoundly deaf infants: Petitto and Marentette (1991); hearing babies exposed to deaf parents' sign language: Petitto et al. (2001).

5. Gestures of deaf children in different cultures: Goldin-Meadow (2003), Goldin-Meadow and Mylander (1998).

6. The emergence of Nicaraguan Sign Language: Senghas *et al.* (2004).

7. Research on deafness and an optimal or critical period for language acquisition: Mayberry *et al.* (2002).

8. The case of Victor: Lane (1977); see also Grimshaw *et al.* (1998); Lenneberg (1967).

9. The case of Genie: Curtiss (1977), especially p. 233 for Genie's conversational competence.

10. The Sally-Anne task: Baron-Cohen *et al.* (1985); the Smarties task: Wimmer and Perner (1983); the fishing task: Custer (1996), Woolfe *et al.* (2002).

11. The view that young children, generally under the age of 4 years, have a conceptual deficit in their ToM: Perner *et al.* (1987), Wellman *et al.* (2001). Exposure to conversation about mental states and enhanced performance on ToM tasks: Dunn (1994) has reported that preschoolers' success on ToM tasks is associated with the frequency with which they exchange mental state terms in conversations with parents, siblings, and friends. Similarly, Lewis *et al.* (1996; see also Peterson, 2001) found that the availability of exposure to mature speakers (adults, older children, and siblings) predicted children's performance on tasks involving ToM. These observations are consistent with the view that the more children are exposed to talk about thoughts and other invisible mental processes, the earlier they develop a ToM of other persons' mental states. Fonagy *et al.* (2007) provide an examination of the importance of caregivers for children's mentalizing.

12. It has long been noted that children who are isolated in their contact with others have specific difficulty in adopting the perspectives of others (Hollos and Cowan 1973). Work on ToM and culture: Avis and Harris (1991), Callaghan *et al.* (2005), Sabbagh *et al.* (2006), Yazdi *et al.* (2006).

13. ToM tests and language comprehension: Bloom and German (2000).

14. The performance of 3-year-olds on 'look first' tasks: Joseph (1998), Nelson *et al.* (2003), Siegal and Beattie (1991), Surian and Leslie (1999), Yazdi *et al.* (2006).

15. Responses of infants and toddlers on measures of visual attention to false beliefs: Onishi and Baillargeon (2005), Southgate *et al.* (2007), Surian *et al.* (2007). These findings are consistent with reports that 1-year-olds can imitate a model on the basis of the model's intentions rather than his or her overt behavior: Gergely *et al.* (2002), Meltzoff (1995).

16. Selection Processor: Leslie *et al.* (2004). Also Friedman and Leslie (2004), Leslie (1994, 2000), Leslie, German, and Polizzi (2005), Scholl and Leslie (1999); very simple ToM: Fodor (1992); also Fodor (1983).

17. Development of executive functioning (EF): Diamond *et al.* (2002) tested report conditions under which 4-year-olds can inhibit a habitual or prepotent response on the day–night task that requires them to say "night" to a picture of the sun and "day" to a picture of the moon. This task is easier when children are asked to delay their answers, or to respond not with "night" or "day" but with words that are unrelated to the pictures such as "dog" and "pig." EF requires updating of relevant information and resistance to irrelevant distractions: Dibbets and Jolles (2006). ToM reasoning has often been found to be associated with EF measures: Frye *et al.* (1995), Moses (2001), Perner and Lang (1999).

18. The right frontal cortex and the neural substrate of ToM reasoning: Siegal and Varley (2002), Stuss *et al.* (2001). EF and the development of right frontal lobe activation from childhood to adulthood: Bunge *et al.* (2002). Aron *et al.* (2003) have reported an impressive association between a measure of EF and damage to areas of the right frontal cortex, especially the right inferior frontal gyrus. ToM impairment in adults with damage to the right hemisphere: Surian and Siegal (2001), Siegal and Varley (2006).

19. Neural substrate of irony in children: Wang *et al.* (2006b). Research on EF and impairment in pragmatics: Martin and McDonald (2003).

20. Mental states that have no concrete referent: Marschark (1993); Morford and Goldin-Meadow (1997). Deaf children with deaf parents converse as readily as hearing children with hearing parents: Meadow et al. (1981).

21. Tyron Woolfe's research: Woolfe et al. (2002). Receptive Skills Test in British Sign Language: Herman et al. (1999).

22. Difficulties of deaf children to communicate in a hearing environment without access to a sign language: Harris (1992), Lederberg and Everhart (1998), Marschark, (1993), Spencer and Meadow-Orlans (1966), Vaccari and Marschark (1997).

23. The situation involving communication with deaf children who have received cochlear implants or hearing aids may be somewhat different. Moeller and Schick (2006) studied the mothers of a group of American late signing deaf children aged 7–10 years, many of whom wore hearing aids or had received cochlear implants, and attended schools where both sign and spoken English were encouraged. The mothers had acquired advanced signing skills through access to continuous sign instruction and early intervention programs. Their children scored well on ToM tasks that hearing children often pass by the age of 4 years.

24. Late-signing deaf children and "conversationally-supported" ToM questions: Peterson and Siegal (1995, 1999).

25. Shared grounding for communication: Clark and Brennan (1991); function of conversational experience: Harris (1996).

26. Link between early use of mental state verbs in language directed at infants and performance on ToM measures: Meins et al. (2002); Swedish research on ToM in early nonnative signers: Falkman et al. (2007). Scottish research revealing persistent lack of expression of ToM reasoning abilities in adolescence: Russell et al. (1998). ToM in the Nicaraguan deaf: Morgan and Kegl (2006).

27. ToM abilities of the deaf in generating stories about acquaintances: Marschark et al. (2000).

28. Swedish studies on ToM in nonvocal children with cerebral palsy: Dahlgren et al. (2003); keeping different perspectives in mind during conversation: Clark (1997).

29. Position that grammar supports ToM: Astington and Jenkins (1999), Smith *et al.* (2003). Position that sentence complementation supports ToM: De Villiers and Pyers (2002), Plaut and Karmiloff-Smith (1993), Schick *et al.* (2007); position that language generally supports ToM and that there is no specific role for complementation: Ruffman *et al.* (2003), Tardif *et al.* (2007); see review by Milligan *et al.* (2007). Spontaneous production of sentence complements before success on standard ToM reasoning tasks: Custer (1996). Training sentence complementation to determine the effects on ToM task performance: Hale and Tager-Flusberg (2003), Lohmann and Tomasello (2003).

30. ToM in patients with aphasia following brain damage, and grammar seen as a "co-opted" system that can support the expression of ToM: Siegal and Varley (2002), Varley and Siegal (2000).

31. Grammar and ToM as autonomous modular systems: Sperber (1996).

32. ToM and how children learn the meaning of words: Bloom (2000), Diesendruck and Markson (2002); example from Gelman and Ebeling (1998).

33. Mark Baker's position: Baker (2001). I also have Baker to thank for the observation that there are spoken and sign language that have clausal adjuncts.

34. Main functions of culture: Premack and Hauser (2001).

35. Birds hiding food from others: Emery and Clayton (2001), Raby *et al.* (2007); sheep remembering faces: Kendrick *et al.* (2001).

Chapter 3: Astronomy and geography

1. Vosniadou's account: Vosniadou (1991, 1994b), Vosniadou and Brewer (1992).

2. Follow-up studies: Vosniadou and Brewer (1994), Samarapungavan *et al.* (1996).

3. The Copernican revolution: Kuhn (1957).

4. The problem of whether an object can be eaten: Toyama (2000).

5. Differences between the drawings of children and adults: Blades and Spencer (1994), Ingram and Butterworth (1989), Jolley *et al.* (2000), Kosslyn *et al.* (1977), Pemberton (1990). Vosniadou's findings are consistent with a number of other studies using similar methods in which structured interviews, coupled with drawings, model selection or construction of clay representations, have allowed children to be classified into groups according to their different mental models (e.g., Nussbaum, 1979). The earth's shape in India: Samarapungavan *et al.* (1996).

6. The effects of repeated questioning on children's answers: Siegal (1999).

7. Swedish research on children's astronomy: Schoultz *et al.* (2001).

8. Some of Peter Newcombe's PhD work: Newcombe and Siegal (1996, 1997). Re-examination of what children can know: Siegal *et al.* (2004).

9. Cultural differences in religiosity between England and America: Kelemen (2003).

10. Curriculum in Queensland: http://www.qsa.qld.edu.au/yrs1_10/kla/science/syllabus.html; in England: http://www.nc.uk.net.

11. Astonishingly, despite cultural differences in the extent to which children have been exposed to astronomy, if at all, Vosniadou and her team (Vosniadou *et al.* 2004) claim that "we are not interested in finding out whether children have been exposed to the scientific information about the shape of the earth and the day/night cycle. We know they have. Rather we are interested in finding out whether they fully understand this information."

12. Fragmentation and lack of systematization in children's early scientific knowledge: di Sessa (1988).

13. Research involving card-sorting of possible shapes of the earth: Nobes *et al.* (2003, 2005).

14. Adults' drawings of the shape of the earth: Panagiotaki (2003).

15. Visuospatial memory in Aboriginal Australians: Kearins (1981).

16. Placeholders: S. A. Gelman (2000), Medin (1989).

17. Misconceptions involving interactions: Chi (2005).

18. Counting that occurs spontaneously: Geary (1995).

19. Intuitive or modular constraints: Shweder *et al.* (1998).

20. Australian training study on the shape of the earth: Hayes *et al.* (2003).

21. Heavenly talk: Schoultz *et al.* (2001).

Chapter 4: Biology, food and hygiene

1. These statistics come from an Australian source that has assembled information from various websites: SBS World Guide (2003).

2. Carey's approach: Carey (1985, 1995, 2000).

3. Children immersed in conversations about whether food is dirty: Toyama (2000).

4. Bodily functions of the buried: Slaughter *et al.* (1999).

5. Conservative vs nonconservative conceptual change: Thagard (1999).

6. Piagetian view on the development of children's beliefs about the transmission of illness: Bibace and Walsh (1981). Immanent justice in the child: Piaget (1932).

7. Rejection of naughtiness as a cause of colds: Siegal (1988). Recognition of illness susceptibility rather than misbehavior: Inagaki and Hatano (2002: 91).

8. Colds transmitted by poisons or irritants: Solomon and Cassimatis (1999); no incubation period for illness: Kalish (1997); germs grow like tumors: Au *et al.* (1999).

9. Germs as physical agents of contamination: Kalish (1999: 108).

10. Contaminated by a cockroach at snack time: Siegal and Share (1990).

11. Reports of results showing that young children have a knowledge of contamination: Au *et al.* (1993), Keil *et al.* (1999), Rosen and Rozin (1993), Springer and Belk (1994); Springer and Keil (1991).

12. Germs of the cute vs the unloved: Nemeroff and Rozin (1994).

13. Discriminating the basis for movement of animate and inanimate objects: Massey and Gelman (1988).

14. Western training programs on the microscopic nature of infection: Au *et al.* (1999), Solomon and Johnson (2000).

15. Laws of sympathetic magic: Frazer (1890/1959), Mauss (1902/1972), Nemeroff and Rozin (2000), Tylor (1871/1974).

16. The cultural and psychological significance of food and cuisine: Rozin (1996); see also Kass (1994).

17. The mouth as the principal incorporative organ and associational contamination: Fallon *et al.* (1984), Rozin (1990), Springer and Belk (1994).

18. Dowayo drinking habits: Barley (1983, p. 69).

19. Three models of contagion: Nemeroff and Rozin (1994, 2000).

20. Food and culture in Indian society: Appadurai (1981), Marriott (1968).

21. Details of the study on contagious essence and conceptions of purification in Hindu Indian and American children: Hejmadi *et al.* (2004).

22. Poor sanitation and polio in India: Grassly *et al.* (2006).

23. Knowledge of health and hygiene in the Third World: Curtis and Biran (2001), Curtis *et al.* (2000, 2001).

24. Learning about biology through caring for living things: Hatano and Inagaki (1994). A tribute to the work of the influential Japanese cultural psychologist, Giyoo Hatano, appears in a 2007 issue of the journal *Human Development, 50*, 1–82.

Chapter 5: Life and death

1. Understanding of biological inheritance: Solomon *et al.* (1996).

2. Hirschfeld (1995: 239) raises issues about the methodology used in the Solomon *et al.* study. He observes that children were asked to make many more judgments about traits that are environmentally as opposed to biologically transmitted. This procedure may have prompted children to respond that even biological traits such as eye color are the result of adoptive parentage.

3. Research with the Vezo: Astuti (2001). The similarity in the concepts of American and Vezo adults is consistent with the proposal that there is cross-cultural universality in beliefs about certain areas of biological knowledge compatible with innate conceptual representations: Medin and Atran (2004). Whereas American children by the age of 7 years differentiate between physical attributes that are transmitted biologically and beliefs that are socially transmitted, for the most part Vezo children and even adolescents do not. Although adult Vezo do differentiate, they still profess to observers, for example, that a baby looks like a person his mother befriended when she was pregnant: Astuti *et al.* (2004).

4. Children's knowledge of seeds for plants: Hickling and Gelman (1994). Naive theory of kinship: Springer (1995, 1999), Springer and Keil (1991).

5. Knowledge of genetic disorders and contagious illnesses: Raman and Gelman (2005).

6. Infants' expectations about persons and objects: Bonatti *et al.* (2002), Legerstee (2000).

7. Voluntary and involuntary processes: Inagaki and Hatano (1993); infant anger attached to voluntary refusal to give toys: Behne *et al.* (2005).

8. Biological functions and the death interview: Slaughter *et al.* (1999). For example, of 18 non-life-theorizer children, the numbers who claimed that dead people need food, need to excrete, need air, move, need water, dream, and have cuts heal were 8, 5, 8, 1, 5, 6, and 10 respectively. Comparable figures for 20 life-theorizer children were 1, 1, 0, 0, 2, 2, and 8.

9. Vitalism: Inagaki and Hatano (2006); conception of the stomach as taking in vital energy from food: Morris *et al.* (2000); training to think vitalistically: Slaughter and Lyons (2003: 28).

10. Dead versus asleep: Barrett and Behne (2005).

11. Transcending the termination of life: Bering and Bjorkland (2004: 232).

12. Living on in a form of heaven (or hell): Barrett and Keil (1996). Religion and after-life beliefs: Atran (2002, 2006); Boyer (2002). New Guinea funeral rites: Meigs (1983).

13. Chomsky's views on numbers believing in religious miracles: http://www.brainyquote.com/quotes/authors/n/noam_chomsky. html.

14. Religious beliefs about the afterlife as an adaptation to a hostile social environment: Bering (2006). A fine example comes from the case of the Portuguese diplomat Aristides de Sousa Mendes who in 1940 single-handedly saved an estimated 30,000 people considered undesirable by the Nazis, by issuing them with visas to travel to Portugal in defiance of instructions from his superiors and at great personal cost following the war. It was his religious faith that led him to endure the consequences of his actions.

Chapter 6: Number and arithmetic

1. Bryson on science at school: Bryson (2003: 21–22).

2. There is a fine discussion of the concept of numerosity in Butterworth (2005).

3. Counting principles: Gelman and Gallistel (1978); counting and grabbing: Wynn (1990; 1992b); skill at predicting and checking numerosities and detecting others' inaccurate counts: Gelman (2006). Piaget's views on children's number concepts: Piaget (1952), Piaget *et al.* (1960).

4. Number in the Amazon: Gordon (2004).

5. Linguistic determinism: Whorf (1956); the Whorfian hypothesis and the myth of Inuit words for snow a.k.a. The Great Eskimo Vocabulary Hoax: Pinker (1994).

6. Acquiring counting following imitation and reinforcement, Fuson (1988); acquiring counting through an object-tracking system and linguistic bootstrapping: Carey (2001).

7. Support for the independence of language from number: Gelman and Butterworth (2005); infant dishabituation and sensitivity to correspondence between dots and sounds: Starkey *et al.* (1983); sensitivity to changes in the ratio size of objects: Brannon *et al.* (2006); counting before having words for number: Starkey (1992).

8. Debate on infants' arithmetic and abilities to discriminate number: the views of Wynn (1992a, 2002) and those of others

(Clearfield and Mix 1999; Cohen and Marks 2002; Gao *et al.* 2000; Wakely *et al.* 2000; Xu *et al.* 2005).

9. Concept of numerosity in monkeys: Brannon and Terrace (1999). Using stimuli similar to those shown to monkeys, Brannon and her team report fMRI studies indicating that nonsymbolic number processing is accompanied by activation in the intraparietal sulcus for both 4-year-olds and adults: Cantlon *et al.* (2006).

10. Agrammatic but numerate: Varley *et al.* (2005).

11. Children's understanding that number words have exact meanings: Sarnecka and Gelman (2004). Rips *et al.* (2006) observe that such findings and the fact that a bootstrap does not convey to the child the sequence of natural numbers apart from a nonequivalent sequence makes the bootstrap unnecessary.

12. The effects of repeated questioning on conservation of number: Siegal *et al.* (1988). Repeated questioning doesn't provide a complete explanation for why children answer incorrectly on conservation problems but attention to the way children are questioned significantly boosts their success.

13. Inhibition of responses in conservation problems: Dehaene (1999).

14. Language and costs in numerical calculations: Hodent *et al.* (2005), Hunt and Agnoli (1991), Miller *et al.* (1995).

15. Work on dyscalculia: Butterworth (1999), Landerl *et al.* (2004).

16. Children's judgments of part–whole relations: Sharpe *et al.* (1999).

17. Addition and subtraction strategies in young children: Canobi (2005), Canobi *et al.* (2003), Resnick and Ford (1981).

18. Children's adeptness at nonnumerical representations of proportions and fractions: Mix *et al.* (1999), Sophian (2000). Children's difficulties with the numerical symbols for fractions: Bialystok and Codd (2000), Siegal and Smith (1997). Teachers' assessments of what students know: Gearhart and Saxe (2004). Position that entrenchment of children's problem-solving strategies impairs their understanding of number: McNeil and Alibali (2005), Rittle-Johnson *et al.* (2001);

children's particular difficulties with fractions: Harnett and Gelman (1998).

19. Relation between understanding that both number and physical matter are infinitely divisible: Smith *et al.* (2005).

20. Infinity in literature: Borges (1964), Joyce (1916/1964).

21. Japanese method of teaching fractions to children: Ginbayashi (1984), Kobayashi (1988), Inagaki *et al.* (1998).

22. According to Vygotsky (1962), a primary goal of education is to bridge what children are capable of achieving by themselves and what they may achieve through formal instruction within a culture of learning.

23. Conrad and mathematics: Conrad (1912).

Chapter 7: Autism and disorders of development

1. Critique of the autism epidemic: Gernsbacher *et al.* (2005). Estimates based on broad and narrow definitions of autism: Baird *et al.* (2006).

2. Case study of Michael: Anderson *et al.* (1999); of E.C.: Mottron and Belleville (1993).

3. Enhanced perceptual functioning: Mottron *et al.* (2006).

4. Inability of children with autism to respond on simplified ToM tasks: Surian and Leslie (1999). To distinguish between knowing and believing: Dennis *et al.* (2002). To define *friend:* Lord and Paul (1997).

5. Executive functioning in autism: Hill (2004); variability in autism and the position that a single explanation is not possible: Happé *et al.* (2006), Pellicano *et al.* (2006). Modeling multicausality in developmental disorders such as autism: Morton (2004).

6. Prevalence of language and communication disorders in ASD: Bailey, Philips, and Rutter (1996), Frith (2003), Joseph *et al.* (2002), Kanner (1943).

7. Word learning in autism: Baron-Cohen *et al.* (1997), Preissler and Carey (2004). Neural basis of gaze in autism: Senju *et al.* (2005) have reported abnormalities in the activity of the

occipital–temporal lobe of people with autism during eye direction processing in a study on event-related potentials. Occipito–temporal negativity was bilaterally distributed in children with autism whereas it was lateralized in the right hemisphere in the typically developing controls. Moreover the amplitude of this negativity was affected by eye direction (averted vs direct) in typically developing children but not in children with autism.

8. View that grammar and phonology may be affected in autism: Rapin and Dunn (2003); position that such impairments are due to general retardation: Frith (2003), Tager-Flusberg (2004). One pragmatic misunderstanding I remember well from my days as a student in Oxford involved a student who had recently come from South Africa. He kept complaining to me, "This gown! This gown! Isn't it terrible?" I commiserated with him saying, "Yes, isn't it terrible that they make us wear these things." He shot back, "No, that's not it. I want a long gown like everyone else." Though he had graduated with a BA from his university in South Africa, he was reading for a second BA and so he was given a short undergraduate gown to wear rather than the long gown of a graduate student. It had never occurred to me to pay attention to gown length as the conversational context for his remarks.

9. Just getting pragmatics off the ground: Tager-Flusberg (1994) carried out a study of 6 boys with autism aged 3–7 years who showed pronoun reversals but yet appeared to have mastered syntax.

10. Autism and the Gricean maxims: Surian *et al.* (1996).

11. Difficulties associated with pragmatic deficits in autism: Capps *et al.* (1998), Happé, 1993, Mitchell *et al.* 1997, Ziatis *et al.* (2003). Prosody in autism: Rutherford *et al.* (2002), Shriberg *et al.* (2001). Wang *et al.* (2006b) reported that children with ASD were less accurate than typically developing controls in deciding whether an utterance was meant to be ironic. In an fMRI investigation of this process, greater activity of the right inferior temporal gyrus occurred in the children with ASD. This result contrasts with previous findings that reported hypoactivations of the same areas during ToM and pragmatic

reasoning tasks. The hyperactivation found by Wang and colleagues suggests greater effort in performing an explicit task, while the hypoactivation found in previous studies could be due to the fact that subjects were not explicitly required to engage in mental states attributions.

12. Infant auditory attention: Mendleson and Haith (1976).

13. Auditory dominance in preschoolers: Napolitano and Sloutsky (2004); Robinson and Sloutsky (2004).

14. Joint attention as a "pivotal skill" in autism: Charman (2003). Autism and the ability to detect speech from noise: Bebko *et al.* (2006), Khalfa *et al.* (2001); and signals from masking sounds: Boddaert *et al.* (2003), Foxton *et al.* (2003), Plaisted *et al.* (2003).

15. In a study that used cortical event-related brain potentials to examine auditory processing in autism, Ceponiene *et al.* (2003), 9 children with autism aged 6 to 12 years (mean, 8 years, 9 months) were exposed to tone and vowel stimuli. Three types of electrophysiological measurements were recorded: auditory sensory event-related potentials (ERPs), the mismatch negativity component, and the P3a component. The auditory sensory ERP measure is assumed to reflect sound frequency or intensity, the mismatch negativity component to elicit infrequent "deviant" sounds as distinct from repetitive "standard" sounds, and the P3a component to indicate the involuntary orientation of attention to events salient in the environment. Differences in auditory sensory ERPs between the children with autism and a normal control group were not quite significant and there was no significant difference on mismatch negativity. However, for the children with autism, unlike for the control group, changes in vowel pitch (though not tones) elicited no significant P3a. On this basis, Ceponiene *et al.* conclude that impairment in auditory processing is at the attentional rather than the sensory level and that children with autism may have an attentional deficit in orienting to the "speechness" quality of sounds as represented by vowels. In a magnetoencephalography (MEG) study of autism, Gage *et al.* (2003) report a similar pattern of results suggesting abnormal development of the auditory system.

16. The superior temporal sulcus as a voice selective area: Gervais *et al.* (2004).

17. The discovery of TMS: Barker *et al.* (1985). Implications of TMS for cognitive neuroscience: Walsh and Pascual-Leone (2003).

18. The effects of TMS on discriminating one's own face from familiar other faces: Uddin *et al.* (2006). The proposal that the left TPJ is necessary for ToM: Samson *et al.* (2004). The proposal that the left HIPS is necessary for exact calculation: Dehaene *et al.* (2003).

19. Early diagnosis of autism before the age of two: Osterling *et al.* (2002).

20. Proposals on the nature of abnormal brain activation in autism: Courchesne and Pierce (2005), Rubenstein and Merzenrich (2003). Mirror neuron dysfunction in children with autism: Dapretto *et al.* (2006); difficulties of preschoolers with autism in using voices to recognize faces and to attend to speakers in conversation: Baranek *et al.* (2006), Klin (1992), Lord (1995). Responses of older children with autism to voices: Boucher *et al.* (2000).

21. Abnormal electrophysiological and behavioural responses to speech in preschoolers with ASD: Kuhl *et al.* (2005).

22. Lack of response to names by children with ASD: Nadig *et al.* (2007). Impairment in 'episodic' memory in autism or memory for personally experienced events: Walenski *et al.* (2006); performance on visuospatial tasks in autism: Mitchell and Ropar (2004), Mottron *et al.* (2006), O'Riordan (2001). However, skill on spatial tasks may not extend to the ability to detect coherent motion in following the direction of moving dots in a kinematogram: Milne *et al.* (2002).

23. Impairment in autism on ToM tasks: Siegal and Peterson (in press); Surian and Leslie (1999). A related matter is that many schizophrenics also have difficulties in ToM and in processing information in the auditory modality that is associated with hallucinations. ToM in schizophrenia: Brune (2005), Frith and Corcoran (1996), Langdon *et al.* (2006). Auditory hallucinations: Hunter *et al.* (2006). Paradoxically, as Kanner pointed out, auditory hallucinations are absent in autism.

24. Dyslexia, culture, and the ability to analyze speech sounds: Tan *et al.* (2005). Reading and training in sound discrimination: Temple *et al.* (2003).

25. Whereas research to date has shown the effectiveness of training sound discrimination in 8- to 10-year-olds (Moore *et al.* 2005) and in adults (Armitay *et al.* 2006), there is a need to develop tests for much younger children aged 2 and 3 years and then to relate their performance to reading success.

26. Controversy over gastrointestinal disorders in autism: *BMJ* paper: Black *et al.* (2002).

27. Indiana review of gastrointestinal factors in autism: Erickson *et al.* (2005). Also Molloy and Manning-Courtney (2003) and Valicenti-McDermott *et al.* (2006).

Chapter 8: Culture, communication, and what children know

1. My discussion of cultural variations in children's achievement is similar to that provided by Hatano (1990) and Shweder *et al.* (1998).

2. Distinctions between lies and mistakes: Siegal and Peterson (1998). Language acquisition and trust: Koenig, Clement and Harris (2004), Koenig and Harris (2005), Jaswal and Neely (2006); see also Bergstrom, Muehlmann and Boyer (2006). Behaviors judged as wrong even if there were no prohibition: Nucci and Turiel (1978). The moral "side effect": Leslie *et al.* (2006); also Hauser (2006).

3. Knowledge as incomplete or inflexible: Woolley (2006), drawing from Siegler (2000).

4. Studies of extracting speaker meaning: Carston (1998, 2002), Clark (1996), Gazdar (1999), Glucksberg (2003), Hilton (1995), Horn (1989), Levinson (2000), Ninio and Snow (1996), Sperber and Wilson (1995),Wilson and Sperber (2004), Winner (1988). Grice's account of "logic in communication": Grice (1975, 1989).

5. Children's strategies in answering questions: Donaldson (1978); Siegal (1999). Eyewitness testimony and children's resistance to

suggestive questions: Bright-Paul, Jarrold, and Wright (2005), Howie, Sheehan, Mojarrad, and Wrzesinska (2004), Pipe, Lamb, Orbach, and Esplin (2004). Reporting the original rather than a distorted version of an event: Newcombe and Siegal (1996, 1997).

6. A conceptual deficit in understanding language contradictions: Osherson and Markman (1975). The distinction between literal meaning and speaker's meaning: Beal and Flavell (1984), Robinson *et al.* (1983).

7. Children's responses to yes–no questions: Fritzley and Lee (2003); also Waterman *et al.* (2001, 2004).

8. Scalar implicatures: Mill (1867, p. 561), Grice (1975). Studies suggesting that young children do not make SIs: Braine and Rumain (1981), Smith (1980).

9. Papafragou's work on SIs: Papafragou and Musolino (2003). Follow-up study: Papafragou and Tantalou (2004). Relevance Theory (Sperber and Wilson, 1995; Wilson and Sperber, 2004) proposes that all SIs are effortful as these are derived when the hearer is trying to compute an optimally relevant interpretation of the utterance. Although controversial (Levinson, 2000), research with adults would seem to support this position. For example, Bott and Noveck (2004; see also Breheny, Katsos and Williams 2006), asked adult subjects to comprehend and evaluate infelicitous sentences such as "Some elephants are mammals." Those who rejected them (i.e., they interpreted the items by assigning the meaning "Some but not all elephants are mammals") took significantly longer to answer, indicating that those who were interpreting these items pragmatically were engaged in effortful inferential processing aimed at deriving an implicature. A range of studies have documented children's ability to draw conversational implicatures when "computational effort" is reduced: Gualmini, Crain and Meroni. (2001), Surian (1995), Surian and Job (1987).

10. Differences between children and adults in attending to the context of language: Trueswell, Sekerina and Hill (1999). Eye-gaze research: Sekerina, Stromswold and Hestvik (2004), Trueswell *et al.* (1999). Distractions to adult attention: Keysar and Henly (2002), Nadig and Sedivy (2002).

11. Children's ability to compile plans: Meroni and Crain (2003); also Mattei (1981), Hamburger and Crain (1984).

12. Using an "order-of-mention" reaction that overlooks the second part of a statement: Fay and Klahr (1996), Morris and Sloutsky (2002). Striving to extract meaning from contradictory statements by using "local" conversational concerns: Scholnick and Wing (1991), Sharpe, Eakin and Saragovi (1996).

13. Logic, conversation, and schooling: Artman, Cahan and Auni-Babad (2006), Scribner and Cole (1973).

14. Bruner (1966) sought to block children from responding incorrectly on a conversation of liquids task by having 4- to 6-year-olds predict the water level in glass that was hidden behind a screen. Sigel (1993) emphasized the importance of "distancing behaviours ... that place demands on the child to separate himself or herself from the ongoing field of observable events through representations in space and time" and to "anticipate outcomes, recall events, and attend to transformations of objects or phenomena." The longitudinal research of Mischel and his coworkers has documented continuities in behavior that involves "delay of gratification" and outcomes that involve focused attention such as school achievement: Mischel *et al.* (1989), Eigsti *et al.* (2006).

15. Hauser (1999) has made the point that it is necessary to distinguish between "affective perseveration" in EF processes in which a failure to inhibit emotions interferes with reasoning and perseverative reasoning errors that are due to a conceptual difficulty and requires conceptual change to be overcome.

16. Components of EF: Miyake *et al.* (2000).

17. EF and bilingualism: Bialystok and Martin (2004), Bialystok and Senman (2004), Costa *et al.* (2008), Goetz (2003).

18. Variety of terms for bilingualism: adopted from Wei (2000: 6).

19. EF and ToM in Chinese and American children: Sabbagh *et al.* (2006); in hard-to-manage children: Hughes *et al.* (1998). Absence of relation between EF and ToM tasks: Tardif *et al.* (2007), Woolfe *et al.* (2002).

References

Anderson, M., O'Connor, N. and Hermelin, B. (1999). A specific calculating ability. *Intelligence, 26*, 383–403.

Appadurai, A. (1981). Gastro-politics in Hindu South Asia. *American Ethologist, 8*, 494–511.

Armitay, S., Irwin, A. and Moore, D. R. (2006). Discrimination learning induced by training with identical stimuli. *Nature Neuroscience, 9*, 1446–1448.

Aron, A. R. *et al.* (2003). Stop-signal inhibition disrupted by damage to right inferior frontal gyrus in humans. *Nature Neuroscience, 6*, 115–116.

Artman, L., Cahan, S. and Avni-Babad, D. (2006). Age, schooling and conditional reasoning. *Cognitive Development, 21*, 131–145.

Astington, J. W. and Jenkins, J. M. (1999). A longitudinal study of the relation between language and theory-of-mind development. *Developmental Psychology, 35*, 1311–1320.

Astuti, R. (2001). Are we all natural dualists? A cognitive developmental approach. *Journal of the Royal Anthropological Institute, 7*, 429–447.

Astuti, R., Solomon, G. E. A. and Carey, S. (2004). Constraints on conceptual development. *Monographs of the Society for Research in Child Development, 69, Serial No. 277*.

Atran, S. (2002). *In gods we trust*. New York: Oxford University Press.

Atran, S. (2006). *Religion's innate origins*. In P. Carruthers, S. Laurence and S. Stich (eds), *The innate mind: Culture and cognition* (pp. 302–317). New York: Oxford University Press.

Au, T. K., Sidle, A. L. and Rollins, K. (1993). Developing an understanding of conservation and contamination: Invisible particles as a plausible mechanism. *Developmental Psychology, 29*, 286–299.

Au, T. K-F., Romo, L. F. and DeWitt, J. E. (1999). Folkbiology in health education. In M. Siegal and C. C. Peterson (eds), *Children's understanding of biology and health* (pp. 209–234). New York: Cambridge University Press.

Avis, J. and Harris, P. L. (1991). Belief-desire reasoning among Baka children: Evidence for a universal conception of mind. *Child Development, 62*, 460–467.

Bailey, A., Phillips, W. and Rutter, M. (1996). Autism: Towards an integration of clinical, genetic, neuropsychological and neurobiological perspectives. *Journal of Child Psychology and Psychiatry, 37*, 89–126.

Baird, G. *et al.* (2006). Prevalence of disorders of the autism spectrum in a population cohort of children in South Thames: the Special Needs and Autism Project (SNAP). *The Lancet, 368*, 210–215.

Baker, M. A. (2001). *The atoms of language.* New York: Basic Books.

Baranek, G. T. *et al.* (2006). The Sensory Experiences Questionnaire: Discriminating response patterns in young children with autism, developmental delays and typical development. *Journal of Child Psychology and Psychiatry, 47,* 591–601.

Barker, A. T., Jalinous, R. and Freeston, I. L. (1985). Non-invasive magnetic stimulation of human motor cortex. *The Lancet, 1*(8437), 1106–1107.

Barley, N. (1983). *The innocent anthropologist: Notes from a mud hut.* Harmondsworth, UK: Penguin.

Baron-Cohen, S., Baldwin, D. and Crowson, M. (1997). Do children with autism use the Speaker's Direction of Gaze (SDG) strategy to crack the code of language? *Child Development, 68,* 48–57.

Baron-Cohen, S., Leslie, A. M. and Frith, U. (1985). Does the autistic child have theory of mind? *Cognition, 21,* 37–46.

Barrett, H. C. and Behne, T. (2005). Children's understanding of death as the cessation of agency: A test using sleep versus death. *Cognition, 96,* 93–108.

Barrett, H. C. and Kurzban, R. (2006). Modularity in cognition: Framing the debate. *Psychological Review, 113,* 628–647.

Barrett, J. L. and Keil, F. (1996). Conceptualizing a nonnatural entity: Anthropomorphism in God concepts. *Cognitive Psychology, 31,* 219–247.

Bate, J. (1997). *The genius of Shakespeare.* London: Picador.

Beal, C. R. and Flavell, J. H. (1984). Development of the ability to distinguish communicative intention and literal message meaning. *Child Development, 55,* 920–928.

Bebko, J. M. *et al.* (2006). Discrimination of temporal synchrony in intermodal events by children with autism and children with developmental disabilities without autism. *Journal of Child Psychology and Psychiatry, 47,* 88–98.

Behne, T., M., Carpenter, M., Call, J. and Tomasello, M. (2005). Unwilling versus unable: Infants' understanding of intentional action. *Developmental Psychology, 41,* 328–337.

Bergstrom, B., Moehlmann, B. and Boyer, P. (2006). Extending the testimony problem: Evaluating the truth, scope and source of cultural information. *Child Development, 77,* 531–538.

Berguno, G. and Bowler D. M. (2004). Communicative interactions, knowledge of a second language and theory of mind in young children. *Journal of Genetic Psychology, 165,* 293–309.

Bering, J. M. (2006). The folk psychology of souls. *Behavioral and Brain Sciences, 29,* 453–462.

Bering, J. M. and Bjorklund, D. F. (2004). The natural emergence of reasoning about the afterlife as a developmental regularity. *Developmental Psychology, 40,* 217–233.

Bialystok, E. and Codd, J. (2000). Representing quantity beyond whole numbers: Some, none and part. *Canadian Journal of Experimental Psychology, 54*, 117–128.

Bialystok, E. and Martin, M. M. (2004). Attention and inhibition in bilingual children: evidence from the dimensional change card sort task. *Developmental Science, 7*, 325–339.

Bialystok, E. and Senman, L. (2004). Executive processes in appearance-reality tasks: The role of inhibition of attention and symbolic representation. *Child Development, 75*, 562–579.

Bibace, R. and Walsh, M. E. (1981). Children's conceptions of illness. In R. Bibace and M. E. Walsh (eds), *New directions for child development: Children's conceptions of health, illness and bodily functions, No. 14* (pp.31–48). San Francisco, CA: Jossey-Bass.

Black, C., Kaye, J. A. and Jick, H. (2002). Relation of childhood gastrointestinal disorders to autism: nested case-control study using data from the UK General Practice. *British Medical Journal, 325*, 419–421.

Blades, M. and Spencer, C. (1994). The development of children's ability to use spatial representations. In H. W. Reese (ed.), *Advances in Child Development, Vol. 25* (pp. 157–199). San Diego, CA: Academic Press.

Bloom, P. (2000). *How children learn the meaning of words.* Cambridge, MA: MIT Press.

Bloom, P. and German, T. P. (2000). Two reasons to abandon the false belief task as a test of theory of mind. *Cognition, 77*, B25–B31.

Boddaert, N. *et al.* (2003). Perception of complex sounds: Abnormal pattern of cortical activation in autism. *American Journal of Psychiatry, 160*, 2057–2060.

Bonatti, L., Frot, E., Zangl, R. and Mehler, J. (2002). The human first hypothesis: Identification of conspecifics and individuation of objects in the young infant. *Cognitive Psychology, 44*, 388–426.

Borges, J. L. (1964). *Labyrinths.* New York: New Directions.

Bott, L. and Noveck, I. A. (2004). Some utterances are underinformative: The onset and time course of scalar implicatures. *Journal of Memory and Language, 51*, 437–457.

Boucher, J., Lewis, V. and Collis, G. (2000). Voice processing abilities in children with autism, children with specific language impairments and young typically developing children. *Journal of Child Psychology and Psychiatry, 41*, 847–857.

Boyer, P. (2002). *Religion explained.* New York: Basic Books.

Braine, M. and Rumain, B. (1981). Children's comprehension of 'or': Evidence for a sequence of competences. *Journal of Experimental Child Psychology, 31*, 46–70.

Brannon, E. M. and Terrace, H. S. (1998). Ordering of the numerosities 1–9 by monkeys. *Science, 282*, 746–749.

Brannon, E. M., Lutz, D. and Cordes, S. (2006). The development of area discrimination and its implications for number representation in infancy. *Developmental Science, 9,* F59–F64.

Breheny, R., Katsos, N. and Williams, N. (2006) Are generalised scalar implicatures generated by default? An on-line investigation into the role of context in generating pragmatic inferences. *Cognition, 100,* 434–463.

Bright-Paul, A., Jarrold, C. and Wright, D. B. (2005). Age-appropriate cues facilitate source-monitoring and reduce suggestibility in 3-to 7-year-olds. *Cognitive Development, 20,* 1–18.

Brown, R. and Hanlon, C. (1970). Derivational complexity and order of acquisition in child speech. In J. R. Hayes (ed.), *Cognition and the development of language* (pp. 11–54). New York: Wiley.

Brune, M. (2005). Theory of mind in schizophrenia: A review of the literature. *Schizophrenia Bulletin, 31,* 21–42.

Bruner, J. S. (1966). On the conservation of liquids. In J. S. Bruner, R. R. Olver and P. M. Greenfield (eds), *Studies in cognitive growth* (pp. 183–207). New York: Wiley.

Bryson, B. (2003). *A short history of nearly everything.* London: Doubleday.

Bunge, S. A. *et al.* (2002). Immature frontal lobe contributions to cognitive control in children: Evidence from fMRI. *Neuron, 33,* 301–311.

Butterworth, B. (1999). *The mathematical brain.* London: Macmillan.

Butterworth, B. (2005). The development of arithmetical abilities. *Journal of Child Psychology and Psychiatry, 46,* 3–18.

Canobi, K. H. (2005). Children's profiles of addition and subtraction understanding. *Journal of Experimental Child Psychology, 92,* 220–246.

Canobi, K. H., Reeve, R. A. and Pattison, P. E. (2003). Patterns of knowledge in children's addition. *Developmental Psychology, 39,* 521–534.

Cantlon, J. F., Brannon, E. M., Carter, E. J. and Pelphrey, K. A. (2006) Functional imaging of numerical processing in adults and 4-y-old children. *PloS Biology, 4,* e125.

Capps, L., Kehres, J. and Sigman, M. (1998). Conversational abilities among children with autism and children with developmental delays. *Autism, 2,* 325–344.

Caramazza, A. and Mahon, B. Z. (2006). The organization of conceptual knowledge in the brain: The future's past and some future directions. *Cognitive Neuropsychology, 23,* 13–38.

Carey, S. (1985). *Conceptual change in childhood.* Cambridge, MA: MIT Press.

Carey, S. (1995). On the origin of causal understanding. In D. Sperber, D. Premack and A. J. Premack (eds), *Causal cognition* (pp. 268–301). Oxford: Oxford University Press.

Carey, S. (1999). Sources of conceptual change. In E. K. Scholnick, K. Nelson, S. A. Gelman and P. H. Miller (eds), Sources of conceptual change.

Conceptual development: Piaget's legacy (pp. 293–326). Mahwah, NJ: Erlbaum.

Carey, S. (2000). Science education as conceptual change. *Journal of Applied Developmental Psychology, 21,* 13–19.

Carey, S. (2001). Cognitive foundations of arithmetic: Evolution and ontogenesis. *Mind and Language, 16,* 37–55.

Carruthers, P., Laurence, S. and Stich, S. (eds) (2005). *The innate mind: Structure and contents.* New York: Oxford University Press.

Carruthers, P., Laurence, S. and Stich, S. (eds) (2006). *The innate mind: Culture and cognition.* New York: Oxford University Press.

Carruthers, P., Laurence, S. and Stich, S. (eds) (in press). *The innate mind: Reflections and future directions.* New York: Oxford University Press.

Carston, R. (1998). Informativeness, relevance and scalar implicature. In R. Carston and S. Uchida (eds), *Relevance theory: Applications and implications* (pp. 179–236). Amsterdam: Benjamins.

Carston, R. (2002). *Thoughts and utterances: The pragmatics of explicit communication.* Oxford: Blackwell.

Ceponiene, R. *et al.* (2003). Speech–sound-selective auditory impairment in children with autism: They can perceive but do not attend. *Proceedings of the National Academy of Sciences, 100,* 5567–5572.

Charman, T. (2003) Why is joint attention a pivotal skill in autism? *Philosophical Transactions of the Royal Society, London, Series B, 358,* 315–324.

Cheour, M. *et al.* (2002). Speech sounds learned by sleeping newborns. *Nature, 415,* 599–600.

Chi, M. T. H. (2005). Commonsense conceptions of emergent processes: Why misconceptions are robust. *The Journal of the Learning Sciences, 14,* 161–199.

Chomsky, N. (1980). *Rules and Representations.* Oxford: Blackwell.

Clark, E. V. (1997) Conceptual perspective and lexical choice in acquisition. *Cognition 64,* 1–37.

Clark, H. H. (1996). *Using language.* New York: Cambridge University Press.

Clark, H. H. and Brennan, S. E. (1991). Grounding in communication. In L. B. Resnick, J. M. Levine and S. Behrens (eds), *Perspectives on socially shared cognition* (pp.127–149). Washington, DC: American Psychological Association.

Clearfield, M. W. and Mix, K. S. (1999). Number versus contour length in infants discrimination of small visual sets. *Psychological Science, 10,* 408–411.

Cohen, L. B. and Marks, K. S. (2002). How infants process addition and subtraction events. *Developmental Science, 5,* 186–201.

Conrad, R. (1912). *A personal record.* New York: Harper.

Costa, A., Hernandez, M. and Sebastián-Gallés, N. (2008). Bilingualism aids conflict resolution: Evidence from the ANT task. *Cognition, 106,* 59–86.

Courchesne, E. and Pierce, K. (2005). Why the frontal cortex in autism might be talking only to itself: Local over-connectivity but long-distance disconnection. *Current Opinion in Neurobiology, 15,* 225–230.

Courtin, C. and Melot, A-M (2005). Metacognitive development of deaf children: Lessons from the appearance-reality and false belief tasks. *Developmental Science, 8,* 16–25.

Cowie, F. (1998). *What's within? Nativism reconsidered.* New York: Oxford University Press.

Crain, S. and Pietroski, P. (2001). Nature, nurture and universal grammar. *Linguistics and Philosophy, 24,* 139–186.

Curtis, V. and Biran, A. (2001). Dirt, disgust and disease – is hygiene in our genes? *Perspectives in Biology and Medicine, 44,* 17–31.

Curtis, V. *et al.* (2001). Evidence of behaviour change following a hygiene promotion programme in Burkina Faso. *Bulletin of the World Health Organization, 79,* 518–527.

Curtis, V., Cairncross S. and Yonli, R. (2000). Domestic hygiene and diarrhoea – pinpointing the problem. *Tropical Medicine and International Health, 5,* 22–32.

Curtiss, S. (1977). *Genie: A psycholinguistic study of a modern-day 'wild child'.* New York: Academic Press.

Custer, W. L. (1996). A comparison of young children's understanding of contradictory representations in pretense, memory and belief. *Child Development, 67,* 678–688.

Dahlgren, S., Sandberg, A. D. and Hjelmquist, E. (2003). The non-specificity of theory of mind deficits: Evidence from children with communicative disabilities. *European Journal of Cognitive Psychology, 15,* 129–155.

Dalton, K. M. *et al.* (2005). Gaze fixation and the neural circuitry of face processing in autism. *Nature Neuroscience, 8,* 519–526.

Dapretto, M. *et al.* (2006). Understanding emotions in others: Mirror neuron dysfunction in autism. *Nature Neuroscience, 9,* 28–30.

De Villiers, J. G. and Pyers, J. E. (2002). Complements to cognition: A longitudinal study of the relationship between complex syntax and false-belief understanding. *Cognitive Development, 17,* 1037–1060.

Deák, G. O. (2006). Do children really confuse appearance and reality? *Trends in Cognitive Sciences, 10,* 546–550.

Deák, G. O. and Enright, K. (2006). Choose and choose again:Appearance-reality errors, pragmatics and logical ability. *Developmental Science, 9,* 323–333.

Deák, G. O., Ray, S. D. and Brenneman, K. (2003). Children's perseverative appearance-reality errors are related to emerging language skills. *Child Development, 74,* 944–964.

Dehaene, S. (1999). *The number sense: How the mind creates mathematics.* New York: Oxford University Press.

Dehaene, S., Piazza, M., Pinel, P. and Cohen, L. (2003). *Cognitive Neuropsychology*, *20*, 487–506.

Dehaene-Lambertz, G., Dehaene, S. and Hertz-Pannier, L. (2002). Functional neuroimaging of speech perception in infants. *Science, 298*, 2013–2015.

Dehaene-Lambertz, G., Pena, M., Christophe, A. and Landrieu, P. (2004). Phoneme perception in a neonate with a left sylvian infarct. *Brain and Language, 88*, 26–38.

Dennis, M., Lazenby, A. L. and Lokyer, L. (2002). Inferential language in high function children with autism. *Journal of Autism and Developmental Disorders, 31*, 47–54.

DeVries, R. (1969). Constancy of generic identity in the years three to six. *Monographs of the Society for Research in Child Development, 34*, Serial No. 127.

Di Sessa, A. A. (1988). Knowledge in pieces. In G. Forman and P. B. Pufall (eds), *Constructivism in the computer age* (pp. 49–70). Hillsdale, NJ: Erlbaum.

Diamond, A., Kirkham, N. and Amso, D. (2002). Conditions under which young children CAN hold two rules in mind and inhibit a prepotent response. *Developmental Psychology, 38*, 352–362.

Dias, M. G. and Harris, P. L. (1988). The effect of make-believe play on deductive reasoning. *British Journal of Developmental Psychology, 6*, 207–221.

Dibbets, P. and Jolles, J (2006). The Switch Task for Children: Measuring mental flexibility in young children. *Cognitive Development, 21*, 60–71.

Diesendruck, G. and Markson, L. (2001). Children's avoidance of lexical overlap: A pragmatic account. *Developmental Psychology, 37*, 630–641.

Donaldson, M. (1978). *Children's minds*. Glasgow, UK: Fontana.

Dunn, J. (1994). Changing minds and changing relationships. In C. Lewis and P. Mitchell (eds), *Origins of an understanding of mind* (pp. 297–310). Hove, UK: Erlbaum.

Eigsti, I. *et al.* (2006). Predictive cognitive control from preschool to late adolescence and young adulthood. *Psychological Science, 17*, 478–484.

Ellis, A. E. and Oakes, L. M. (2006). Infants flexibly use different dimensions to categorize objects. *Developmental Psychology, 42*, 1000–1011.

Elman, J. L. *et al.* (1996). *Rethinking innateness: A connectionist perspective on development*. Cambridge, MA: MIT Press.

Emery, N. J. and Clayton, N. S. (2001) Effects of experience and social context on prospective caching strategies by scrub jays. *Nature, 414*, 443–446.

Erickson, C. A. *et al.* (2005). Gastrointestinal factors in autistic disorder: A critical review. *Journal of Autism and Developmental Disorders. 35*, 713–727.

Falkman, K., Roos, C. and Hjelmquist, E. (2007). Mentalizing skills of non-native, early signers: A longitudinal perspective. *European Journal of Developmental Psychology, 4*, 178–197.

Fallon, A. E., Rozin, P. and Pliner, P. (1984). The child's conception of food: The development of food rejections with special reference to disgust and contamination sensitivity. *Child Development, 55*, 566–575.

Fay, A. L. and Klahr, D. (1996). Knowing about guessing and guessing about knowing: Preschoolers' understanding of indeterminacy. *Child Development, 67*, 689–716.

Flavell, J. H. (1963). *The developmental psychology of Jean Piaget.* Princeton, NJ: Van Nostrand.

Flavell, J. H. (1999). Cognitive development: Children's knowledge about the mind. *Annual Review of Psychology, 50*, 21–45.

Flavell, J. H., Flavell, E. R. and Green, F. L. (1983). Development of the appearance-reality distinction. *Cognitive Psychology, 15*, 95–120.

Flavell, J. H., Green, F. L. and Flavell, E. R. (1986). Development of the appearance-reality distinction. *Monographs of the Society for Research in Child Development, 51. Serial No. 212.*

Fodor, J. (2000). *The mind doesn't work that way: The scope and limits of computational psychology.* Cambridge, MA: MIT Press.

Fodor, J. A. (1983). *The modularity of mind.* Cambridge, MA: Bradford/MIT Press.

Fodor, J. A. (1992). A theory of the child's theory of mind. *Cognition 44*, 283–296.

Fonagy, P., Gergely, G. and Target, M. (2007). The parent–infant dyad and the construction of the subjective self. *Journal of Child Psychology and Psychiatry, 48*, 288–328.

Foxton, J. M. *et al.* (2003). Absence of auditory 'global interference' in autism. *Brain, 126*, 2703–2709.

Frazer, J. G. (1890/1959). *The golden bough: A study in magic and religion.* New York: Macmillan. (reprint of 1922 abridged edition, edited by T. H. Gaster; original work published 1890).

Friedman, O. and Leslie, A. M. (2004). Mechanisms of belief-desire reasoning. *Psychological Science, 15*, 547–552.

Frith, C. D. and Corcoran, R. (1996). Exploring 'theory of mind' in people with schizophrenia. *Psychological Medicine, 26*, 521–530.

Frith, U. (2003). *Autism: Explaining the enigma, 2nd edn.* Oxford: Blackwell.

Frith, U. and Happé, F. (1998). Why specific developmental disorders are not specific: On-line and developmental effects in autism and dyslexia. *Developmental Science, 1*, 267–272.

Fritzley, V. H. and Lee, K. (2003). Do young children always say yes to yes–no questions? A metadevelopmental study of the affirmation bias. *Child Development, 74*, 1297–1313.

Frye, D., Zelazo, P. D. and Palfai, T. (1995). Theory of mind and rule-based reasoning. *Cognitive Development, 10*, 483–527.

Fuson, K. C. (1988). *Children's counting and concepts of number*. New York: Springer Verlag.

Gage, N. M., Siegel, B. and Roberts, T. P. L. (2003). Cortical auditory system maturational abnormalities in children with autism disorder: An MEG investigation. *Developmental Brain Research, 144*, 201–209.

Gao, F., Levine, S. C. and Huttenlocher, J. (2000). What do infants know about continuous quantity? *Journal of Experimental Child Psychology, 77*, 20–29.

Gauvain, M. and Greene, J. K. (1994). What do children know about objects? *Cognitive Development, 9*, 311–329.

Gazdar, G. (1979). *Pragmatics*. New York: Academic Press.

Gearhart, M. and Saxe, G. B. (2004). When teachers know what students know: Integrating mathematics assessment. *Theory Into Practice, 43*, 304–313.

Geary, D. (1995). Reflections on evolution and culture in children's cognition: Implications for mathematical development and instruction. *American Psychologist, 50*, 24–35.

Gelman, R. (2000). The epigenesis of mathematical thinking. *Journal of Applied Developmental Psychology, 21*, 27–37.

Gelman, R. (2006). Young natural-number arithmeticians. *Current Directions in Psychological Science, 15*, 193–197.

Gelman, R. and Butterworth, B. (2005). Number and language: How are they related? *Trends in Cognitive Sciences, 9*, 6–10.

Gelman, R. and Gallistel, C. R. (1978). *The child's understanding of number*. Cambridge, MA: Harvard University Press.

Gelman, R. and Williams, E. M. (1998). Enabling constraints for cognitive development and learning: Domain specificity and epigenesis. In D. Kuhn and R. Siegler (eds), *Handbook of Child Psychology, 5th* edn, Volume 2: Cognition, perception and language (pp.575–630). New York: Wiley.

Gelman, S. A. (2000). The role of essentialism in children's concepts. *Advances in Child Development and Behavior, 27*, 55–98.

Gelman, S. A. (2003). *The essential child*. New York: Oxford University Press.

Gelman, S. A. and Ebeling, K. S. (1998). Shape and representational status in children's early naming. *Cognition, 66*, 35–47.

Gergely, G., Bekkering, H. and Kiraly, I. (2002). Rational imitation in preverbal infants. *Nature, 415*, 755.

Gernsbacher, M. A., Dawson, M. and Goldsmith, H. H. (2005). Three reasons not to believe in an autism epidemic. *Current Directions in Psychological Science, 14*, 55–58.

Gervais, H. *et al.* (2004). Abnormal cortical voice processing in autism. *Nature Neuroscience, 7*, 801–802.

Ginbayashi, K. (1984). *Principles of mathematics education*. Tokyo: Association of Mathematical Instruction.

Glucksberg, S. (2003) The psycholinguistics of metaphor. *Trends in Cognitive Sciences, 7,* 92–96.

Goetz, P. J. (2003). The effects of bilingualism on theory of mind development. *Bilingualism, 6,* 1–15.

Goldin-Meadow, S. (2003). *The resilience of language.* New York: Psychology Press.

Goldin-Meadow, S. and Mylander, C. (1998). Spontaneous sign systems created by deaf children in two cultures. *Nature, 391,* 279–281.

Goldin-Meadow, S., Gelman, S. A. and Mylander, C. (2005). Expressing generic concepts with and without a language model. *Cognition, 96,* 109–126.

Gopnik, A. (1996). The scientist as child. *Philosophy of Science, 63,* 485–514.

Gopnik, A. and Wellman, H. M. (1994). The theory theory. In L. A. Hirschfeld and S. A. Gelman (eds), *Mapping the mind: Domain specificity in culture and cognition* (pp. 257–293). New York: Cambridge University Press.

Gordon, P. (2004). Numerical cognition without words: Evidence from Amazonia. *Science, 306,* 496–499.

Grassly, N. C. *et al.* (2006). New strategies for the elimination of polio from India. *Science, 314,* 1150–1153.

Grice, H. P. (1975). Logic and conversation. In P. Cole and J. L. Morgan (eds), *Syntax and semantics, Vol. 3, Speech acts* (pp. 41–58). New York: Academic.

Grice, H. P. (1989). *Studies in the way of words.* Cambridge, MA: Harvard University Press.

Grimshaw, G. M., Adelstein, A., Bryden, M. P. and MacKinnon, G. E. (1998). First-language acquisition in adolescence: Evidence for a critical period for verbal language development. *Brain and Language, 63,* 237–255.

Gualmini, A., Crain, S., Meroni, L. and Chierchia, G. (2001). At the semantic/pragmatic interface in child language. *Proceedings of Semantics and Linguistic Theory, 11,* 231–247.

Hale, C. M. and Tager-Flusberg, H. (2003). The influence of language on theory of mind: A training study. *Developmental Science, 6,* 346–359.

Hamburger, H. and Crain, S. (1984). Acquisition of cognitive compiling. *Cognition 17,* 85–136.

Happé, F. (1993). Communicative competence and theory of mind in autism: A test of relevance theory. *Cognition, 48,* 101–119.

Happé, F., Ronald, A. and Plomin, R. (2006). Time to give up on a single explanation for autism. *Nature Neuroscience, 9,* 1218–1220.

Harnett, R. and Gelman, R. (1998). Early understandings of numbers: Paths or barriers to the contruction of new understandings? *Learning and Instruction, 8,* 341–374.

Harris, M. (1992). *Language experience and early language development.* Hove, UK: Erlbaum.

Harris, P. L. (1996). Desires, beliefs and language. In P. Carruthers and P. K. Smith, *Theories of theory of mind* (pp. 200–220). New York: Cambridge University Press.

Harris, P. L. (2000). *The work of the imagination.* Oxford: Blackwell.

Harris, P. L., de Rosnay, M. and Pons, F. (2005). Language and children's understanding of mental states. *Current Directions in Psychological Science,* *14,* 69–73.

Hatano, G. (1990). Toward a cultural psychology of mathematical cognition. Commentary on H. W. Stevenson and S-Y Lee, *Contexts of achievement: A study of American, Chinese and Japanese children. Monographs of the Society for Research in Child Development, 55 (1/2),* 108–115.

Hatano, G. and Inagaki, K. (1994). Young children's naive theory of biology. *Cognition, 50,* 171–188.

Hauser, M. D. (1999). Perseveration, inhibition and the prefrontal cortex: a new look. *Current Opinion in Neurobiology, 9,* 214–222.

Hauser, M. D. (2006). *Moral minds.* New York: Ecco (HarperCollins).

Hayes, B. K., Goodhew, A., Heit, E. and Gillan, J. (2003). The role of diverse instruction in conceptual change. *Journal of Experimental Child Psychology, 86,* 253–276.

Hejmadi, A., Rozin, P. and Siegal, M. (2004). Once in contact, always in contact: Conceptions of essence and purification in Hindu Indian and American children. *Developmental Psychology, 40,* 467–476.

Herman, R., Holmes, S. and Woll, B. (1999). *Assessing BSL Development: Receptive Skills Test.* Forest Books: London.

Hickling, A. K. and Gelman, S. A. (1994). How does your garden grow? Early conceptualization of seeds and their place in the plant growth cycle. *Child Development, 66,* 856–876.

Hill, E. (2004). Executive dysfunction in autism. *Trends in Cognitive Sciences, 8,* 26–32.

Hilton, D. J. (1995). The social context of reasoning: Conversational inference and rational judgment. *Psychological Bulletin, 118,* 248–271.

Hirschfeld, L. A. (1995). Do children have a theory of race? *Cognition,* *54,* 209–252.

Hirschfeld, L. A. and Gelman, S. A. (eds) (1994). *Mapping the mind: Domain specificity in culture and cognition.* New York: Cambridge University Press.

Hodent, C., Bryant, P. and Houdé, O. (2005). Language-specific effects on numerical computation in toddlers. *Developmental Science, 8,* 420–423.

Hollos, M. and Cowan, P. (1973). Social isolation and cognitive development: Logical operations and role-taking abilities in three Norwegian school settings. *Child Development, 44,* 630–641.

Holowka, S. and Petitto, L. A. (2002). Left hemisphere cerebral specialization for babies while babbling. *Science, 297,* 1515.

Horn, L. R. (1989). *A natural history of negation*. Chicago, IL: University of Chicago Press.

Howie, P., Sheehan, M., Mojarrad, T. and Wrzesinska, M. (2004). 'Undesirable' and 'desirable' shifts in children's responses to repeated questions: Age differences in the effect of providing a rationale for repetition. *Applied Cognitive Psychology, 18,* 1161–1180.

Hughes, C., Dunn, J. and White, A. (1998). Trick or treat?: Uneven understanding of mind and emotion and executive dysfunction in 'hard-to-manage' preschoolers. *Journal of Child Psychology and Psychiatry, 39,* 981–994.

Hunt, E. and Agnoli, F. (1991). The Whorfian hypothesis: A cognitive psychology perspective, *Psychological Review, 98,* 377–389.

Hunter, M. D. *et al.* (2006). Neural activity in speech-sensitive auditory cortex during silence. *Proceedings of the National Academy of Sciences, 103,* 189–194.

Inagaki, K. and Hatano, G. (1993). Young children's understanding of the mind-body distinction. *Child Development, 8,* 503–526.

Inagaki, K. and Hatano, G. (2002). *Young children's naive thinking about the biological world*. New York: Psychology Press.

Inagaki, K. and Hatano, G. (2006). Young children's conception of the biological world. *Current Directions in Psychological Science, 15,* 177–181.

Inagaki, K., Hatano, G. and Morita, E. (1998). Construction of mathematical knowledge through whole-class discussion. *Learning and Instruction, 64,* 1534–1549.

Ingram, N. and Butterworth, G. E. (1989). The young child's representation of depth in drawing: process and product. *Journal of Experimental Child Psychology, 47,* 356–369.

Jaswal, V. K. and Neely, L. A. (2006). Adults don't always know best: Preschoolers use past reliability over age when learning new words. *Psychological Science, 17,* 757–758.

Jenkins, M. W. and Curtis, V. (2005). Achieving the 'good life': Why some people want latrines in rural Benin. *Social Science and Medicine, 61,* 2446–2459.

Jolley, R., Knox, E. and Foster, S. (2000). The relationship between children's production and comprehension of realism in drawing. *British Journal of Developmental Psychology, 18,* 557–582.

Joseph, R. M. (1998). Intention and knowledge in preschoolers' conception of pretend. *Child Development, 69,* 966–980.

Joseph, R. M., Tager-Flusberg, H. and Lord, C. (2002). Cognitive profiles and social-communicative functioning in children with autism spectrum disorder. *Journal of Child Psychology and Psychiatry, 43,* 807–822.

Joyce, J. (1916/1964). *A portrait of the artist as a young man*. London: Jonathan Cape.

Kalish, C. W. (1997). Preschoolers' understanding of mental and bodily reactions to contamination: What you don't know can hurt you, but cannot sadden you. *Developmental Psychology, 33*, 79–91.

Kalish, C. W. (1999). What young children's understanding of contamination and contagion tells us about their concepts of illness. In M. Siegal and C. C. Peterson (eds), *Children's understanding of biology and health* (pp. 99–130). Cambridge: Cambridge University Press.

Kaminski, J., Call, J. and Fischer, J. (2004). Word learning in a domestic dog: Evidence for "fast mapping". *Science, 304*, 1682–1683.

Kanner, L. (1943). Autistic disturbances of affective contact. *Nervous Child, 2*, 217–250.

Kass, L. (1994). *The hungry soul*. Chicago, IL: University of Chicago Press.

Kearins, J. (1981). Visual-spatial memory in Australian Aboriginal children of desert regions. *Cognitive Psychology, 13*, 434–460.

Keil, F. C., Levin, D. T., Richman, B. A. and Gutheil, G. (1999). Mechanism and explanation in the development of biological thought: The case of disease. In D. Medin and S. Atran (eds), *Folkbiology* (pp. 285–319). Cambridge, MA: MIT Press.

Kelemen, D. (2003). British and American children's preferences for teleo-functional explanations of the natural world. *Cognition, 88*, 201–221.

Kendrick, K. M. *et al.* (2001). Sheep don't forget a face. *Nature, 414*, 165–166.

Keysar, B. and Henly, A. S. (2002). Speakers' overestimation of their effectiveness. *Psychological Science, 13*, 207–212.

Khalfa, S. *et al.* (2001). Peripheral auditory asymmetry in infantile autism. *European Journal of Neuroscience, 13*, 628–632.

Klin, A. (1992). Listening preferences in regard to speech in four children with developmental disabilities. *Journal of Child Psychology and Psychiatry, 33*, 763–769.

Kobayashi, M. (1988). *New ideas of teaching mathematics in Japan*. Tokyo: Chuo University Press.

Koenig, M. A. and Harris, P. L. (2005). Preschoolers mistrust ignorant and inaccurate speakers. *Child Development, 76*, 1261–1277.

Koenig, M. A., Clément, F. and Harris, P. L. (2004). Trust in testimony: Children's use of true and false statements. *Psychological Science, 17*, 757–758.

Kohlberg, L. (1966). A cognitive-developmental analysis of children's sex-role concepts and attitudes. In E. E. Maccoby (ed.), *The development of sex differences*, (pp. 82–173). Stanford, CA: Stanford University Press.

Kosslyn, S. M., Heldmeyer, K. H. and Locklear, E. P. (1977). Children's drawings as data about internal representations. *Journal of Experimental Child Psychology, 23*, 191–211.

Kuhl, P. K., Coffey-Corina, S., Padden, D. and Dawson, G. (2005). Links between social and linguistic processing of speech in preschool children with autism: Behavioral and electrophysiological measures. *Developmental Science, 8*, F1–12.

Kuhn, T. S. (1957). *The Copernican revolution.* Cambridge, MA: Harvard University Press.

Kuhn, T. S. (1962). *The structure of scientific revolutions.* Chicago: University of Chicago Press.

Landerl, K., Bevan, A. and Butterworth, B. (2004). Developmental dyscalculia and basic numerical capacities: A study of 8–9-year-old students. *Cognition, 93*, 99–125.

Lane, H. (1977). *The wild boy of Aveyron.* New York: Bantam Books.

Langdon, R., Coltheart, M. and Ward, P. B. (2006). Empathetic perspective-taking is impaired in schizophrenia: Evidence from a study of emotion attribution and theory of mind. *Cognitive Neuropsychiatry, 11*, 133–155.

Laurence, S. and Margolis, E. (2001). The poverty of the stimulus argument. *British Journal for the Philosophy of Science, 52*, 217–276.

Lederberg, A. R. and Everhart, V. S. (1998). Communication between deaf children and their hearing mothers: The role of language, gesture and vocalizations. *Journal of Speech, Language and Hearing Research, 41*, 887–899.

Legerstee, M. (2000). Precursors to the development of intention at 6 months: Understanding people and their actions. *Developmental Psychology, 36*, 627–63.

Lenneberg, E. H. (1967). *Biological foundations of language.* New York: Wiley.

Leslie, A. M. (1994). ToMM, ToBy and Agency: core architecture and domain specificity. In L. A. Hirschfeld and S. A. Gelman (eds), *Mapping the mind.* Cambridge: Cambridge University Press.

Leslie, A. M. (2000). 'Theory of mind' as a mechanism of selective attention. In M. S. Gazzaniga (ed.), *The new cognitive neurosciences, 2nd edn* (pp. 1235–1247). Cambridge, MA: MIT Press.

Leslie, A. M., Friedman, O. and German, T. P. (2004). Core mechanisms in 'theory of mind'. *Trends in Cognitive Sciences, 8*, 528–533.

Leslie, A. M., German, T. P. and Polizzi P. (2005). Belief-desire reasoning as a process of selection. *Cognitive Psychology, 50*, 45–85.

Leslie, A. M., Knobe, J. and Cohen, A. (2006). Acting intentionally and the side-effect. *Psychological Science, 17*, 421–427.

Levinson, S. (2000). *Presumptive meanings.* Cambridge, MA: MIT Press.

Lewis, C., Freeman, N. H., Kyriakidou, C., Maridaki-Kassotaki, K. and Berridge, D. M. (1996). Social influences on false belief access: specific sibling influences or general apprenticeship? *Child Development, 67*, 2930–2947.

Lidz, J., Waxman, S. and Freedman, J. (2003). What infants know about syntax but couldn't have learned: Experimental evidence for syntactic structure at 18 months. *Cognition, 89*, B65–B73.

Lohmann, H. and Tomasello, M. (2003). The role of language in the development of false belief understanding: A training study. *Child Development, 74,* 1130–1144.

Lord, C. (1995). Follow-up of two-year-olds referred for possible autism. *Journal of Child Psychology and Psychiatry, 36,* 1365–1382.

Lord, C. and Paul, R. (1997). Language and communication in autism. In D. J. Cohen and F. J. Volkmar (eds), *Handbook of autism and persuasive developmental disorders,* 2nd edn (pp. 195–225). New York: Wiley.

Ma, L. and Lillard, A. S. (2006). Where is the real cheese? Young children's ability to discriminate between real and pretend acts. *Child Development, 77,* 1762–1777.

Macnamara, J. (1999). *Through the rearview mirror: Reflections on psychology.* Cambridge, MA: MIT Press.

Mandler, J. M. (2004). *The foundations of mind: Origins of conceptual thought.* New York: Oxford University Press.

Marcus, G. (2004). *The birth of the mind.* New York: Basic Books.

Mareschal, D. and Tan, S. H. (2007). Flexible and context-dependent categorization by 18-month-olds. *Child Development, 78,* 19–37.

Marriott, M. (1968). Caste reading and food transactions: A metric analysis. In M. Singer and B. S. Cohn (eds), *Structure and change in Indian society* (pp. 133–142). Philadelphia, PA: Institute for the Study of Human Issues.

Marschark, M. (1993). *Psychological development of deaf children.* New York: Oxford University Press.

Marschark, M., Green, V., Hindmarsh, G. and Walker, S. (2000). Understanding theory of mind in children who are deaf. *Journal of Child Psychology and Psychiatry, 41,* 1067–1073.

Martin, C. L., Ruble, D. N. and Szkrybalo, J. (2002). Cognitive theories of early gender development. *Psychological Bulletin, 128,* 903–933.

Martin, I. and McDonald, S. (2003). Weak central coherence, no theory of mind, or executive dysfunction? Solving the puzzle of pragmatic language disorders. *Brain and Language, 85,* 451–466.

Massey, C. and Gelman, R. (1988). Preschoolers' ability to decide whether a pictured unfamiliar object can move itself. *Developmental Psychology, 24,* 307–317.

Matthei, E. M. (1981). The acquisition of prenominal modifier sequences. *Cognition, 11,* 301–332.

Mauss, M. (1902/1972). *A general theory of magic* (R. Brain, Trans.). New York: W. W. Norton. Original work published 1902. Esquisse d'une théorie generale de la magie. *L'Année Sociologique,* 1902–1903.

Mayberry, R. I., Lock, E. and Hazmi, H. (2002). Linguistic ability and early language exposure. *Nature, 417,* 38.

McNeil, N. M. and Alibali, M. W. (2005). Why won't you change your mind? Knowledge of operational patterns hinders learning and performance on equations. *Child Development, 76,* 883–899.

Meadow, K. P., Greenberg, M. T., Erting, C. and Carmichael, H. (1981). Interactions of deaf mothers and deaf preschool-children – Comparisons with three other groups of deaf and hearing dyads. *American Annals of the Deaf, 126,* 454–468.

Medin, D. L. (1989). Concepts and conceptual structure. *American Psychologist, 44,* 1469–1481.

Medin, D. L. and Atran, S. (2004). The native mind: Biological categorization and reasoning in development and across cultures. *Psychological Review, 111,* 960–983.

Meigs, A. S. (1983). *Food, sex and pollution: A New Guinea religion.* New Brunswick, NJ: Rutgers University Press.

Meins, E., Fernyhough, C., Wainwright, R., Gupta, M., Fradley, E. and Tuckey, M. (2002). Maternal mind-mindness and attachment security as predictors of theory-of-mind understanding. *Child Development, 73,* 1715–1726.

Meltzoff, A. N. (1995). Understanding the intentions of others: Re-enactment of intended acts by 18-month-old children. *Developmental Psychology, 31,* 838–850.

Mendleson, M. J. and Haith, M. M. (1976). The relation between audition and vision in the newborn. *Monographs of the Society for Research in Child Development, 41,* Serial No. 167.

Meroni, L. and Crain, S. (2003). On not being led down the Kindergarten path. *Proceedings of the 25th Annual Boston University Conference on Language Development.* Somerville, MA: Cascadilla Press.

Mill, J. S. (1867). *An examination of Sir William Hamilton's philosophy,* 3rd edn. London: Longman.

Miller, K. F., Smith, C. M., Zhu, J. and Zhang, H. (1995). Preschool origins of cross-national differences in mathematical competence: The role of number-naming systems. *Psychological Science, 6,* 56–60.

Milligan, K., Astington, J. W. and Dack, L. A. (2007). Language and Theory of Mind: Meta-analysis of the relation between language ability and false-belief understanding. *Child Development, 78,* 622–646.

Milne, E. *et al.* (2002). High motion coherence thresholds in children with autism. *Journal of Child Psychology and Psychiatry, 43,* 255–264.

Mischel, W., Shoda, Y. and Rodriguez, M. L. (1989). Delay of gratification in children. *Science, 244,* 933–938.

Mitchell, P. and Ropar, D. (2004). Visuo-spatial abilities in autism: A review. *Infant and Child Development, 13,* 185–198.

Mitchell, P., Saltmarsh, R. and Russell, J. (1997). Overly literal interpretations of speech in autism: Understanding that messages arise from minds. *Journal of Child Psychology and Psychiatry, 38,* 685–691.

Mix, K., Levine, S. and Huttenlocher, J. (1999). Early fraction calculation ability. *Developmental Psychology, 35,* 164–174.

Miyake, A. *et al.* (2000). The unity and diversity of executive functions and their contributions to complex "frontal lobe" tasks: A latent variable analysis. *Cognitive Psychology, 41,* 49–100.

Moeller, M. P. and Schick, B. (2006). Relations between maternal input and theory of mind understanding in deaf children. *Child Development, 77,* 751–766.

Molloy, C. A. and Manning-Courtney, P. (2003). Prevalence of chronic gastrointestinal symptoms in children with autism and autistic spectrum disorder. *Autism, 7,* 165–171.

Moore, D. R., Rosenberg, J. F. and Coleman, J. S. (2005). Discrimination training of phonemic contrasts enhances phonological processing in mainstream school children. *Brain and Language, 94,* 72–85.

Morford, J. P. and Goldin-Meadow, S. (1997). From here and now to there and then: The development of displaced reference in Homesign and English. *Child Development, 68,* 420–435.

Morgan, G. and Kegl, J. (2006). Theory of Mind and late access to language: Evidence from users of Nicaraguan Sign Language. *Journal of Child Psychology and Psychiatry, 47,* 811–819.

Morris, B. J. and Sloutsky, V. (2002). Children's solutions of logical versus empirical problems: What's missing and what develops? *Cognitive Development, 16,* 907–928.

Morris, S. C., Taplin, J. E. and Gelman, S. A. (2000). Vitalism in naïve biological thinking. *Developmental Psychology, 36,* 582–595.

Morton, J. (2004). *Understanding developmental disorders: A causal modelling approach.* Oxford: Blackwell.

Moses, L. J. (2001). Executive accounts of theory of mind development. *Child Development, 72,* 688–690.

Mottron, L. and Belleville, S. (1993). A study of perceptual analysis in a high-level autistic subject with exceptional graphic abilities. *Brain and Cognition, 23,* 279–309.

Mottron, L., Dawson, M., Soulieres, I., Hubert, B. and Burack, J. (2006). Enhanced perceptual functioning in autism: An update,and eight principles of autistic perception. *Journal of Autism and Developmental Disorders, 36,* 27–43.

Nadig, A. S. and Sedivy J. C. (2002). Evidence of perspective-taking constraints in children's on-line reference resolution. *Psychological Science, 13,* 329–336.

Nadig, A. S. *et al.* (2007). A prospective study of response to name in infants at risk for autism. *Archives of Pediatrics and Adolescent Medicine, 161,* 378–383.

Naito, M. and Miura, H. (2001). Japanese children's numerical competencies: Age- and schooling-related influences on the development of number concepts and addition skills. *Developmental Psychology, 37,* 217–230.

Napolitano, A. C. and Sloutsky, V. M. (2004). Is a picture worth a thousand words? Part II: The flexible nature of modality dominance in young children. *Child Development, 75,* 1850–1870.

Nelson, K. *et al.* (2003). Entering a community of minds: An experiential approach to 'theory of mind'. *Human Development, 46,* 24–46.

Nemeroff, C. and Rozin, P. (2000). The makings of the magical mind. In K. S. Rosengren, C. N. Johnson and P. L. Harris (eds), *Imagining the impossible: magical, scientific and religious thinking in children* (pp. 1–34). New York: Cambridge University Press.

Nemeroff, C. J. and Rozin, P. (1994). The contagion concept in adult thinking in the United States: Transmission of germs and of interpersonal influence. *Ethos: Journal of Psychological Anthropology, 22,* 158–186.

Newcombe, P. A. and Siegal, M. (1996). Where to look first for suggestibility in children's memory. *Cognition, 59,* 337–356.

Newcombe, P. A. and Siegal, M. (1997). Explicitly questioning the nature of suggestibility in preschoolers' memory and retention. *Journal of Experimental Child Psychology, 67,* 185–203.

Newport, E. L. (1990). Maturational constraints on language learning. *Cognitve Science,14,* 11–28.

Ninio, A. and Snow, C. E. (1996). *Pragmatic development.* Boulder, CO: Westview Press.

Nobes, G. *et al.* (2003). Children's understanding of the earth in a multicultural community: Mental models or fragments of knowledge? *Developmental Science, 6,* 74–87.

Nobes, G., Martin, A. E. and Panagiotaki, G. (2005). The development of scientific knowledge of the earth. *British Journal of Developmental Psychology. 23,* 47–64.

Nucci, L. and Turiel, E. (1978). Social interactions and the development of social concepts in preschool children. *Child Development, 49,* 400–407.

Nussbaum, J. (1979). An assessment of children's concepts of the earth using structured interviews. *Science Education, 63,* 83–93.

O'Riordan, M. A., Plaisted, K. C., Driver, J. and Baron-Cohen, S. (2001). Superior visual search in autism. *Journal of Experimental Psychology: Human Perception and Performance, 27,* 719–730.

Onishi, K. and Baillargeon, R. (2005). Do 15-month-old infants understand false beliefs? *Science, 308,* 255–258.

Osherson, D. and Markman, E. (1975). Language and the ability to evaluate contradictions and tautologies. *Cognition, 86,* 213–226.

Osterling, J. A., Dawson, G. and Munson, J. (2002) Early recognition of 1-year-old infants with autism spectrum disorder versus mental retardation. *Development and Psychopathology, 14,* 239–251.

Pan, Y., Gauvain, M., Liu, Z. and Cheng, L. (2006). American and Chinese parental involvement in young children's mathematics learning. *Cognitive Development, 21,* 17–35.

Panagiotaki, G. (2003). Is the earth flat or round? Knowledge acquisition in the domain of astronomy. D.Phil. thesis, University of Sussex.

Panksepp, J. (2005). Beyond a joke: From animal laughter to human joy. *Science, 308,* 62–63.

Papafragou, A. and Musolino, J. (2003). Scalar implicatures: experiments at the semantics–pragmatics interface. *Cognition, 86,* 253–282.

Papafragou, A. and Tantalou, N. (2004). Children's computation of implicatures. *Language Acquisition, 12,* 71–82.

Pellicano, E., Maybery, M., Durkin, K. and Maley, A. (2006). Multiple cognitive capabilities/ deficits in children with an autism spectrum disorder: 'weak' central coherence and its relationship to theory of mind and executive control. *Developmental Psychopathology, 18,* 77–98.

Pemberton, E. F. (1990). Systematic errors in children's drawings. *Cognitive Development, 5,* 395–404.

Perner, J. (1991). *Understanding the representational mind.* Cambridge, MA: MIT Press.

Perner, J. and Lang, B. (1999). Development of theory of mind and executive control. *Trends in Cognitive Sciences, 3,* 337–344.

Perner, J., Leekam, S. R. and Wimmer, H. (1987). Three year olds' difficulty with false belief: The case for a conceptual deficit. *British Journal of Developmental Psychology, 5,* 125–137.

Peterson, C. C. (2001). Kindred spirits: Influences of siblings' perspectives on theory of mind. *Cognitive Development, 15,* 435–455.

Peterson, C. C. and Siegal, M. (1995). Deafness, conversation and theory of mind. *Journal of Child Psychology and Psychiatry, 36,* 459–474.

Peterson, C. C. and Siegal, M. (1999). Representing inner worlds: Theory of mind in autistic, deaf and normal hearing children. *Psychological Science, 10,* 126–129.

Petitto, L. A. and Marentette, P. F. (1991). Babbling in the manual mode: Evidence for the ontogeny of language. *Science, 251,* 1493–1496.

Petitto, L. A., Holowska, S., Sergio, J. E. and Ostry, D. (2001). Language rhythms in baby hand movements. *Nature, 413,* 35–36.

Piaget, J. (1929). *The child's conception of the world.* London: Routledge and Kegan Paul.

Piaget, J. (1930). *The child's conception of physical causality.* London: Routledge and Kegan Paul.

Piaget, J. (1932). *The moral judgement of the child.* London: Routledge and Kegan Paul.

Piaget, J. (1952). *The child's conception of number.* London: Routledge and Kegan Paul.

Piaget, J. (1954). *The construction of reality in the child.* New York: Basic Books.

Piaget, J. (1962). *Play, dreams and imitation.* London: Routledge and Kegan Paul.

Piaget, J., Inhelder, B. and Szeminska, A. (1960). *The child's conception of geometry.* London: Routledge and Kegan Paul.

Pinker, S. (1994). *The language instinct.* New York: William Morrow.

Pinker, S. (2002). *The blank slate: The modern denial of human nature.* New York: Viking.

Pipe, M. E., Lamb, M. E., Orbach, Y. and Esplin, P. W. (2004). Recent research on children's testimony about experienced and witnessed events. *Developmental Review, 24,* 440–468.

Plaisted, K. *et al.* (2003). Towards an understanding of the mechanisms of weak central coherence effects: Experiments in visual configural learning and auditory perception. *Philosophical Transactions of the Royal Society of London, B, 358,* 375–386.

Plato (1961). *The collected dialogues of Plato.* Edited by E. Hamilton and H. Cairns. Princeton, NJ: Princeton University Press.

Plaut, D. C. and Karmiloff-Smith, A. (1993). Representational development and theory-of-mind computations. *Behavioral and Brain Sciences, 16,* 70–71

Plimmer, M. and King, B. (2004). *Beyond coincidence.* Cambridge, UK: Icon Books.

Preissler, M. A. and Carey, S. A. (2004). The role of inferences about the referential intent in word learning: Evidence from autism. *Cognition, 97,* B13–B23.

Premack, D. and Hauser, M. D. (2001). A whale of a tale: Calling it culture doesn't help. *Behavioral and Brain Sciences, 24,* 350–351.

Premack, D. and Premack, A. (2003). *Original intelligence.* New York: McGraw-Hill.

Raby, C. R., Alexis, D. M., Dickinson, A. and Clayton, N. S. (2007). Planning for the future by western scrub-jays. *Nature, 445,* 919–921.

Raman, L. and Gelman. S. (2005). Children's understanding of the transmission of genetic disorders and contagious illnesses. *Developmental Psychology, 41,* 171–182.

Ramus, F. *et al.* (2003).Theories of developmental dyslexia: insights from a multiple case study of dyslexic adults. *Brain, 126,* 841–865.

Rapin, I. and Dunn, M. (2003). Update on the language disorders of individuals on the autistic spectrum. *Brain and Development, 25,* 166–172.

Resnick, L. B. and Ford, W. W. (1981). *The psychology of mathematics for instruction.* Hillsdale, NJ: Lawrence Erlbaum Associates.

Richards, C. A. and Sanderson, J. A. (1999). The role of imagination in facilitating deductive reasoning in 2-, 3- and 4-year-olds. *Cognition, 72,* B1–B9.

Rips, L. J., Asmuth, J. and Bloomfield, A. (2006). Giving the boot to the bootstrap: How not to learn the natural numbers. *Cognition, 101,* B51–B60.

Rittle-Johnson, B., Siegler, R. S. and Alibali, M. W. (2001). Developing conceptual understanding and procedural skill in mathematics: An iterative process. *Journal of Educational Psychology, 93,* 346–362.

Robinson, C. W. and Sloutsky, V. M. (2004). Auditory dominance and its change in the course of development. *Child Development, 75,* 1387–1401.

Robinson, E. J., Goelman, H. and Olson, D. (1983). Children's understanding of the relation between expressions (what was said) and intentions (what was meant). *British Journal of Developmental Psychology, 1,* 75–86.

Rogers, S. J. and Ozonoff, S. (2005). Annotation: What do we know about sensory dysfunction in autism? A critical review of the empirical evidence. *Journal of Child Psychology and Psychiatry, 46,* 1255–1268.

Rosen, A. B. and Rozin, P. (1993). Now you see it ... now you don't: The preschool child's conception of invisible particles in the context of dissolving. *Developmental Psychology, 29,* 300–311.

Rozin, P. (1976). The evolution of intelligence and access to the cognitive unconscious. In J. A. Sprague and A. N. Epstein (eds), *Progress in psychobiology and physiological psychology, Volume 6* (pp. 245–280). New York: Academic Press.

Rozin, P. (1990). Social and moral aspects of eating. In I. Rock (ed.), *The legacy of Solomon Asch: Essays in cognition and social psychology* (pp. 97–110). Potomac, MD: Lawrence Erlbaum.

Rozin, P. (1996). Towards a psychology of food and eating: From motivation to model to meaning, morality and metaphor. *Current Directions in Psychological Science, 5,* 1–7.

Rozin, P. (2006). About 17 (+/– 2) potential principles about links between the innate mind and culture: Preadaptation, predispositions, preferences, pathways and domains. In P. Carruthers, S. Laurence and S. Stich (eds), *The innate mind: Culture and cognition.* New York: Oxford University Press.

Rozin, P. and Fallon, A. E. (1987). A perspective on disgust. *Psychological Review, 94,* 23–41.

Rozin, P., Fallon, A. E. and Augustoni-Ziskind, M. (1985). The child's conception of food: The development of contamination sensitivity to "disgusting" substances. *Developmental Psychology, 21,* 1075–1079.

Rubenstein, J. L. and Merzenich, M. M. (2003). Model of autism: Increased ratio of excitation/inhibition in key neural systems. *Genes, Brain and Behavior, 2,* 255–267.

Ruffman, T., Slade, L., Rowlandson, K., Rumsey, C. and Garnham, A. (2003). How language relates to belief, desire and emotion understanding. *Cognitive Development, 18,* 139–158.

Russell, P. A. *et al.* (1998). The development of theory of mind in deaf children. *Journal of Child Psychology and Psychiatry, 39,* 903–910.

Rutherford, M. D., Baron-Cohen, S. and Wheelwright, S. (2002). Reading the mind in the voice: A study with normal adults and adults with Asperger syndrome and high functioning autism. *Journal of Autism and Developmental Disorders, 32,* 189–194.

Sabbagh, M. A., Xu, F., Carlson, S. M., Moses, L. J. and Lee, K. (2006). The development of executive functioning and theory-of-mind: A comparison of Chinese and U. S. preschoolers. *Psychological Science, 17,* 74–81.

Samarapungavan, A., Vosniadou, S. and Brewer, W. F. (1996). Mental models of the earth, sun and moon: Indian children's cosmologies. *Cognitive Development, 11,* 491–521.

Samson, D., Apperly, I. A., Chiavarino, C. and Humphreys, G. W. (2004). The left temporo-parietal junction is necessary for representing someone else's belief. *Nature Neuroscience, 7,* 449–500.

Samson, F., Mottron, L., Jemel, B., Belin, P. and Ciocca, V. (2006). Can spectro-temporal complexity explain the autistic pattern of performance on auditory tasks? *Journal of Autism and Developmental Disorders, 36,* 65–76.

Sapp F., Lee K. and Muir, D. (2000). Three-year-olds' difficulty with the appearance–reality distinction: Is it real or is it apparent? *Developmental Psychology, 36,* 547–560.

Sarnecka, B. W. and Gelman, S. A. (2004). *Six* does not just mean *a lot*: preschoolers see number words as specific. *Cognition, 92,* 329–352.

SBS World Guide, 11th edn (2003). Melbourne, Australia: Hardie Grant Books.

Schick, B., de Villiers, P., de Villiers, J. and Hoffmeister, R. (2007). Language and Theory of Mind: A study of deaf children. *Child Development, 78,* 376–396.

Scholl, B. J. and Leslie, A. M. (1999). Modularity, development and 'Theory of Mind'. *Brain and Language, 14,* 131–153.

Scholnick, E. K. and Wing, C. S. (1991). Speaking deductively: Preschoolers use of *If* in conversation and in conditional inference. *Developmental Psychology, 27,* 249–258.

Schoultz, J., Säljö, R. and Wyndhamn, J. (2001). Heavenly talk: Discourse, artifacts and children's understanding of elementary astronomy. *Human Development, 44,* 103–118.

Scribner, S. and Cole, M. (1973). Cognitive consequences of formal and informal education. *Science, 182,* 553–559.

Sekerina, I. A., Stromswold, K. and Hestvik, A. (2004). How do adults and children process referentially ambiguous pronouns? *Journal of Child Language, 31,* 123–152.

Senghas, A., Kita, S. and Özyürek, A. (2004). Children creating core components of language: Evidence from an emerging sign language. *Science, 305,* 1779–1782.

Senju, A., Tojo, Y., Yaguchi, K. and Hasegawa, T. (2005). Deviant gaze processing in children with autism: an ERP study. *Neuropsychologia, 43,* 1297–1306.

Shallice, T. (1982). Specific impairments of planning. *Philosophical Transactions of the Royal Society of London, B298,* 199–209.

Sharpe, D., Coté, M. H. and Eakin, L. (1999). Reasoning about a structured object: Three- and four-year-olds' grasp of a borderline case and an unexcluded middle. *Child Development, 70,* 866–871.

Sharpe, D., Eakin, L., Saragovi, C. and Macnamara, J. (1996). Adults' and preschoolers' ability to cope with non-classical negation. *Journal of Child Language, 23,* 675–691.

Shriberg, L., Paul, R., McSweeny, J., Klin, A. and Cohen, D. (2001). Speech and prosody characteristics of adolescents and adults with high-functioning autism and Asperger syndrome. *Journal of Speech, Language and Hearing Research, 44,* 1097–1115.

Shriberg, L., Paul, R., McSweeny, J., Klin, A. and Cohen, D. (2001). Speech and prosody characteristics of adolescents and adults with high-functioning autism and Asperger syndrome. *Journal of Speech, Language and Hearing Research, 44,* 1097–1115.

Shweder, R. *et al.* (1998). Cultural psychology of human development: One mind, many mentalities. In R. Lerner (volume ed.), *Handbook of child psychology, Fifth edition, vol. 1* (pp. 865–939). New York: Wiley.

Siegal, M. (1988). Children's knowledge of contagion and contamination as causes of illness. *Child Development, 59,* 1353–1359.

Siegal, M. (1997). *Knowing children: Experiments in conversation and cognition,* 2nd edn. Hove, UK: Psychology Press.

Siegal, M. (1999). Language and thought: The fundamental significance of conversational awareness for cognitive development. *Developmental Science, 2,* 1–14.

Siegal, M. and Beattie, K. (1991). Where to look first for children's knowledge of false beliefs. *Cognition, 38,* 1–12.

Siegal, M. and Peterson, C. C. (1996). Breaking the mold: A fresh look at questions about children's understanding of lies and mistakes. *Developmental Psychology, 32,* 322–334.

Siegal, M. and Peterson, C. C. (1998). Children's understanding of lies and innocent and negligent mistakes. *Developmental Psychology, 34,* 332–343.

Siegal, M. and Peterson, C. C. (eds) (1999). *Children's understanding of biology and health.* New York: Cambridge University Press.

Siegal, M. and Peterson, C. C. (in press). Language and theory of mind in atypical children: Evidence from studies of deafness, blindness and autism. In C. Sharp, P. Fonagy and I. Goodyer (eds), *Social cognition and developmental psychopathology.* New York: Oxford University Press.

Siegal, M. and Robinson, J. (1987). Order effects in children's gender-constancy responses. *Developmental Psychology, 23,* 283–286.

Siegal, M. and Share, D. L. (1990). Contamination sensitivity in young children. *Developmental Psychology, 26,* 455–458.

Siegal, M. and Smith, J. A. (1997). Toward making representation count in children's conceptions of fractions. *Contemporary Educational Psychology, 22,* 1–22.

Siegal, M. and Surian, L. (2006). Modularity in language and theory of mind: What is the evidence? In P. Carruthers, S. Laurence and S. Stich (eds), *The innate mind: Culture and cognition* (pp. 133–148). New York: Oxford University Press.

Siegal, M. and Surian, L. (2007). Conversational understanding in young children. In E. Hoff and M. Shatz (eds), *Blackwell handbook of language development* (pp. 304–323). Oxford: Blackwell.

Siegal, M. and Varley, R. (2002). Neural systems underlying theory of mind. *Nature Reviews Neuroscience, 3,* 463–471.

Siegal, M. and Varley, R. (2006). Aphasia, language and theory of mind. *Social Neuroscience, 1,* 167–174.

Siegal, M., Butterworth, G. and Newcombe, P. A. (2004). Culture and children's cosmology. *Developmental Science, 7,* 308–324.

Siegal, M., Varley, R. and Want, S. C. (2001). Mind over grammar: Reasoning in aphasia and development. *Trends in Cognitive Sciences, 5,* 296–301.

Siegal, M., Waters, L. J. and Dinwiddy, L. S. (1988). Misleading children: Causal attributions for inconsistency under repeated questioning. *Journal of Experimental Child Psychology, 45,* 438–456.

Siegler, R. S. (1986). *Children's thinking.* Englewood Cliffs, NJ: Prentice-Hall.

Siegler, R. S. (2000). The rebirth of children's learning. *Child Development, 71,* 26–35.

Sigel, I. E. (1993). The centrality of a distancing model for the development of representational competence. In R. R. Cocking and K. A. Renninger (eds), *The development and meaning of psychological distance* (pp. 141–158). Hillsdale, NJ: Lawrence Erlbaum Associates Inc.

Slaby, R. G. and Frey, K. S. (1975). Development of gender constancy and selective attention to same sex models. *Child Development, 46,* 849–856.

Slaughter, V., Jaakkola, R. and Carey, S. (1999). Constructing a coherent theory: Children's biological understanding of life and death. In M. Siegal and C. C. Peterson (eds), *Children's understanding of biology and health* (pp. 71–96). Cambridge: Cambridge University Press.

Slaughter, V. and Lyons, M. (2003). Learning about life and death in early childhood. *Cognitive Psychology, 46,* 1–30.

Smith, C. (1980) Quantifiers and question-answering in young children. *Journal of Experimental Child Psychology, 30,* 191–205.

Smith, C. L., Solomon, G. E. A. and Carey, S. (2005). Never getting to zero: Elementary school students' understanding of the infinite divisibility of number and matter. *Cognitive Psychology, 51,* 101–140.

Smith, M., Apperly, M. and White, V. (2003). False belief reasoning and the acquisition of relative clauses. *Child Development, 74,* 1709–1719.

Solomon, G. E. A. and Cassimatis, N. L. (1999). On facts and conceptual systems: Young children's integration of their understandings of germs and contagion. *Developmental Psychology, 35,* 113–126.

Solomon, G. E. A. and Johnson, S. C. (2000). Conceptual change in the classroom: Teaching young children to understand biological inheritance. *British Journal of Developmental Psychology, 18,* 81–96.

Solomon, G. E. A., Johnson, S. C., Zaitchik, D. and Carey, S. (1996). Like father, like son: Young children's understanding of how and why offspring resemble their parents. *Child Development, 67,* 151–171.

Sophian, C. (2000). Perceptions of proportionality in young children. *Cognition, 75,* 145–170.

Southgate, V., Senju, A. and Csibra, G. (2007). Action attribution through anticipation of false beliefs by two-year-olds. *Psychological Science, 7,* 587–592.

Spencer, P. E. and Meadow-Orlans, K. P. (1996). Play, language and maternal responsiveness: A longitudinal study of deaf and hearing children. *Child Development, 67,* 3176–3191.

Sperber, D. (1996). Explaining culture: A naturalistic approach. Oxford: Blackwell.

Sperber, D. and Wilson, D. (1995). *Relevance: Communication and Cognition* (2nd ed.) Oxford: Blackwell.

Sperber, D. and Wilson, D. (2002). Pragmatics, modularity and mindreading. *Mind and Language, 17,* 3–23.

Springer, K. (1995). Acquiring a naive theory of kinship through inference. *Child Development, 66,* 547–558.

Springer, K. (1999). How a naïve theory of biology is acquired. In M. Siegal and C. C. Peterson (eds), *Children's understanding of biology and health* (pp. 45–70). Cambridge: Cambridge University Press.

Springer, K. and Belk, A. (1994). The role of physical contact and association in early contamination sensitivity. *Developmental Psychology, 30,* 864–868.

Springer, K. and Keil, F. C. (1991). Early differentiation of causal mechanisms appropriate to biological and non-biological kinds. *Child Development, 62,* 767–781.

Starkey, P. (1992). The early development of numerical reasoning. *Cognition, 43,* 93–126.

Starkey, P., Spelke, E. S. and Gelman, R, (1983). Detection of intermodal number correspondences by human infants. *Science, 222,* 179–181.

Stromwold, K. (2000). The cognitive neuroscience of language acquisition. In M. S. Gazzaniga (ed.), *The new cognitive neurosciences, 2nd edn* (pp. 902–932). Cambridge, MA: MIT Press.

Stuss, D. T., Gallup, G. G. and Alexander, M. P. (2001). The frontal lobes are necessary for 'theory of mind'. *Brain 124,* 279–286.

Surian, L. (1995) Children's ambiguous utterances – a reexamination of processing limitations on production. *Journal of Child Language, 22*, 151–169.

Surian, L. and Job, R. (1987). Children's use of conversational rules in a referential communication task. *Journal of Psycholinguistic Research, 16*, 369–382.

Surian, L. and Leslie, A. M. (1999). Competence and performance in false belief understanding: A comparison of autistic and normal 3-year-old children. *British Journal of Developmental Psychology, 17*, 141–155.

Surian, L. and Siegal, M. (2001). Sources of performance on theory of mind tasks in right hemisphere damaged patients. *Brain and Language, 78*, 224–232.

Surian, L., Baron-Cohen, S. and van der Lely, H. (1996). Are children with autism deaf to Gricean maxims? *Cognitive Neuropsychiatry, 1*, 55–71.

Surian, L., Caldi, S. and Sperber, D. (2007). Attribution of beliefs by 13-month-old infants. *Psychological Science, 1*, 580–586.

Tager-Flusberg, H. (1994). Dissociations in form and function in the acquisition of language by autistic children, in H. Tager-Flusberg (ed.), *Constraints on language acquisition: Studies of atypical children.* Hillsdale, NJ: Erlbaum.

Tager-Flusberg, H. (2004). Strategies for conducting research on language in autism. *Journal of Autism and Developmental Disorders, 34*, 75–80.

Tan, L. H. *et al.* (2005). Reading depends on writing, in Chinese. *Proceedings of the National Academy of Sciences, 102*, 8781–8785.

Tardif, T., So, C. W.C. and Kaciroti, N. (2007). Language and false belief: Evidence for general, not specific, effects in Cantonese-speaking preschoolers. *Developmental Psychology, 43*, 318–340.

Temple, E. *et al.* (2003). Neural deficits in children with dyslexia ameliorated by behavioral remediation: Evidence from functional MRI. *Proceedings of the National Academy of Sciences, 100*, 2860–2865.

Thagard, P. (1999). *How scientists reason about disease.* Princeton, NJ: Princeton University Press.

Thatcher, R. W. (1992). Cyclic cortical organization during early childhood. *Brain and Cognition, 20*, 24–50.

Toyama, N. (2000). Young children's awareness of socially mediated rejection of food: Why is food dropped at the table "dirty"? *Cognitive Development, 15*, 523–541.

Trueswell, J. C., Sekerina, I., Hill, N. M. and Logrip, M. L. (1999). The kindergarten-path effect: studying on-line sentence processing in young children. *Cognition, 73*, 89–134.

Tylor, E. B. (1871/1974). *Primitive culture: Researches into the development of mythology, philosophy, religion, art and custom.* New York: Gordon Press. (Original work published 1871).

Uddin, L. Q., Molnar-Szakacs, I., Zaidel, E. and Iacoboni, M. (2006). rTMS to the right inferior parietal lobule disrupts self–other discrimination. *Social, Cognitive and Affective Neuroscience, 1,* 65–71.

Vaccari, C. and Marschark, M.(1997). Communication between parents and deaf children: Implications for social-emotional development, *Journal of Child Psychology and Psychiatry, 38,* 793–801.

Valicenti-McDermott, M. *et al.* (2006). Frequency of gastrointestinal symptoms in children with autistic spectrum disorders and association with family history of autoimmune disease. *Journal of Developmental and Behavioral Pediatrics 27,* S128-S136

Varley, R. and Siegal, M. (2000). Evidence for cognition without grammar from causal reasoning and 'theory of mind' in an agrammatic aphasic patient. *Current Biology, 10,* 723–726.

Varley, R., Klessinger, N., Romanowski, C. A.J. and Siegal, M. (2005). Agrammatic but numerate. *Proceedings of the National Academy of Sciences, 102,* 3519–3524.

Varley, R., Siegal, M. and Want, S. C. (2001). Severe grammatical impairment does not preclude 'theory of mind'. *Neurocase, 7,* 489–493.

Vosniadou, S. (1991). Designing curricula for conceptual restructuring: Lessons from the study of knowledge acquisition in astronomy. *Journal of Curriculum Studies, 23,* 219–237.

Vosniadou, S. (1994a). Capturing and modelling the process of conceptual change. *Learning and Instruction, 4,* 45–69.

Vosniadou, S. (1994b). Universal and culture-specific properties of children's mental models of the earth. In L. A. Hirschfeld and S. A. Gelman (eds), *Mapping the mind: Domain-specificity in culture and cognition* (pp. 412–430). New York: Cambridge University Press.

Vosniadou, S. and Brewer, W. F. (1992). Mental models of the earth: A study of conceptual change in childhood. *Cognitive Psychology, 24,* 535–585.

Vosniadou, S. and Brewer, W. F. (1994). Mental models of the day/night cycle. *Cognitive Science, 18,* 123–183.

Vosniadou, S., Skopeliti, I. and Ikospentaki, K. (2004). Modes of knowing and ways of reasoning in elementary astronomy. *Cognitive Development, 19,* 203–222.

Vouloumanos, A. and Werker, J. F. (2004). Tuned to the signal: the privileged status of speech for young infants. *Developmental Science, 7,* 270–276.

Vygotsky, L. S. (1962). *Thought and language.* Cambridge, MA: MIT Press.

Wakeley, A., Rivera, S. and Langer, J. (2000). Can young infants add and subtract? *Child Development, 71,* 1525–1534.

Walenski, M., Tager-Flusberg, H. and Ullman, M. T. (2006). Language in Autism. In S. O. Moldin and J. L. R. Rubenstein (eds), *Understanding autism: From basic neuroscience to treatment* (pp. 175–203). Boca Raton, FL: Taylor and Francis Books.

Walsh, V. and Pascual-Leone, A. (2003). *Transcranial magnetic stimulation: A neurochronometrics of mind*. Cambridge, MA: MIT Press.

Wang, A. T., Lee, S. S., Sigman, M. and Dapretto, M. (2006a). Developmental changes in the neural basis of interpreting communicative intent. *Social, Cognitive and Affective Neuroscience, 1,* 107–121.

Wang, A. T., Lee, S. S., Sigman, M. and Dapretto, M. (2006b). Neural basis of irony comprehension in children with autism: The role of prosody and context. *Brain, 129,* 932–943.

Waterman, A. H., Blades, M. and Spencer, C. (2001) Interviewing children and adults: The effect of question format on the tendency to speculate. *Applied Cognitive Psychology, 15,* 1–11.

Waterman, A. H., Blades, M. and Spencer, C. (2004) Indicating when you do not know the answer: The effect of question format and interviewer knowledge on children's 'don't know' responses. *British Journal of Developmental Psychology, 22,* 335–348.

Wei, L. (2000). *The bilingualism reader*. London: Routledge.

Wellman, H. M. (2002). Understanding the psychological world: Developing a theory of mind. In U. Goswami (ed.), *Blackwell handbook of childhood cognitive development* (pp. 167–187). Malden, MA: Blackwell.

Wellman, H. M., Cross, D. and Watson, J. (2001). Meta-analyses of theory-of-mind development. *Child Development, 72,* 655–684.

Whorf, B. (1956). *Language, thought and reality*. Cambridge, MA: MIT Press.

Wilson, D. and Sperber, D. (2004). Relevance theory. In G. Ward and L. Horn (eds), *Handbook of pragmatics* (pp. 607–632). Oxford: Blackwell.

Wimmer, H. and Perner, J. (1983). Beliefs about beliefs: representation and constraining function of wrong beliefs in young children's understanding of deception. *Cognition, 13,* 103–128.

Winkler, I. *et al.* (2003). Newborn infants can organize the auditory world. *Proceedings of the National Academy of Sciences, 100,* 11812–11815.

Winner, E. (1988). *The point of words: Children's understanding of metaphor and irony*. Cambridge, MA: Harvard University Press.

Woolfe, T., Want, S. C. and Siegal, M. (2002). Signposts to development: Theory of mind in deaf children. *Child Development, 73,* 768–778.

Woolfe, T., Want, S. C. and Siegal, M. (2003). Siblings and theory of mind in deaf native signing children. *Journal of Deaf Studies and Deaf Education, 8,* 340–347.

Woolley, J. D. (2006). Verbal-behavioral dissociations in development. *Child Development, 77,* 1539–1553.

Wynn, K. (1990). Children's understanding of counting. *Cognition, 36,* 155–193.

Wynn, K. (1992a). Addition and subtraction by human infants. *Nature, 358,* 749–750.

Wynn, K. (1992b). Children's acquisition of the number words and the counting system. *Cognitive Psychology, 24,* 220–251.

Wynn, K. (2002). Do infants have numerical expectations or just perceptual preferences? Commentary. *Developmental Science, 5,* 207–209.

Xu, F., Spelke, E. S. and Goddard, S. (2005). Number sense in human infants. *Developmental Science, 8,* 88–101.

Yazdi, A. A., German, T. P., Defeyer, M. and Siegal, M. (2006). Competence and performance in belief-desire reasoning across two cultures: The truth, the whole truth and nothing but the truth about false belief? *Cognition, 100,* 343–368.

Ziatas, K., Durkin, K. and Pratt C. (2003). Differences in assertive speech acts produced by children with autism, Asperger syndrome, specific language impairment and normal development. *Development and Psychopathology, 15,* 73–94.

Further reading

Barrett, H. C. and Kurzban, R. (2006). Modularity in cognition: Framing the debate. *Psychological Review, 113,* 628–647. A theoretical article far-reaching in scope that sets out the issues for conceptualizing modularity and its importance for the study of cognition and cognitive development.

Bloom, P. (2000). *How children learn the meaning of words.* Cambridge, MA: MIT Press. A fine discussion of children's use of their knowledge of speakers' mental states to infer the correspondence between words and things and to learn new words.

Bloom, P. and German, T. P. (2000). Two reasons to abandon the false belief task as a test of theory of mind. *Cognition, 77,* B25–B31. A provocatively titled article that demonstrates how false belief tasks are liable to measure more than children's understanding of false beliefs.

Butterworth, B. (2005). The development of arithmetical abilities. *Journal of Child Psychology and Psychiatry, 46,* 3–18. A thoughtful examination of the basis underlying milestones in children's number and the nature of dyscalculia.

Carey, S. (1985). *Conceptual change in childhood.* Cambridge, MA: MIT Press. A landmark volume that aims to document the extent to which children's concepts of biology undergo change during their development.

Carruthers, P., Laurence, S. and Stich, S. (eds) (2005). *The innate mind: Structure and contents.* New York: Oxford University Press.

Carruthers, P., Laurence, S. and Stich, S. (eds) (2006). *The innate mind: Culture and cognition.* New York: Oxford University Press.

Carruthers, P., Laurence, S. and Stich, S. (eds) (in press). *The innate mind: Reflections and future directions.* New York: Oxford University Press. This trilogy on the issue of innateness contains state-of-the-art essays by philosophers, anthropologists and psychologists, including Susan Gelman, Paul Rozin, Elizabeth Spelke, and Dan Sperber.

Deák, G. O. (2006). Do children really confuse appearance and reality? *Trends in Cognitive Sciences, 10*, 546–550. A probing examination of children's AR knowledge.

Donaldson, M. (1978). *Children's minds*. Glasgow, UK: Fontana. A concise, easily readable account of an alternative, conversational approach to the interpretation of children's answers to questions in Piaget's experiments. Though 30 years old, this work is still important to research on cognitive development.

Flavell, J. H., Green, F. L. and Flavell, E. R. (1986). Development of the appearance–reality distinction. *Monographs of the Society for Research in Child Development, 51. Serial No. 212*. A pioneering investigation in this area that has had a significant impact on child development research over the past 20 years.

Fodor, J. A. (1983). *The modularity of mind*. Cambridge, MA: Bradford/MIT Press.

Frith, U. (2003). *Autism: Explaining the enigma*, 2nd edn. Oxford: Blackwell. A perceptive, balanced account of the main issues in defining and explaining autism.

Fritzley, V. H. and Lee, K. (2003). Do young children always say yes to yes–no questions? A metadevelopmental study of the affirmation bias. *Child Development, 74*, 1297–1313.

Gelman, R. and Butterworth, B. (2005). Number and language: How are they related? *Trends in Cognitive Sciences, 9*, 6–10. An insightful account of the development and nature of mathematical cognition in terms of the extent to which it is supported by language.

Gelman, R. and Gallistel, C. R. (1978). *The child's understanding of number*. Cambridge, MA: Harvard University Press. Possibly the most influential book on this subject in modern times, Gelman and Gallistel set the agenda for research on children's numerical understanding – including the proposal of five principles for counting.

Gelman, S. A. (2003). *The essential child*. New York: Oxford University Press. An original summary of research pointing, even in very young children, to the presence of essentialism – the notion that people and objects retain essential properties even if these undergo superficial perceptual transformations that change their appearances.

Goldin-Meadow, S. (2003). *The resilience of language*. New York: Psychology Press. A perceptive examination of how deaf children strive to communicate in a highly degraded language environment.

Grice, H. P. (1989). *Studies in the way of words*. Cambridge, MA: Harvard University Press. Sets out a highly influential framework describing the nature of communication in which we retrieve meaning from inferences derived through violations of conversational conventions.

Harris, P. L. (2000). *The work of the imagination*. Oxford: Blackwell. Provides a comprehensive account of young children's pretending and imagination and explores the implications for child development.

Hirschfeld, L. A. and Gelman, S. A. (eds) (1994). *Mapping the mind: Domain specificity in culture and cognition*. New York: Cambridge University Press. A very useful collection of articles on this theme, including contributions by Susan Carey, Alison Gopnik and Henry Wellman, and Stella Vosniadou.

Inagaki, K. and Hatano, G. (2002). *Young children's naive thinking about the biological world*. New York: Psychology Press. A searching exploration of what children know about biology and health with a cultural emphasis that makes the case for a belief in vitalism.

Kuhn, T. S. (1962). *The structure of scientific revolutions*. Chicago, IL: University of Chicago Press. Among the most important books in philosophy and cognitive science, this text puts forth a discontinuity thesis for the way in which science advances.

Leslie, A. M., Friedman, O. and German, T. P. (2004). Core mechanisms in 'theory of mind'. *Trends in Cognitive Sciences*, 8, 528–533. An important elucidation of what develops in the process by which children come to express a ToM, including the proposal that manifestations of ToM take place along the same lines as color vision.

Macnamara, J. (1999). *Through the rearview mirror: Reflections on psychology.* Cambridge, MA: MIT Press. A unique account of centuries of deliberation since ancient Greek times that has led up to present concerns with the nature of modularity and conceptual change.

Piaget, J. (1952). *The child's conception of number.* London: Routledge and Kegan Paul.

Piaget, J. (1954). *The construction of reality in the child.* New York: Basic Books.

Piaget, J. (1962). *Play, dreams and imitation.* London: Routledge and Kegan Paul. These sources represent Piaget's painstaking experiments in cognitive development, much of which is expressed through anecdotes and interviews with individual children.

Pinker, S. (1994). *The language instinct.* New York: William Morrow. An extremely readable and very entertaining account of how language comes about and its implications for cognition.

Premack, D. and Premack, A. (2003). *Original intelligence.* New York: McGraw-Hill. A distinguished research program on comparisons between the intelligence of nonhuman primates and humans.

Rozin, P. (1976). The evolution of intelligence and access to the cognitive unconscious. In J. A. Sprague and A. N. Epstein (eds), *Progress in Psychobiology and Physiological Psychology, Volume 6* (pp. 245–280). New York: Academic Press. A highly scholarly and accessible examination of intelligence in terms of adaptive solutions that is central to contemporary debates about the nature of modularity today.

Senghas, A., Kita, S. and Özyürek, A. (2004). Children creating core components of language: Evidence from an emerging sign language. *Science, 305,* 1779–1782. An account of the emergence of sign language in Nicaragua without a prior language model.

Siegal, M. and Peterson, C. C. (eds) (1999). *Children's understanding of biology and health.* New York: Cambridge University Press.

Includes chapters on topics such as children's knowledge of contagion and contamination, their understanding of pain, the effectiveness of instructional programs to prevent AIDS and the ability of children to consent to medical procedures.

Sperber, D. and Wilson, D. (1995). *Relevance: Communication and cognition*, 2nd edn. Oxford: Blackwell. In this treatise on conversational understanding, it is proposed that the goal of extracting meaning involves the need to compute the relevance of a speaker's message.

Surian, L., Caldi, S. and Sperber, D. (2007). Attribution of beliefs by 13-month-old infants. *Psychological Science* 7, 580–586. An incisive demonstration, based on visual attention, of infants' abilities to attend to mental states involving false beliefs.

Thagard, P. (1999). *How scientists reason about disease*. Princeton, NJ: Princeton University Press. A very readable description of varieties of conceptual change in this area supported by historical and psychological evidence.

Index